⚛ METAPHILOSOPHY

Volume 34, Nos. 1/2   January 2003

SPECIAL ISSUE
MORAL AND EPISTEMIC VIRTUES

GUEST EDITORS
MICHAEL S. BRADY and DUNCAN PRITCHARD

CONTENTS

ARtICLES

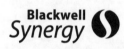

This journal is available online.
Contact your librarian or visit
www.blackwell-synergy.com

METAPHILOSOPHY
Vol. 34, Nos. 1/2, January 2003
0026-1068

MORAL AND EPISTEMIC VIRTUES

MICHAEL S. BRADY AND DUNCAN PRITCHARD

I

The past thirty years have seen a revival of interest in the moral virtues, which has been motivated, to a large extent, by dissatisfaction with consequentialist and Kantian approaches to normative moral theory. One source of dissatisfaction is the seemingly intractable nature of the disagreement among these other theories; another, however, is that the theories appear to leave us with an impoverished view of rightness (and wrongness) and goodness (and badness). For, *contra* these theories, it seems that more things matter to the moral assessment of an action than the fact that it has good consequences or that it accords with duty; and more things contribute to the moral evaluation of a person than the fact that she reliably makes the world a better place or is moved to act by thoughts of her duty.

Taking these in turn, and simplifying somewhat, the thought is that in its assessment of behaviour consequentialism is too "act-based," in that it defines rightness wholly in terms of an act's possessing some "external" feature (that is, the feature of bringing about the best consequences); the theory therefore fails to allow for the possibility that "internal" features of the agent (that is, her reasons or motives) can affect our assessment of what she did. Kantian deontology is less susceptible to this criticism, since it explicitly holds that the moral *worth* of an action depends upon whether or not it was performed from the motive of duty. Nevertheless, this theory is (famously) open to the charge that it fails to allow for the possibility that *other* motives matter for moral assessment, and so is thought to have an over-narrow view of right or worthy action.

When it comes to the assessment of agents, the theories are again regarded as too focused on what agents *do*, since each holds the concept of a right (or dutiful) action to be primary and proceeds to define a good person as one who reliably (or conscientiously) performs such acts. Now even if we agree with their accounts of right action, this might strike us as too narrow: there are, after all, good character traits that are not typically expressed in, or defined in terms of, right action at all.[1] But the core objection here is that good people are not those who *merely* bring about good

---

[1] See, for instance, the account of "spiritual virtues" offered by Trianosky (1987, especially 134).

consequences, or who *merely* do the right thing because it's the right thing to do. Our common-sense understanding of a good character involves an ideal of appropriate feelings, emotions, and sentiments, where these are not (obviously) susceptible to a consequentialist interpretation and not (obviously) subservient to the motive of conscientiousness.[2]

Virtue-theoretic approaches shift the emphasis away from *acts* and on to *agents* – or, more specifically, to the character traits that constitute virtues and vices – and in this way aim to avoid the problems that beset consequentialism and Kantian deontology. In particular, they suppose that a closer focus on the virtues will allow for a richer account of rightness (and wrongness), and a more plausible or developed account of goodness (and badness), than is possible under the rival approaches. Virtue theory is, however, a very broad church, and the idea that we should be more concerned with the virtues is about *all* that the multitude of theories taken to fall under its roof have in common. For instance, virtue-ethical accounts differ with regard to the precise relation between virtue and rightness: some views hold that the virtues are necessary so that we might see the right action in our particular circumstances, but they contend that rightness is not dependent upon virtue in any stronger sense;[3] other views maintain, instead, that rightness and virtue are *interdependent*, such that neither enjoys any priority over the other.[4] (As we shall see, there are more radical departures from the traditional neo-Aristotelian conception than this.) There are, in addition, different views on what *makes* some trait a virtue, on the kind of trait a virtue *is*, on the relation of such traits to (the goodness of) states of affairs, and so on.[5]

There is another way in which virtue theory has a wide scope. Philosophers have begun to be interested in the possibility of virtue-theoretical approaches to *epistemology* and in particular have become concerned with parallel questions as to the nature of *intellectual* virtues (such as open-mindedness and intellectual courage),[6] and with how these might figure in the evaluation of *beliefs*. On these issues virtue epistemology appears to be even broader than its ethical counterpart, because when this kind of approach started to appear in the literature some twenty years ago, it was not modelled on the kind of Aristotelian lines common in virtue ethics; it took its cue instead from a more inclusive sense of virtue that has

---

[2] There is a need for qualification here, as one upshot of the revival of interest is that consequentialists and Kantians alike have sought ways in which their accounts can accommodate these kinds of criticisms. See, for instance, Korsgaard 1996, Baron 1997 and Driver 1998.

[3] This, for instance, is a plausible reading of Aristotle's view.

[4] See, for instance, McDowell 1997.

[5] For useful overviews of the many different types of virtue theory, see, for instance, Trianosky 1990, Montague 1992 and Slote 1997.

[6] Given that the revival in virtue ethics has followed broadly Aristotelian lines, it seems puzzling that it took a while for contemporary philosophers to pick up on the possibility of virtue epistemology; after all, Aristotle himself did not restrict his discussion to the moral virtues alone.

long been all but lost to antiquity. As a result, the focus was less on the (broadly, Aristotelian) virtues of the agent than on her "faculties." Here, for instance, is Ernest Sosa, who outlined an early and influential version of virtue epistemology that took this form:

> For example, it may be one's faculty of sight operating in good light that generates one's belief in the whiteness and roundness of a facing snowball. Is possession of such a faculty a "virtue"? Not in the narrow Aristotelian sense, of course, since it is no disposition to make deliberate choices. But there is a broader sense of "virtue," still Greek, in which anything with a function – natural or artificial – does have virtues. The eye does, after all, have its virtues, and so does a knife. And if we include grasping the truth about one's environment among the proper ends of a human being, then the faculty of sight would seem in a broad sense a virtue in human beings; and if grasping the truth is an intellectual matter then that virtue is also in a straightforward sense an intellectual virtue. (Sosa 1991, 271)

There are good reasons for this emphasis on the faculties rather than on the (Aristotelian) virtues, and they lie in the fact that despite the obvious analogies between ethics and epistemology, there are also some key disanalogies. For one thing, the focus in epistemology is on *beliefs* rather than *acts*, and although one can identify a sense of belief that can be modelled on the notion of an act (the state of acceptance is one possibility), when it comes to the most basic cases of belief that have long been the focus of epistemological debate, such as perceptual belief, they seem to be completely unlike acts, possessing a force and spontaneity that appears to exempt them from the realm of responsibility altogether. As Sosa puts the point, our perceptual faculties may be regarded as having, in one sense, their virtues, but since the beliefs that they generate are not typically the product of "deliberate choices," they cannot be easily thought of as *Aristotelian* virtues.

In any case, the early virtue-theoretic epistemological theories were turning to virtue theory primarily to meet certain problems that were facing the (naturalistically minded) process reliabilist accounts of justification and knowledge that are most often associated with Alvin Goldman (1986). The difficulty with these early reliabilist accounts was that they tended to cast the net too wide: they allowed reliable processes to count as knowledge conducive even though the reliability in question was clearly of the wrong sort. For example, an agent might form beliefs in a reliable fashion even though the reliability in question was due to the world for some reason tracking her beliefs rather than vice versa, or to her being the victim of a cognitive "malfunction" that nevertheless somehow manages to lead her reliably to form true beliefs.[7] The task set for early faculty-based virtue

---

[7] Greco (1999) discusses examples of both these sorts and explains how a faculty-based reliabilism (what he terms an "agent reliabilism") can meet the problems posed by these examples.

theories was thus to restrict the class of reliable processes relevant to knowledge in a principled way in order to meet these difficulties, and this was done by making stable cognitive dispositions of the agent central to the theory. In this way, for example, one could explain why it is important to knowledge possession that an agent's beliefs should reliably track the truth rather than vice versa, and why "malfunctions," even if as it happens they turn out to be reliable, were not knowledge conducive. In both cases the reliability at issue does not arise out of a stable cognitive disposition of the agent.

II

The most recent developments in moral and epistemic virtue theory have something very interesting in common: each would seem to involve a *rejection* of the general position upon which the revival of interest in the virtues was centred. Thus, epistemology has seen the re-emergence of an Aristotelian account of the intellectual virtues that marks a definitive break with the earlier faculty-based view, and a number of articles in this collection reflect this. Perhaps the most influential of these neo-Aristotelian views has been the one proposed by Linda Zagzebski (1996), who attempts to offer a unified account of both the moral and intellectual virtues. For Zagzebski, the "sub-personal" nature of the faculties at issue in the faculty-based virtue epistemologies makes them poor candidates to support genuine knowledge possession. Her claim is that we should focus instead upon that species of belief that can be modelled on action, and that can thus be understood as voluntary in the relevant manner (at least where the voluntary is distinguished from the intentional). In this way an Aristotelian account of the virtues is possible where agents are (in some sense) responsible for their virtues (and thus the lack of them), and are as a consequence also responsible for the products of those virtues (such as beliefs).

In her contribution to this collection, Zagzebski further argues that unless we interpret knowledge along these lines then it is unclear just what is valuable about the possession of knowledge, as opposed to merely true belief. In particular, she argues that the "machine-product" model that reliabilists (even faculty-based reliabilists) work with leaves it a mystery why we should value knowledge at all. After all, as she points out, the reliability of a machine (faculty) at producing a certain product (in this case true belief) does not add to the value of what is produced. Just as it makes no difference to the value of my espresso whether or not it comes from a reliable espresso maker, there is no reason to think that a true belief acquired via a reliable faculty should be any more valuable than one that isn't. In contrast, she argues that a fully fledged Aristotelian account of the moral and intellectual virtues can evade this problem, since on this account the good of knowledge is derived from the good of the intellectual virtues and they in turn are explicitly understood as "components of a life of flourishing" (p. 25).

Philip Percival responds to Zagzebski's paper by arguing (*inter alia*) that reliabilist views need not be committed to the supposedly problematic machine-product analogy in the way that Zagzebski claims, and as a result he maintains that there is a lacuna in her argument. Furthermore, he contends that even if this analogy is thought to hold in the problematic respects, it remains that her argument is inconclusive. For although it might be true of an espresso that its value is not improved by the value of the machine that produces it, this example is misleading because there are other products where the value of the machine used to produce the product *does* improve the product's value. He illustrates this point by offering the example of two identical books, one of which is more valuable than the other because it was produced on the world's first printing press.

Juli Eflin also takes issue with Zagzebski's proposal. Her claim is that what we should seek is a "pluralistic" and context-bound virtue-centred epistemology that takes the ultimate end of epistemological inquiry to be understanding. Eflin compares her view to a number of the main epistemological theories in the literature (both virtue and non-virtue based), and she argues that her account has a number of advantages over the more traditional views: (i) it is not hierarchical (in that there are no basic theoretical elements from which all else is derived); (ii) it is not complete, in that not "everything in the theory's domain is accounted for in terms of the basic concepts" (52); (iii) it is not concerned (in the main) with sceptical worries; (iv) it does not appeal to the notion of an "idealised knower" and hence does not ignore the context of particular individuals; and (v) it makes room for both rules or procedures and the epistemic virtues.

Andrew McGonigal argues, in his response, that the aims of traditional epistemology are misconstrued by Eflin and that as a result her case against traditional theories, insofar as it rests upon such a reading, is undermined. McGonigal points out, against (iii) and (iv), that traditional epistemology is *not* primarily concerned with refuting scepticism (at least not in the sense that Eflin alleges) and neither does it ignore the particular contexts in which knowers find themselves. He then proceeds to cast doubt upon Eflin's positive account, arguing that its appeal to rules *and* virtues suggests that pluralistic virtue epistemology *is* hierarchical and complete, and that this puts it in conflict with the theoretical virtue of simplicity.

Whereas Zagzebski emphasises the *voluntary* aspect of the epistemic act of belief, Christopher Hookway's main contention is that virtue theory can be employed to accommodate the psychological *immediacy* of belief (at least regarding certain subject matters), a property of belief that is often thought to imply that it is in a certain sense *in*voluntary. Hookway thus emphasises the role of our cognitive faculties in our acquisition of knowledge in a way that has more in common with the faculty-based view of Sosa than with Zagzebski's Aristotelian model. Nevertheless, his view is not a faculty-based version of virtue epistemology, for although he sees a close connection between our epistemic virtues and our cognitive skills,

© Metaphilosophy LLC and Blackwell Publishing Ltd. 2003

capacities and faculties, he clearly resists the suggestion that the epistemic virtues are *nothing but* such faculties.[8]

Hookway's aim in his article is to show how one can use virtue theory in order to model our acquisition of knowledge and justified belief in terms of a stable and reliable pattern of immediate *felt* responses to the relevant beliefs or propositions that need not involve conscious inference or even reflection. He sees in this account of knowledge and justification a way of responding to problems concerning scepticism and induction as well as a means to allow emotions to play a role in our epistemology which is analogous to the role that they play in ethics. In order to highlight and support his point, he offers the example of the character trait of being observant.

Marie McGinn responds to Hookway by querying his claim that the approach to the epistemic virtues that he advocates can offer us respite from the problem posed by the radical sceptic. In particular, she argues that by making our immediate emotional responses central to our epistemic assessment of beliefs we actually *exacerbate* the sceptical challenge rather than weaken it. As she puts it, "There is something prima facie perverse in trying to answer the philosophical sceptic by appeal to the essential role of emotional responses in our epistemic evaluations, in so far as we do not normally regard the emotions as having any special or privileged connection with veridicality" (101). More generally, the problem facing any account of the epistemic virtues that incorporates a pivotal role for involuntary emotional responses is to explain why we should regard an agent's involuntary responses as contributing to the epistemic status of that agent's beliefs at all.

The contrast between neo-Aristotelian virtue epistemologies and their faculty-based counterparts reappears in Duncan Pritchard's contribution to this volume. He traces the source of the contrast back to how these theories respond in different ways to the demand that knowledge should be incompatible with luck. Whilst faculty-based views focus on what he terms "veritic" luck, the neo-Aristotelian theories emphasise the need to eliminate "reflective" luck. The problem, Pritchard argues, is that one does not need a faculty-based theory in order to eliminate veritic luck, and there is no fully adequate way of eliminating reflective luck. In so far as it is the problem of epistemic luck, in both its guises, that is motivating the adoption of virtue epistemology, then the view is curiously ill-motivated.

The moral sphere has also been marked by a move away from recent tradition, although in this case it is neo-Aristotelianism that has been the default position. Perhaps the most influential figure here has been Michael Slote, who rejects a neo-Aristotelian account of the moral virtues as epistemically necessary (but not metaphysically sufficient) for right action, favouring instead a more radical agent-based account according to which

[8] Indeed, Hookway explicitly endorses an Aristotelian reading of the epistemic virtues, arguing that it is the virtues that "*guide* the use we make of our skills and capacities in carrying out inquiries effectively" (91; our italics).

the rightness of some action *consists in* the fact that it expresses a virtuous motivation. What is more, Slote appears to reject a neo-Aristotelian understanding of the virtues as components of *eudaimonia* or human flourishing, preferring instead to understand them as autonomously justified (because *intrinsically valuable*) character traits.[9]

In his contribution to this collection Slote takes an agent-based (or sentimentalist) virtue-ethical approach even further, and he shows in outline how it can apply in both the metaethical and normative realms. He argues that we can, by appealing to the motive of empathic caring, accommodate intuitions about the strength of our moral obligations. For instance, we intuitively feel that we have greater obligations to help those who are suffering now as opposed to (possibly a greater number of) people who will suffer in the future, and this can be explained if we invoke the fact that we are empathically sensitive to "temporal immediacy." In the same vein, Slote appeals to our empathic sensitivity to *causal* immediacy in order to show how a sentimentalist theory can capture deontological constraints on killing. Finally, he describes how we might appeal to empathic responses in order to "fix the reference" of our moral terms, resulting in an intuitively plausible sentimentalist account of the nature and meaning of moral judgements. Slote is thus optimistic about the prospects for a unified or integrated normative and metaethical sentimentalism.

In his response to Slote's article, Michael Brady raises doubts about each of these claims. He contends that Slote's agent-based standard of rightness needs to be qualified in order to be plausible but that this puts it in tension with Slote's sentimentalist metaethics. Furthermore, Brady questions whether our common-sense understanding of deontological constraints can really be captured by appeal to the kind of causal immediacy that Slote invokes, and finally whether Slote's account of moral judgements is ultimately as externalist as he claims.

III

Whereas the articles by Zagzebski, Eflin, Hookway, Pritchard and Slote all primarily deal with the general theoretical issues surrounding virtue-theoretic approaches to ethics and epistemology, the remaining articles in this collection focus upon how those theories can be applied to specific problems of both an epistemological and (broadly) ethical dimension.

Miranda Fricker's article brings to the fore the kind of issue regarding epistemic immediacy that Hookway examines in his essay, although this time in the context of a specific debate concerning how one should understand the epistemology of testimony. She uses virtue theory in order to evade an impasse common to debates concerning testimony between those who argue that testimony should only be accepted when one can adduce

---

[9] See Slote 2001.

grounds in its favour and those who maintain that, as a default position at least, such grounds are unnecessary. Like Hookway, Fricker sees the problem here as relating to how neither conception of testimony is able to accommodate how it could be that one can have an immediate, trusting and, in one sense at least, *groundless* response to testimony which is nevertheless a response that is the product of a stable and reliable sensitivity to the facts at issue. She offers a virtue-based account of what she terms our "testimonial sensibility" in order to meet this challenge. Furthermore, she argues that a general virtue-theoretic approach to testimony can also accommodate the less discussed *moral* dimension to testimony, such as occurs, for example, when agents are the victims of what she calls the "epistemic injustice" of not having their testimony taken seriously enough.

In her response to Fricker's article, Sandra Marshall points out that any account of a virtue of testimonial sensibility also needs to accommodate cases where the virtues come into conflict. She gives the example of loyalty in this regard, where such a virtue might demand trust even when one's testimonial sensibility would ordinarily dictate suspicion. Furthermore, she takes issue with Fricker's claim that agents can sometimes be in historical or cultural situations that prevent them from correcting their faulty responses to another's testimony, thereby leading to epistemic injustice.

A further application of virtue theory in the contemporary philosophical literature is to the field of jurisprudence, and the collection closes with an exchange on this topic from two of the leading figures working in this area. Lawrence Solum proposes and defends a virtue-centred theory of judging that has affinities to the agent-based model familiar from the work of Slote. The first part of Solum's article consists in his presentation of a "thick" account of the judicial vices and virtues, in order to identify the qualities necessary for someone to be a reliably good judge. These include temperance, courage, temperament, intelligence, wisdom and justice (all of which are qualified as *judicial* virtues). He then proceeds to explain and defend his virtue-centred theory, the central thesis of which is that lawful (or legally correct) decisions are defined in terms of the judicial virtues, and that justice is simply a matter of what the virtuous person would decide. Solum argues that this approach is in agreement with common sense concerning decisions that accord with legal rules (and, moreover, can explain and justify such decisions), and that it enjoys an advantage over other normative theories of judging in cases which require equity, that is, where legal rules clash with justice (as fairness). For Solum, equity as a practice requires equity as a virtue, and so is best accommodated in a judicial system by a virtue-centred theory of judging.

Antony Duff, whilst sympathetic to the idea that notions of virtue and vice have a contribution to make to theories of judging, remains sceptical about Solum's virtue-centred theory. Although he has some worries about the content of Solum's survey of the judicial virtues and vices – Duff argues that, *contra* Solum, avarice is not equivalent to corruption and nor is it the case that the corresponding virtue is temperance – his main criticism is that a virtue-centred account of judging is neither plausible nor proven. In support of the former, he argues that sometimes a decision which expresses a judge's corruption or vice can nevertheless be right, which is something that Solum is at pains to deny; in support of the latter, he claims that even though the virtues might be epistemically necessary for one to discern justice, Solum gives no argument for the more radical thesis that virtuous decisions make outcomes just. In any case, Duff thinks that this latter view is implausible on independent grounds: it is the salient features of the particular case, rather than her own virtuous nature, that a judge would appeal to in order to explain and justify her decision, in which case it will be these features, rather than her own virtues, that make her decision just (if it is).

Department of Philosophy
University of Stirling
Stirling FK9 4LA
United Kingdom
m.s.brady@stir.ac.uk
d.h.pritchard@stir.ac.uk

Acknowledgments

With the exception of the articles by Eflin and Pritchard and the responses by Brady and McGonigal, all of these articles were presented in an earlier form at a conference held at the University of Stirling in March 2002, entitled "Virtues: Moral and Epistemic." We would like to thank the following organisations for providing financial assistance for the conference: the Analysis Trust; Basil Blackwell; the British Academy; the Faculty of Arts and the Department of Philosophy at the University of Stirling; the Mind Association; and the Scots Philosophical Club. We would also like to thank all those at *Metaphilosophy* for their help in the preparation of this collection.

References

Baron, M. 1997. "Kantian Ethics." In *Three Methods of Ethics*, edited by M. Baron, P. Pettit and M. Slote, 3–91. Oxford: Basil Blackwell.
Baron, M., P. Pettit and M. Slote, editors. 1997. *Three Methods of Ethics*. Oxford: Basil Blackwell.
Crisp, R., and M. Slote, editors. 1997. *Virtue Ethics*. Oxford: Oxford University Press.
Driver, J. 1998. "The Virtues and Human Nature." In *How Should One Live?*, edited by R. Crisp, 111–30. Oxford: Oxford University Press.
Goldman, A. 1986. *Epistemology and Cognition*. Cambridge, Mass.: Harvard University Press.

Greco, J. 1999. "Agent Reliabilism." *Philosophical Perspectives* 13: 273–96.
Korsgaard, C. 1996. "From Duty and for the Sake of the Noble: Kant and Aristotle on Morally Good Action." In *Aristotle, Kant, and the Stoics*, edited by S. Engstrom and J. Whiting, 203–36. Cambridge, U.K.: Cambridge University Press.
McDowell, J. 1997. "Virtue and Reason." In *Virtue Ethics*, edited by R. Crisp and M. Slote, 141–62. Oxford: Oxford University Press.
Montague, P. 1992. "Virtue Ethics: A Qualified Success Story." *American Philosophical Quarterly* 29: 53–61.
Slote, M. 1997. "Agent-Based Virtue Ethics." In *Virtue Ethics*, edited by R. Crisp and M. Slote, 239–62. Oxford: Oxford University Press.
———. 2001. *Morals from Motives*. Oxford: Oxford University Press.
Sosa, E. 1991. *Knowledge in Perspective: Selected Essays in Epistemology*. Cambridge, U.K.: Cambridge University Press.
Trianosky, G. 1987. "Virtue, Action, and the Good Life." *Pacific Philosophical Quarterly* 68: 124–47.
———. 1990. "What Is Virtue Ethics All About?" *American Philosophical Quarterly* 27: 335–44.
Zagzebski, L. 1996. *Virtues of the Mind: An Inquiry into the Nature of Virtue and the Ethical Foundations of Knowledge*. Cambridge, U.K.: Cambridge University Press.

Select Bibliography of Virtue Epistemology

Note: The literature on virtue ethics is now so vast that it cannot be usefully summarised. What follows is thus a select bibliography of the main texts on virtue epistemology only.

Surveys and Introductions
Axtell, G. 1997. "Recent Work on Virtue Epistemology." *American Philosophical Quarterly* 34: 1–26.
Greco, J. 1992. "Virtue Epistemology." In *A Companion to Epistemology*, edited by J. Dancy and E. Sosa, 520–52. Oxford: Basil Blackwell.
———. 1999. "Virtue Epistemology." In *Stanford Encyclopædia of Philosophy*, http://plato.stanford.edu/entries/epistemology-virtue/.

Articles and Books
Axtell, G. 1998. "The Role of the Intellectual Virtues in the Reunification of Epistemology." *Monist* 81: 488–508.
Axtell, G., editor. 2000. *Knowledge, Belief and Character*. Lanham, Md.: Rowman and Littlefield.
Code, L. 1984. "Toward a 'Responsibilist' Epistemology." *Philosophy and Phenomenological Research* 44: 29–50.
———. 1987. *Epistemic Responsibility*. Hanover, N.H.: University Press of New England and Brown University Press.

DePaul, M., and L. Zagzebski, editors. 2002. *Intellectual Virtue: Perspectives from Ethics and Epistemology.* Oxford: Oxford University Press.

Fairweather, A., and L. Zagzebski, editors. 2001. *Virtue Epistemology: Essays on Epistemic Virtue and Responsibility.* Oxford: Oxford University Press.

Goldman, A. 1993. "Epistemic Folkways and Scientific Epistemology." *Philosophical Issues* 3: 271–84.

Greco, J. 1993. "Virtues and Vices of Virtue Epistemology." *Canadian Journal of Philosophy* 23: 413–32.

———. 1994. "Virtue Epistemology and the Relevant Sense of 'Relevant Possibility.'" *Southern Journal of Philosophy* 32: 61–77.

———. 1999. "Agent Reliabilism." *Philosophical Perspectives* 13: 273–96.

———. 2000. *Putting Skeptics in Their Place: The Nature of Skeptical Arguments and Their Role in Philosophical Inquiry.* Cambridge, U.K.: Cambridge University Press.

Hookway, C. 1994. "Cognitive Virtues and Epistemic Evaluations." *International Journal of Philosophical Studies* 2: 211–27.

Kvanvig, J. 1992. *The Intellectual Virtues and the Life of the Mind: On the Place of Virtues in Epistemology*: Savage, Md.: Rowman and Littlefield.

Montmarquet, J. 1987. "Epistemic Virtue." *Mind* 96: 487–97.

———. 1993. *Epistemic Virtue and Doxastic Responsibility.* Lanham, Md.: Rowman and Littlefield.

Plantinga, A. 1988. "Positive Epistemic Status and Proper Function." *Philosophical Perspectives* 2: 1–50.

———. 1993. *Warrant and Proper Function.* New York: Oxford University Press.

———. 1993. "Why We Need Proper Function." *Noûs* 27: 66–82.

Sosa, E. 1991. *Knowledge in Perspective: Selected Essays in Epistemology* Cambridge, U.K.: Cambridge University Press.

———. 1993. "Proper Functionalism and Virtue Epistemology." *Noûs* 27: 51–65.

Steup, M., editor. 2002. *Knowledge, Truth, and Duty: Essays on Epistemic Justification, Responsibility, and Virtue.* Oxford: Oxford University Press.

Zagzebski, L. 1996. *Virtues of the Mind: An Inquiry into the Nature of Virtue and the Ethical Foundations of Knowledge.* Cambridge, U.K.: Cambridge University Press.

———. 1997. "Virtue in Ethics and Epistemology." *American Catholic Philosophical Quarterly* 71: 1–17.

———. 1999. "What Is Knowledge?" In *Epistemology*, edited by J. Greco and E. Sosa, 92–116. Oxford: Basil Blackwell.

© Metaphilosophy LLC and Blackwell Publishing Ltd. 2003.
Published by Blackwell Publishing, 9600 Garsington Road, Oxford OX4 2DQ, UK and
350 Main Street, Malden, MA 02148, USA
METAPHILOSOPHY
Vol. 34, Nos. 1/2, January 2003
0026–1068

THE SEARCH FOR THE SOURCE OF EPISTEMIC GOOD

LINDA ZAGZEBSKI

ABSTRACT: Knowledge has almost always been treated as good, better than mere
true belief, but it is remarkably difficult to explain what it is about knowledge that
makes it better. I call this "the value problem." I have previously argued that most
forms of reliabilism cannot handle the value problem. In this article I argue that the
value problem is more general than a problem for reliabilism, infecting a host of
different theories, including some that are internalist. An additional problem is that
not all instances of true belief seem to be good on balance, so even if a given instance
of knowing *p* is better than merely truly believing *p*, not all instances of knowing will
be good enough to explain why knowledge has received so much attention in the
history of philosophy. The article aims to answer two questions: (1) What makes
knowing *p* better than merely truly believing *p*? The answer involves an exploration
of the connection between believing and the agency of the knower. Knowing is an act
in which the knower gets credit for achieving truth. (2) What makes some instances
of knowing good enough to make the investigation of knowledge worthy of so much
attention? The answer involves the connection between the good of believing truths
of certain kinds and a good life. In the best kinds of knowing, the knower not only
gets credit for getting the truth but also gets credit for getting a desirable truth. The
kind of value that makes knowledge a fitting object of extensive philosophical inquiry
is not independent of moral value and the wider values of a good life.

Keywords: epistemology, reliabilism, value, virtues.

Philosophers have traditionally regarded knowledge as a highly valuable
epistemic state, perhaps even one of the great goods of life. At a minimum,
it is thought to be more valuable than true belief. Contemporary proposals
on the nature of knowledge, however, make it difficult to understand why
knowledge is good enough to have received so much attention in the history
of philosophy. Some of the most common theories cannot even explain why
knowledge is better than true belief. I propose that the search for the source
of epistemic value reveals some constraints on the way knowledge can be
defined. I believe it will also show that the common view that epistemic
good is independent of moral good is largely an illusion.

1. What Makes Knowledge Better Than True Belief?

It is almost always taken for granted that knowledge is good, better than
true belief *simpliciter*, but it is remarkably difficult to explain what it is

about knowledge that makes it better. I call this "the value problem."[1] I have previously argued that most forms of reliabilism have a particularly hard time handling the value problem.[2] According to standard reliabilist models, knowledge is true belief that is the output of reliable belief-forming processes or faculties. But the reliability of the source of a belief cannot explain the difference in value between knowledge and true belief. One reason it cannot do so is that reliability per se has no value or disvalue. A reliable espresso maker is good because espresso is good. A reliable water-dripping faucet is not good because dripping water is not good. The good of the product makes the reliability of the source that produces it good, but the reliability of the source does not then give the product an additional boost of value. The liquid in this cup is not improved by the fact that it comes from a reliable espresso maker. If the espresso tastes good, it makes no difference if it comes from an unreliable machine. If the flower garden is beautiful, it makes no difference if it was planted by an unreliable gardener. If the book is fascinating, it makes no difference if it was written by an unreliable author. If the belief is true, it makes no difference if it comes from an unreliable belief-producing source.

This point applies to any source of a belief, whether it be a process, faculty, virtue, skill – any cause of belief whose value is thought to confer value on the true belief that is its product, and which is thought to confer value because of its reliability. If knowledge is true belief arising out of the exercise of good traits and skills, it cannot be the reliability of the agent's traits and skills that adds the value. Those traits or skills must be good for some reason that does not wholly derive from the good of the product they produce: true belief. As reliabilism has matured, the location of reliability has shifted from processes to faculties to agents.[3] There are advantages in this progression, but if the good-making feature of a belief-forming process or faculty or agent is only its reliability, then these versions of reliabilism all share the same problem; being the product of a reliable faculty or agent does not add value to the product.[4] Hence, if knowledge arises from something like intellectual virtue or intellectually virtuous acts, what makes an intellectual trait good, and hence a virtue, cannot be simply that

[1] For an exception to the almost universal view that knowledge is a better state than true belief, see Sartwell 1992. This move displaces the problem to that of identifying the value of true belief, which will be addressed in the second section.

[2] I mention the value problem briefly in Zagzebski 1996 and discuss it in some detail in Zagzebski 2000. Another version of the value problem is proposed in DePaul 2001.

[3] Sosa's earlier theory is what I call faculty reliabilism. Greco has a theory he calls agent reliabilism. In Greco 1999, he uses the term *agent reliabilism* for a class of theories beyond his own, including Sosa's, Plantinga's, and my early theory.

[4] On the other hand, reliabilists usually have particular faculties and properties of agents in mind, properties they call virtues, e.g., a good memory, keen eyesight, and well-developed powers of reasoning. The goodness of these virtues is not limited to their reliability, and so long as that is recognised, the theory has a way out of the value problem. But for the same reason, it is misleading to call these theories forms of reliabilism.

it reliably leads to true belief. This, then, is the first moral of the value problem: *Truth plus a reliable source of truth cannot explain the value of knowledge.*

It follows that there must be a value in the cause of a true belief that is independent of reliability or truth conduciveness, whether we call it virtue or something else. Suppose we succeed in identifying such a value. Is that sufficient to solve the value problem? Unfortunately, it is not, so long as we think of knowledge as the external product of a good cause. A cup of espresso is not made better by the fact that the machine that produces it is valuable, even when that value is independent of the value of good-tasting espresso. What the espresso analogy shows is not only that a reliable cause does not confer value on its effect but also that there is a general problem in attributing value to an effect because of its causes, even if the value of the cause is independent of the value of the effect. I am not suggesting that a cause can never confer value on its effect. Sometimes cause and effect have an internal connection, such as that between motive and act, which I shall discuss in a moment. My point is just that the value of a cause does not transfer to its effect automatically, and certainly not on the model of an effect as the output of the cause. So even if the cause of true belief has an independent value, that still does not tell us what makes knowledge better than true belief if knowledge is true belief that is good in some way other than its truth. The second moral of the value problem, then, is this: *Truth plus an independently valuable source cannot explain the value of knowledge.*

It follows from the second moral that to solve the value problem it is not enough to find another value in the course of analysing knowledge; one needs to find another value in the right place. Consider Alvin Plantinga's theory of warrant as proper function. A properly functioning machine does not confer value on its product any more than a reliable one does. The problem is not that proper function is not a good thing but that it is not a value in the knowing state itself. The first two morals of the value problem, then, reveal a deeper problem. We cannot explain what makes knowledge more valuable than true belief if we persist in using the machine-product model of belief that is so common in epistemological discourse.[5] Knowledge cannot be identified with the state of true belief that is the output of a valuable cause, whether or not the cause has a value independent of the value of true belief.[6]

In other work I have proposed that in a state of knowledge the agent gets to the truth because of the virtuous features of her belief-forming activity.[7] Wayne Riggs and John Greco's response to the value problem is

---

[5] The machine-product model has been used by Alston, Plantinga, Sosa, Goldman, and others. The word *output* is frequently used, and some of them illustrate their discussion with analogies of machines and their products.

[6] My colleague Wayne Riggs has thought of the location issue as a way out of the value problem. See Riggs 2002.

[7] Zagzebski 1996, part 3.

that the extra value of knowing in addition to true belief is the state of affairs of the epistemic agent's getting credit for the truth that is acquired.[8] Ernest Sosa's response to the value problem is similar. He says that in a state of knowing, the truth is attributable to the agent as his or her own doing.[9] These approaches clearly are similar, but they solve the value problem only if we reject the machine-product model of knowledge.[10] For the same reason that the espresso in a cup is not made better by the fact that it is produced by a reliable espresso maker or a properly functioning espresso maker, it does not get any better if the machine gets credit for producing the espresso. That is to say, the coffee in the cup does not taste any better.

The conclusion is that true belief arising from cognitive activity cannot be like espresso coming out of an espresso maker. Not only is the reliability of the machine insufficient to make the coffee in the cup any better; nothing about the machine makes the product any better. So if knowledge is true belief that is made better by something, knowledge cannot be the external product of the believer in the way the cup of espresso is the external product of the machine.

Let us look at the idea that knowing has something to do with the agent getting credit for the truth, that she gets to the truth because of something about her as a knowing agent – her virtues or virtuous acts. There are theoretical motives for this idea that have nothing to do with the value problem, such as the proposal that it avoids Gettier problems,[11] so it is supported by other constraints on the account of knowledge. But my concern in this article is the way this move can solve the value problem. If I am right that knowing is not an output of the agent, it must be a state of the agent. I am not suggesting that this is the only alternative to the machine-product model,[12] but if we think of a belief as part of the agent, the belief can get evaluative properties from features of the agent in the same way that acts get evaluative properties from the agent. In fact, the idea that in a state of knowing the agent gets credit for getting the truth suggests that her epistemic state is attached to her in the same way her acts

---

[8] See Riggs (1998) and Greco (forthcoming).

[9] See Sosa (forthcoming).

[10] So far as I can tell, Greco and Riggs reject the machine-product model, but Sosa uses it repeatedly, including in Sosa forthcoming, the article in which he proposes his way out of the value problem.

[11] I argued this in Zagzebski 1996. See also Riggs (1998) and Greco (forthcoming). DePaul 2001, note 7, argues that Gettier cases produce another form of the value problem, because we think that the value of the agent's epistemic state in Gettier cases is not as valuable as the state of knowledge.

[12] Another alternative is that knowledge is identified with the entire process culminating in the belief, and it gets value from the value in the process as well as the truth of the end product of the process. I have proposed that it would serve the purposes of Sosa's account of epistemic value to think of knowledge as an organic unity in the sense used by Franz Brentano and G. E. Moore. That would permit the value of the whole to exceed the value of the sum of the parts. See Zagzebski (forthcoming b). DePaul (2001, section 6) also discusses the possibility that knowledge is an organic unity.

© Metaphilosophy LLC and Blackwell Publishing Ltd. 2003

are attached to her. An act is not a product of an agent but is a part of the agent, and the agent gets credit or discredit for an act because of features of the agent. In particular, an agent gets credit for certain good features of an act, for example, its good consequences or the fact that it follows a moral principle – because of features of the act that derive directly from the agent – for example, its intention or its motive. If believing is like acting, we have a model for the way the agent can get credit for the truth of a belief because of features of the belief that derive from the agent. I propose, then, that this is the third moral of the value problem: *Knowing is related to the knower not as product to machine but as act to agent.*[13]

The value problem arises for a group of theories wider than those that are reliabilist or even externalist. Internalists generally do not think of a true belief as the product of what justifies it, and so they accept the first part of the third moral. Nonetheless, some of them are vulnerable to the first moral of the value problem because they analyse justification in such a way that its value is explained by its truth conduciveness. Laurence BonJour does this explicitly in the following passage:

> The basic role of justification is that of a *means* to truth, a more directly attainable mediating link between our subjective starting point and our objective goal. . . . If epistemic justification were not conducive to truth in this way, if finding epistemically justified beliefs did not substantially increase the likelihood of finding true ones, then epistemic justification would be irrelevant to our main cognitive goal and of dubious worth. It is only if we have some reason for thinking that epistemic justification constitutes a path to truth that we as cognitive beings have any motive for preferring epistemically justified beliefs to epistemically unjustified ones. Epistemic justification is therefore in the final analysis only an instrumental value, not an intrinsic one. (BonJour 1985, 7–8)[14]

Notice that in this passage BonJour understands the value of justification the same way the reliabilist does, as something that is good because it is truth conducive. The internality of justification has nothing to do with its value on BonJour's account. But as we have seen, if the feature that converts true belief into knowledge is good just because of its conduciveness to truth, we are left without an explanation of why knowing *p* is better than merely truly believing *p*. And this is the case whether or not that feature is accessible to the consciousness of the believer. BonJour does not appeal to the machine-product model, and so the problem in his case is more subtle than it is for the reliabilist. Nonetheless, the problem is there, because a true belief does not gain any additional good property from justification. In contrast, the traditional account of knowledge as justified true belief does not have the value problem, because the justifying beliefs do

---

[13] I explore the requirement of agency in knowledge in Zagzebski 2001.

[14] DePaul (1993, chap. 2) insightfully discusses the problem of BonJour and others in explaining the value of knowledge. I thank DePaul for bringing this passage to my attention.

not or do not simply produce the belief that is a candidate for knowledge. Instead, they give it a property, justifiedness. They make *it* justified. The conclusion is that if knowing *p* is better than truly believing *p*, there must be something other than the truth of *p* that *makes believing p better*. My proposal is that if believing is like acting, it can be made better by certain properties of the agent.

Consider a few of the ways an act acquires properties because of features of the agent. The class of acts subject to moral evaluation has traditionally been called the voluntary. A voluntary act is an act for which the agent gets credit or blame. The voluntary includes some acts that are intentional and some that are non-intentional. Acts that are voluntary but non-intentional can be motivated, and perhaps always are. My position is that acts of believing are generally in the category of acts that are voluntary but non-intentional, although for the purposes of this article it is not necessary that this position be accepted. What is important is just the idea that beliefs can be and perhaps typically are motivated, and that the motive can affect the evaluation of the belief in a way that is analogous to the way the motive can affect the evaluation of an overt act.

What I mean by a motive is an affective state that initiates and directs action. In my theory of emotion, a motive is an emotion that is operating to produce action. The appreciation for a value is an emotion that can initiate and direct action. When it does, it is a motive in the sense I mean. Acts motivated by appreciation of a value may not be intentional even when they are voluntary. My thesis is that, other things being equal, acts motivated by love of some value are highly valuable.[15]

As I analyse virtue, a motive disposition is a component of a virtue. A virtuous act is an act motivated by the motive of some virtue *V* and is characteristic of acts motivated by *V* in the circumstances in question.[16] An act can be compassionate, courageous, or generous, or unfair, cruel, and so on. The name of the virtue or vice out of which an act is done is typically given by the name of the motive out of which it is done, and the motive is a feature of the agent who performs the act. If believing is like acting, it can be virtuous or vicious. The properties of true believing that make it better than mere true believing are properties that it obtains from the agent in the same way good acts obtain evaluative properties from the

---

[15] I also think that acts motivated by love of some value are more valuable than those that *aim* at the same value but without the motive of love or appreciation for the value. So some nonintentional acts have moral value because they arise from a good motive. In contrast, some intentional acts may aim at a good end but have less value because they do not arise from a good motive. I discuss this in more detail in Zagzebski forthcoming a.

[16] In Zagzebski 1996 I distinguish a virtuous act from an act of virtue. Unlike the latter, a virtuous act need not be successful in its aim. I use *act of virtue* as a term of art to identify an act good in every respect. It is an act that arises out of a virtuous motive, is an act a virtuous person would characteristically do in the circumstances, is successful in reaching the aim of the virtuous motive, and does so because of the other virtuous features of the act.

© Metaphilosophy LLC and Blackwell Publishing Ltd. 2003

agent. In particular, a belief can acquire value from its motive, in addition to the value it may have in being true.

The idea that to know is to act is not very common these days, although it has a lot of precedent in philosophical history.[17] Sometimes the word *judge* is used to distinguish that which can be converted into knowledge from belief, which is commonly understood as a disposition or a passive state rather than as an act. I shall continue to use the word *believe* to refer to an act since I think it is an acceptable use of the term, but some readers might find the substitution of the word *judge* in what follows clearer.

What motives of the agent could make believing better? I have previously argued that it is motives that are forms of the basic motive of love of truth.[18] The motivational components of the individual intellectual virtues such as open-mindedness or intellectual fairness or intellectual thoroughness or caution differ, but they are all based on a general love or valuing of truth or a disvaluing of falsehood.[19] The motivational components of the intellectual virtues are probably more complex than this since, for example, intellectual fairness may consist in part in respect for others as well as in respect or love of truth.[20] But love of truth is plausibly the primary motive underlying a wide range of intellectual virtues.[21] If love of truth is a good motive, it would add value to the intellectual acts it motivates.

What sort of value does love of truth have? Assuming that if something is valuable it is also valuable to appreciate or love it, then love of true belief has value because true belief has value. But the motive of love of truth also derives value from distinctively moral motives. That is because moral permissibility, praise, and blame rest on epistemic permissibility, praise, and blame.[22]

Let me propose a condition for impermissibility. When something of moral importance is at stake when someone performs an act S, then if S is

---

[17] Aquinas and other medieval philosophers seem to have thought of knowing as involving an act of intellect. There may be passages in Plato that suggest this also. See Benson 2000, chap. 9.

[18] I argue this in Zagzebski 1996, part 2, and in more detail in Zagzebski forthcoming a.

[19] I have argued in Zagzebski forthcoming a that loving truth is not the same as hating falsehood, but I do not think the difference makes a difference to the point of this article.

[20] Respect, love, and appreciation in most contexts are quite different, but I do not think the differences make much of a difference in the context of an emotional attitude towards truth. Since most epistemologists do not think *any* emotional attitude towards truth makes any difference to epistemic status, it is quite enough to try to show that one of these attitudes makes a difference.

[21] Some intellectual virtues may aim at understanding rather than truth. I argue that epistemologists have generally neglected the value of understanding in Zagzebski 2001b§. See also Riggs forthcoming.

[22] The *locus classicus* for discussion of the connection between the moral permissibility of acts and the permissibility of beliefs is Clifford's article, "The Ethics of Belief." W. K. Clifford concludes that an unjustified belief is morally impermissible. See also Montmarquet 1993 for a good discussion of the relation between the permissibility of acts and beliefs.

a case of acting on a belief B, it is morally important that B be true. It is, therefore, impermissible for the agent to believe in a way that fails to respect the importance of the truth of B. That implies that the agent must believe out of certain motives. In particular, I suggest that the agent's motives must be such that they include a valuing of truth or, at a minimum, that they do not involve a disvaluing or neglect of truth.[23]

If moral blameworthiness rests on epistemic blameworthiness, then the same reasoning leads to the conclusion that moral praiseworthiness or credit rests on epistemic praiseworthiness or credit.[24] Suppose now that an act S is a case of acting on a belief B and that act S is an instance of an act type that is morally praiseworthy in the right conditions. I propose that act S is credited to the agent only if the truth of belief B is credited to the agent. So if knowing B is something like truly believing when the truth of B is credited to the agent, it follows that the agent gets moral credit for an act S based on belief B only if S knows B.[25]

Suppose also that I am right that there is a motivational requirement for getting credit for the truth that involves love of truth. It follows that the motive of love of truth is a requirement for love of moral goods, or at least is a requirement for love of those moral goods for which one gets praise or blame in one's acts. The praiseworthiness of love of truth is a condition for moral praiseworthiness. There is, therefore, a moral motive to have knowledge. The value that converts true believing into knowing is a condition for the moral value of acts that depend upon the belief.

In spite of the moral importance of having true beliefs, we usually think that true belief is good in itself. The value of true belief is a distinctively epistemic value that allegedly permits epistemologists to treat the domain of belief and knowledge as something independent of acts subject to moral evaluation. This brings us to the deeper value problem of knowledge: In what sense, if any, is true belief good? If true believing is not good, we

---

[23] The issue of what is involved in epistemic permissibility is a difficult one, because of the 'ought implies can' rule. But unless we are willing to say that no belief is impermissible, there must be some things we ought and ought not to believe, so the 'ought implies can' rule does not prohibit us from speaking of epistemic permissibility. I am not going to discuss the extent to which we can control each of our beliefs. My point is just that so long as we do think there are acts of belief that are impermissible, it follows that either we have whatever power over believing is intended in the 'ought implies can' rule or else the 'ought implies can' rule does not apply to these beliefs. In other words, I think the intuition that impermissibility applies in the realm of belief is stronger than the 'ought implies can' rule.

[24] Praiseworthiness differs somewhat from credit in most people's vocabulary, in that deserving praise is a stronger commendation than deserving credit. I think the difference is only one of degree and do not believe that much hangs on the difference.

[25] There is no doubt a variety of qualifications to be made here. For example, the agent generally gets credit of some kind for S even when B is false so long as her intellectual motive sufficiently respects the importance of the truth of B, she does what intellectually virtuous persons characteristically do in her circumstances, and her belief is only false because of her bad luck.

have a much more serious problem than that of finding the value that makes knowing better than true believing.

2. The Value of True Belief

I have been treating knowledge as something the knower earns. It is a state in which the prize of truth is credited to her; perhaps she is even deserving of praise for it. But why should we think that? I have already mentioned that this idea was developed because it avoids Gettier problems, but that objective is surely only a small part of the task of defining knowledge. Knowledge is worth discussing because it is worth having. But the fact that knowledge is valuable does not force us to think of it as something we earn or get credit for or are responsible for or praised for, although that way of looking at it follows from the sports analogies used in discussions of the value problem by Sosa, Greco, and Riggs, and from the analogy of winning a battle used by Michael DePaul.[26] They all treat knowledge as an achievement or points earned in a game rather than the blessings of good fortune. I think they are right about that, but it is worth mentioning that the fact that knowing is a valuable state does not force us to think of it in that way. Some goods are just as good if we do not have to work for them – for example, good health and a safe environment – and some may even be better if we do not have to work for them – for example, love and friend-ship. Good health, safety, love, and friendship are all good in the sense of the desirable. The sense of good that we earn or get credit for is the sense of good as the admirable. I have argued that if we think of knowing as being like acting, it is the sort of thing that can be virtuous or vicious, which is to say, admirable or reprehensible. Knowledge is admirable. But surely knowledge is also desirable because its primary component, true belief, is thought to be desirable. That is to say, we think that true belief is good *for* us.

True belief may be desirable, but it is certainly not admirable. It is not something for which we get credit or praise. That is, true belief by itself does not carry credit with it, although I have said that in cases of know-ing we get credit for the truth because of other features of the belief. The kind of value that makes knowing better than true believing is the admirable, whereas the kind of value true believing has is the desirable. But now we encounter a problem, because surely not all true beliefs are desirable. For one thing, many people have pointed out that some truths are trivial. This is a problem for the value of knowledge, because even if knowing a trivial truth is better than merely truly believing it, how much

---

[26] DePaul 2001, 179. DePaul also uses the example of a commercial for a financial insti-tution in which a pompous gentleman announces, "We make money the old-fashioned way: we earn it." The implication is that it is better to get money by working for it rather than by luck or inheritance. As DePaul points out, that implies that there is something valuable in addition to the money itself.

better can it be? There is only so much good that knowing a trivial truth can have. If it is fundamentally valueless to have a true belief about the number of times the word *the* is used in a McDonald's commercial, it is also valueless to know it. So even if trivial truths are believed in the most highly virtuous, skilful, rational, or justified way, the triviality of the truth makes the knowing of such truths trivial as well. The unavoidable conclusion is that some knowledge is not good for us. Some might even be bad for us. It can be bad for the agent and it can be bad for others – for example, knowing exactly what the surgeon is doing to my leg when he is removing a skin cancer; knowing the neighbour's private life. It follows that either not all knowledge is desirable or some true beliefs cannot be converted into knowledge.

A common response to this problem is to say that truth is conditionally valuable. It is not true belief per se that is valuable but having the answer to our questions. Our interests determine the difference between valuable true beliefs and nonvaluable or disvaluable ones. Sosa gives the example of counting grains of sand on the beach. He says that we do not think that believing the outcome of such a count has value, because it does not serve any of our interests.[27] But, of course, somebody *might* be interested in the number of grains of sand on the beach, yet it seems to me that knowing the count does not get any better if he is. If a truth is trivial, believing it is not improved by the fact that the epistemic agent has peculiar or perverse interests. In fact, the interests may even make it worse, because we add the perversity of the interests to the triviality of the truth.[28]

Perhaps we can appeal to the idea of importance to save the intuition that our interests and goals have something to do with the truths that are valuable to us, by making the value more significant.[29] Maybe some things are just important *simpliciter*, where that means there are truths whose importance is not reducible to what is important to so-and-so. Perhaps there are degrees of distance from the individual in the concept of importance, where some things are important to people in a certain role or in a certain society, and some are important to everybody. But I don't think this move will help us. There are no important 'truths' if a truth is a true proposition, since propositions are not important in themselves, and if truth is a property of propositions, truth is not what is important. Instead, it is the state of truly believing the proposition that is important. So when we say that some truths are important and others are not, what we really mean is that some true *beliefs* are important and others are not. And then to say this means no more than that the value of true beliefs varies. But we already knew that. What we want to know is what makes them vary. The idea of

---

[27] See Sosa 2001.
[28] In addition to Sosa, Christopher Stephens uses our interests as a way to resolve the problem of the two values – getting truth and avoiding falsehood. Goldman 2001 identifies interest as a value that unifies the epistemic virtues.
[29] This idea is briefly discussed by Riggs (forthcoming).

important true beliefs is just another way of posing the problem. It is not a solution to the problem.

Another form of conditional value is instrumental value. It has been argued that satisfaction of our desires or reaching our goals is what reason aims at. True belief is surely a means to reaching our ends, most of which are non-epistemic. A good example of this position is that of Richard Foley, who argues that the epistemic goal of truth is instrumentally valuable as a means to other goals, whose value is left undetermined.[30] Clearly, many true beliefs have instrumental value, but instrumental value is a form of conditional value, since the condition for the value of the means is the value of the end. If the end is disvaluable, so is the means.[31] Conditional value is like a suspected terrorist: someone who is a suspected terrorist may not be a terrorist, and a belief that has conditional value may not have value. No form of conditional value possessed by true belief has the consequence that all true beliefs are valuable.

There is still the possibility that true belief has intrinsic value. Perhaps every true belief has some intrinsic value simply in virtue of being true, whether or not it is good for us. That may well be the case, but I do not see that it will have the consequence that every true belief is valuable on balance, because intrinsicality is unrelated to degree. Intrinsicality pertains to the source of a belief, not to its amount. So even if every true belief has some intrinsic value, it is unlikely that the intrinsic value of every true belief is great enough to outweigh the undesirability or other negative value some true beliefs have from other sources.

The inescapable conclusion is that not every true belief is good, all things considered. Whether we are considering admirability or desirability, or an intrinsic or extrinsic source of value, on balance it is likely that there are some true beliefs that have no value and probably some that have negative value.

Now consider what follows for the value of knowing. In the first section I concluded that knowing is better than true believing only if it is true believing in which the agent gets credit for getting the truth. But if a given true belief is not valuable, how can the agent get credit for it if the truth in that case is not such that it is something someone should be given credit for? So long as some true beliefs are disvaluable, it makes just as much sense to say she is blamed for the truth as that she is praised for it. Assuming that every true belief is intrinsically good, it is good that the agent gets credited with the truth because of what is admirable about the agent's epistemic behaviour – her intellectually virtuous motives and acts. But the truth credited to her may not be much of a prize.

[30] See Foley 2001. Foley seems to be content with allowing the value of the goal to be set by the agent.
[31] A given means could serve more than one end. I would think that the value of a means in a particular case is determined by its end in that case. This is compatible with a means of that type having value when it serves some other end that is good.

Consider also what happens to my proposal that knowledge is better than true belief because it is a case in which the truth is reached by intellectually virtuous motives and acts, the value of which can be traced back to the value of the motive of valuing truth. But if the truth in some cases is not valuable on balance, why should we be motivated to value it? Of course, we are assuming that true belief has some intrinsic value, and we can also assume that true belief is usually good for us, in which case it is reasonable to think that it is good to value it *as* something with some intrinsic value, however slight, as well as something that is usually good for us. But if we are looking for a value that has the potential to be a significant good, we still have not found it.

What is more, so long as some true beliefs are not desirable, the agent's getting the truth can be credited to her even though the agent's getting a *desirable* truth is not credited to her. And even when the truth *is* desirable, it may be a matter of luck that she got a desirable truth rather than an undesirable one. I think this leads us into a problem parallel to the Gettier problem. Gettier cases arise when there is an accidental connection between the admirability of a belief and its truth. Similarly, it is possible that there is an accidental connection between the admirability of a belief and its desirability. I think it is too strong to deny such cases the label of knowledge; nonetheless, they are not as good as they can be. They are not the best instances of knowledge, not the ones that are great goods. The solution to Gettier cases is to close the gap between the admirability of a belief and its truth. The solution to the new value problem is to close the gap between the admirability of a true belief and its desirability. To get a truly interesting value in knowledge, therefore, it should turn out that in some cases of knowing, not only is the truth of the belief credited to the agent but the desirability of the true belief is also credited to the agent. This is a general formula that can be filled out in different ways, just as the formula for the definition of knowledge can be filled out in different ways, depending upon the theorist's conception of credit, and that in turn depends upon a general theory of agent evaluation. In the next section I shall outline the contours of a virtue-theoretic account of knowledge that satisfies the constraints identified in the first two sections of the article.

3. Knowledge, Motives, and *Eudaimonia*

I have claimed that good motives add value to the acts they motivate, and this includes epistemic acts. Motives are complex, and I have not investigated them very far in this article, but a feature of motives that is relevant to our present concern is that they themselves are often motivated by higher-order motives. Higher-order motives are important because they keep our motivational structure compact and aid us in making first-order motives consistent. If good motives can confer value on the acts they motivate, it follows that higher-order motives can confer value on the lower-order motives they motivate the agent to acquire. As we are looking for an additional source of value in some cases of knowledge, it is reasonable to look at the source of the value of the motive of true believing in the particular cases of knowing that are more valuable than ordinary knowing.

We have already seen at least two ways in which the valuing of truth in particular cases is required by other things we value. That is, we have a motive to have the motive for truth because of other good motives. First, if something of moral importance is at stake when we perform an act and that act depends upon the truth of a certain belief, then it is morally important that the belief be true. The motive for true belief in such cases is motivated by the higher-order motive to be moral or to live a good life. Second, since true belief is a means to most practical ends, the motive to value truth in some domain is motivated by the motive of valuing those ends, which is in turn motivated by the desire to have a good life. I propose that the higher-order motive to have a good life includes the motive to have certain other motives, including the motive to value truth in certain domains. The higher-order motive motivates the agent to have the motives that are constituents of the moral and intellectual virtues, and in this way it connects the moral and intellectual virtues together. If knowledge is true belief credited to the agent because of its place in her motivational structure, it gets value not only from the truth motive but also from the higher-order motive that motivates the agent to value truth in some domain or on some occasion. And that motive has nothing to do with epistemic value in particular; it is a component of the motive to live a good life.

My proposal, then, is this. An epistemic agent gets credit for getting a true belief when she arrives at a true belief because of her virtuous intellectual acts motivated by a love of truth. She gets credit for getting a desirable true belief when she arrives at a desirable true belief because of acts motivated by love of true beliefs that are components of a good life. The motive for desirable true beliefs is not the full explanation for the agent's getting credit for acquiring a desirable true belief, for the same reason that the motive for true belief is not the full explanation for the agent's getting credit for acquiring a true belief, but my position is that motives are primary causes of the other valuable features of cognitive activity. When the agent succeeds in getting a desirable true belief because of her admirable intellectual motives, there is a non-accidental connection between the admirability of a belief and its desirability. That connection avoids the parallel to Gettier problems that I mentioned above, and it results in some instances of knowledge being a great good.

Let me review the various ways a belief can be good.

(1) All true beliefs probably have some intrinsic value simply in virtue of being true whether or not they are good for us. When the truth is credited to the agent, the belief is also admirable. That is knowledge.

© Metaphilosophy LLC and Blackwell Publishing Ltd. 2003

(2) Some true beliefs are good for us; they are desirable. They can be desirable whether or not they are admirable. But some true beliefs are undesirable. It is also possible that some false beliefs are desirable, but I have not discussed those cases in this article.

(3) Admirable beliefs are those that are virtuous. Admirable beliefs can be false.

(4) Some true beliefs are both desirable and admirable. The most interesting cases are those in which there is a connection between their admirability and their desirability. A belief is admirable, and given its admirability, it is no accident that the agent has a desirable true belief. These are the most highly valuable instances of knowledge.

The problems we have encountered with the value of true belief indicate, I think, that the standard approach to identifying the value of knowledge is the wrong way round. The issue should be not what is added to true belief to make it valuable enough to be knowledge but what is added to virtuous believing to make it knowledge. And, of course, the answer to that question is obvious: It must be true. When we approach the value problem in this way, the harder question is answered first and the easier one second. That is not the usual order, but I think it is the right one. If we begin in the usual way, by starting with true belief, we are starting with something that may have no value of any kind, neither admirability nor desirability. Furthermore, by starting with the value of virtuous believing we can explain why even false virtuously motivated belief is admirable.

Let me conclude by briefly considering what makes virtue in general a good thing. Suppose that Aristotle is right in thinking of virtuous acts as components of *eudaimonia,* a life of flourishing. If I am also right that believing is a form of acting, it follows that virtuous believings are components of eudaimonia. Eudaimonia is a challenging concept to elucidate for many reasons, but one aspect that contemporary commentators find particularly troublesome is Aristotle's apparent idea that eudaimonia fuses the admirable with the desirable. Nobody disputes the conception of eudaimonia as a desirable life; in fact, eudaimonia is generally defined as a desirable life. It then has to be argued that virtuous – that is, admirable- activity is a component of the desirable life. And that, of course, is hotly disputed. The same problem arises over the value of knowing. Nobody is likely to dispute the claim that some true beliefs are desirable. What can be disputed is whether beliefs that are intellectually virtuous, either in the way I have described or in some other, are also components of a desirable life. The question Why should we want to have admirable beliefs? is really no different from the question Why should we want to do admirable acts? If virtuous acts are desirable, it is because it is more desirable to act in an admirable way. Similarly, if knowing a proposition is more desirable than truly believing it, it is because it is more desirable to believe in an admirable way. But I can see no way to defend that without a general account of eudaimonia, or a good life. That means that the debates currently going on in virtue ethics on the relation between virtuous activity and the good life are relevant to an understanding of an intellectually good life as well as to an understanding of a life that is good *simpliciter*.

4. Conclusion

The question What is knowledge? is not independent of the question Why do we value knowledge? For those who consider the former question prior, compare the pair of questions What is knowledge? and Can we get it? It is common for anti-sceptic naturalistic epistemologists to say that whatever knowledge is, it has to be defined as something we have. We are not interested in a non-existent phenomenon. I say that knowledge has to be defined as something we value. We are not interested in a phenomenon with little or no value. It is possible that no phenomenon roughly coinciding with what has traditionally been called knowledge has the value I have been looking for in this article. If so, we would have to move to an Error theory like that of J. L. Mackie in ethics. But I do not yet see that this will be necessary, since it is possible to give an account of knowledge that both satisfies the usual contemporary constraints and identifies a phenomenon with interesting value. I also think we should conclude that if knowledge is a state worthy of the sustained attention it has received throughout the history of philosophy, it is because its value goes well beyond the epistemic value of truth and what conduces to true belief. Knowledge is important because it is intimately connected to moral value and the wider values of a good life. It is very unlikely that epistemic value in any interesting sense is autonomous.

Department of Philosophy
University of Oklahoma
455 W. Lindsey, Room 605
Norman, OK 73019
USA
lzagzebski@ou.edu

Acknowledgements

I thank Philip Percival, my commentator at the conference at the University of Stirling, for his interesting and helpful comments. Earlier versions of this article were presented at the University of California, Riverside, Tulane University, the University of Oklahoma, and the Eastern Division Meetings of the American Philosophical Association, December 2001. I thank the audiences at those presentations. Particular thanks go to my commentator at the APA session, Michael DePaul, for his help in improving the article.

References

Benson, Hugh. 2000. *Socratic Wisdom*. Oxford: Oxford University Press.

BonJour, Laurence. 1985. *The Structure of Empirical Knowledge*. Cambridge, Mass.: Harvard University Press.

DePaul, Michael. 1993. *Balance and Refinement*. New York: Routledge.

————. 2001. "Value Monism in Epistemology." In *Knowledge, Truth, and Duty*, edited by Matthias Steup. Oxford: Oxford University Press.

Foley, Richard. 2001. "The Foundational Role of Epistemology in a General Theory of Rationality." In *Virtue Epistemology: Essays on Epistemic Virtue and Responsibility*, edited by Abrol Fairweather and Linda Zagzebski. Oxford: Oxford University Press.

Goldman, Alvin. 2001. "The Unity of the Epistemic Virtues." In *Virtue Epistemology: Essays on Epistemic Virtue and Responsibility*, edited by Abrol Fairweather and Linda Zagzebski. Oxford: Oxford University Press.

Greco, John. 1999. "Agent Reliabilism." *Philosophical Perspectives* 13: 273–96.

————. Forthcoming. "Knowledge as Credit for True Belief." In *Intellectual Virtue: Perspectives from Ethics and Epistemology*, edited by Michael DePaul and Linda Zagzebski. Oxford: Oxford University Press.

Montmarquet, James. 1993. *Epistemic Virtue and Doxastic Responsibility*. Lanham, Md.: Rowman and Littlefield.

Riggs, Wayne. 1998. "What Are the 'Chances' of Being Justified?" *Monist* 81: 452–72.

————. 2002. "Reliability and the Value of Knowledge." *Philosophy and Phenomenological Research* 64, no. 1 (January): 79–96.

————. Forthcoming. "Understanding Virtue and the Virtue of Understanding." In *Intellectual Virtue: Perspectives from Ethics and Epistemology*, edited by Michael DePaul and Linda Zagzebski. Oxford: Oxford University Press.

Sartwell, Crispin. 1992. "Knowledge is Merely True Belief." *American Philosophical Quarterly* 28: 157–65.

Sosa, Ernest. 2001. "For the Love of Truth?" In *Virtue Epistemology: Essays on Epistemic Virtue and Responsibility*, edited by Abrol Fairweather and Linda Zagzebski. Oxford: Oxford University Press.

————. Forthcoming. "The Place of Truth in Epistemology." In *Intellectual Virtue: Perspectives from Ethics and Epistemology,* edited by Michael DePaul and Linda Zagzebski. Oxford: Oxford University Press.

Zagzebski, Linda. 1996. *Virtues of the Mind: An Inquiry into the Nature of Virtue and the Ethical Foundations of Knowledge*. Cambridge, U.K.: Cambridge University Press.

Zagzebski, Linda. 2000. "From Reliabilism to Virtue Epistemology." In *Knowledge, Belief, and Character*, edited by Guy Axtell. Lanham, Md.: Rowman and Littlefield.

―――. 2001a. "Must Knowers Be Agents?" In *Virtue Epistemology: Essays on Epistemic Virtue and Responsibility*, edited by Abrol Fairweather and Linda Zagzebski. Oxford: Oxford University Press.

―――. 2001b. "Recovering Understanding." In *Knowledge, Truth, and Obligation*, edited by Matthias Steup. Oxford: Oxford University Press.

―――. Forthcoming a. "Intellectual Motivation and the Good of Truth." In *Intellectual Virtue: Perspectives from Ethics and Epistemology*, edited by Michael DePaul and Linda Zagzebski. Oxford: Oxford University Press.

―――. Forthcoming b. "Epistemic Value Monism." In *Sosa and His Critics*, edited by John Greco. Oxford: Basil Blackwell.

© Metaphilosophy LLC and Blackwell Publishing Ltd. 2003.
Published by Blackwell Publishing, 9600 Garsington Road, Oxford OX4 2DQ, UK and
350 Main Street, Malden, MA 02148, USA
METAPHILOSOPHY
Vol. 34, Nos. 1/2, January 2003
0026–1068

THE PURSUIT OF EPISTEMIC GOOD

PHILIP PERCIVAL

ABSTRACT: *Pace* Zagzebski, there is no route from the value of knowledge to
a non-reliabilist virtue-theoretic epistemology. Her discussion of the value problem is marred by an uncritical and confused employment of the notion of a "state"
of knowledge, an uncritical acceptance of a "knowledge-belief" identity thesis,
and an incoherent presumption that the widely held thought that knowledge is
more valuable than true belief amounts to the view that knowledge is a state of true
belief having an intrinsic property which a state of "mere" true belief lacks. Her
arguments against a "machine-product" conception of knowledge are undermined
by these flaws, while the alternative "agent-act" model she recommends is unat-
tractive, at odds with the knowledge-belief identity thesis she favours, and no solution to the problem of the value of knowledge she poses. I end with the observation
that her version of virtue-theoretic epistemology points in the direction of cognitive decision-theoretic norms, and I briefly discuss the bearing of this fact upon her
viewpoint.

Keywords: belief, cognitive-decision theory, epistemic value, intrinsic property,
knowledge, reliabilism, state of mind, virtue-theoretic epistemology.

The "epistemic good" whose source Linda Zagzebski searches for is the
value of knowledge. Her investigation is premised upon two specific
claims about this value. The first is relative: knowledge is more valuable
than (mere) true belief. The second is absolute: knowledge is *especially*
valuable. She draws two main conclusions: a virtue epistemology according to which the absolute value of knowledge is the value of those intellectually virtuous true beliefs the truth of which is explained (at least in
part) by their virtuousness, and a non-reliabilist claim that this value
derives from the value of moral virtue and the good life.[1] Her argument is
abductive: the explanandum is the value of knowledge, and the explanans
is non-reliabilist virtue-theoretic epistemology and the neo-Aristotelian
account of the value of intellectually virtuous true belief. It is rich and
stimulating.

[1] Zagzebski's virtue epistemology is "non-reliabilist" in so far as it denies that the intellectual virtues have a reliabilist analysis. For more on the distinction between reliabilist and
non-reliabilist virtue theories, see Dancy (1995, 78–83), and the editor's introduction to
Axtell 2000.

Formally, the relative value of knowledge could be accounted for without accounting for the absolute value of knowledge. One might identify something the value of which enhances any value that true belief has in its absence, without identifying something the value of which combines with the value of true belief to yield the absolute value of knowledge. The key to Zagzebski's own explanation of the relative value of knowledge in the first section of her article is that "a [*true*] belief can get evaluative properties from features of the agent in the same way that acts get evaluative properties from the agent [*via motives*]" (15, my italics). Since specifying a motive the value of which might be inherited by true belief says nothing as to the motive's absolute value, and hence nothing as to whether its transfer to belief explains the absolute value of knowledge, the sectional structure of her article tempts one to read her argument in two stages, whereby the two conclusions (non-reliabilist virtue-theoretic epistemology and the link intellectual virtue bears to a morally virtuous and good life) are drawn successively from the two premises – the specific claims regarding the relative and the absolute value of knowledge.

But this reading cannot be sustained. Zagzebski's explanation of the relative value of knowledge in the first section already involves a connection between intellectual and moral virtue. Her explanation is preceded by an anti-reliabilist negative moral: whatever the supplementary ingredient X that converts true belief into knowledge, X's value must go beyond any instrumental value that accrues to X merely on account of its generating true beliefs. But as Zagzebski herself observes, this moral can be applied equally well to her own version of virtue-theoretic epistemology: a valuable motive can account for the relative value of knowledge only if it has a value that goes beyond any instrumental value it has as a means to true beliefs.[2] This observation leads her to suggest immediately that the (most general) motive in question – love of truth – is valuable not just as a means to true belief, but as a precondition of *moral* virtue: "There is, therefore, a moral motive to have knowledge. The value that converts true believing into knowing is a condition for the moral value of acts that depend upon the belief" (19). Thus, her subsequent reflection on the absolute value of knowledge (via a discussion of the absolute value of true belief) in the second section merely attempts to develop and consolidate a connection between intellectual and moral virtue that is already prominent in her discussion of the relative value of knowledge in the first section.

---

[2] Cf. Zagzebski's remark that "[b]eing the product of a reliable faculty or agent does not add value to the product. Hence, if knowledge arises from something like intellectual virtue or intellectually virtuous acts, what makes an intellectual trait good, and hence a virtue, cannot be simply that it reliably leads to true belief" (13–14).

1. The Value Problem

1.1. Zagzebski calls the difficulty of explaining what makes knowledge better than true belief "the value problem." The nature of this problem depends on whether or not a state of knowledge is identical to a state of belief meeting certain non-trivial conditions. If it is not, as, for example, Timothy Williamson (2000, chaps. 1–3) argues, the problem is one of explaining how one thing, knowledge, is better than something entirely different, (true) belief. If it is, the problem is one of explaining how, among the true believings that *p*, those that are knowings that *p* are better than the rest. Exclusively, Zagzebski's discussion is in keeping with the second alternative. So it is best read as a discussion not of the value problem as such but of the constraints this problem imposes on the thesis that a state of knowledge is identical to a state of belief meeting certain non-trivial conditions.

Call the thesis that this identity holds the "knowledge-belief identity thesis." The weight Zagzebski places upon this thesis is evident in her claim that the relative value of knowledge obliges the rejection of a "machine-product" model of knowledge and favours what I shall call an "agent-act" model. The former holds that "knowledge [*is*] *identified with the state of true belief* that is the output of a valuable cause [*that stands to it as a machine stands to its product*]" (14, my italics). The latter holds that "[k]nowing is . . . related to the knower . . . as act to agent" (16), in that "the properties of true believing [*amounting to knowledge*] that make *it* better than *mere* true believing are properties that it obtains from the agent in the same way good acts obtain evaluative properties from the agent" (17, my italics). The knowledge-belief identity thesis is, therefore, built into both of the models of knowledge she discusses in the context of the value problem.

1.2. Zagzebski's focus upon the knowledge-belief identity thesis does not merely limit the scope of her discussion. It distorts her results. Her attack upon the machine-product model of knowledge is taken to be an attack upon "some of the most common [contemporary] theories [of knowledge]." In particular, it is taken to encompass Alvin Plantinga's theory that "proper function" converts true belief into knowledge. But whether or not Zagzebski's exegesis of Plantinga is correct, for two reasons it is tendentious to dismiss the theory that proper function converts true belief into knowledge on the grounds that "[a] properly functioning machine does not confer value on its product any more than a reliable one does" (14).

Firstly, whatever Plantinga's own view, the theory that proper function converts true belief into knowledge is no more committed to the knowledge-belief identity thesis – or, hence, to the machine-product model of knowledge – than is agent reliabilism obliged to choose between this model and Zagzebski's agent-act alternative. Zagzebski herself proposes that agent reliabilism might pursue a third alternative, whereby "knowledge is identified with the entire process culminating in the belief, and [*is held to*] get value from the value in the process as well as the truth of the end product of the process" (footnote 12). Clearly, a similar alternative is available to the theory that proper function converts true belief into knowledge (and even to "standard" [process and faculty] reliabilism). Like agent reliabilism, it too might repudiate the knowledge-belief identity theory, and identify knowledge not with true belief (meeting certain conditions) but with "the entire process culminating in the belief."[3] Although Zagzebski writes as if switching focus from processes and faculties to the agent is obligatory if (what she takes to be) the deficiencies of the machine-product model are to be avoided, theories that focus on processes and faculties need not be committed to the knowledge-belief identity theory this model presupposes.

Secondly, while both standard reliabilism and the theory that proper function converts true belief into knowledge can "identify" knowledge with something without embracing the knowledge-belief identity thesis, they might also avoid any deficiencies of the machine-product model by declining to "identify" knowledge with anything. Whatever the merits of Zagzebski's exegesis, these epistemologies have been developed within a tradition seeking an *analysis* of knowledge. But analysis is not metaphysics. Primarily, it seeks non-trivial necessary and sufficient conditions for an attribution of knowledge, not the identity of any "state" of knowledge. When Zagzebski writes that the problem with Plantinga's theory is "not that proper function is not a good thing but that it is not a value in the knowing state itself" (14), she relies on presuppositions about the metaphysics of knowledge that traditional analyses of knowledge simply bypass. An analysis of knowledge in terms of belief and proper function need have nothing to say about any "knowing *state*." Nor, even, need it be committed to an ontology of states, or to the supposition that knowledge is a state. It simply gives necessary and sufficient conditions for knowledge attributions by means of some such traditional clause as "for agents x and propositions p, x knows that p iff x believes that p, and p is true, and . . ." Nor can Zagzebski's uncritical preoccupation with the knowledge-belief identity thesis be defended by supposing that her concern is simply to investigate constraints that the value of knowledge imposes on theories regarding the identity of the knowledge state. Her concern with the *analysis* of knowledge is explicit when she introduces Plantinga's theory with the observation that "it is not enough to find another value [*in addition to the value of true belief*] in the course of *analysing* knowledge; one needs to find another value in the right place" (14, my italics).

---

[3] On such a view, knowledge *entails* belief even though it is not a state identical to a state of true belief meeting certain conditions.

1.3. Still, let us follow Zagzebski in supposing that knowledge and true belief are states. She claims that the machine-product account of the relationship between these states cannot accommodate the relative value of knowledge: a state of knowledge cannot be a state of true belief that is produced by a machine that is valuable in certain respects, because the value of a machine does not transfer to its products. Her argument for this claim is provided by the "espresso analogy": "A cup of espresso is not made better by the fact that the machine that produces it is valuable, even when that value is independent of the value of good-tasting espresso" (14). She takes this much to show that "the value of a cause does not transfer to its effect automatically, and certainly not on the model of an effect as the output of the cause" (14).

In some respects the espresso analogy is misleading. Ordinarily, "[i]f the espresso tastes good, it makes no difference if it comes from an unreliable [*or otherwise non-valuable*] machine" (13, my italics). But "it makes no difference" only because, ordinarily, the value of an espresso is determined by its taste.[4] Once other values are envisaged, so that the possibility genuinely arises that the product might be valuable in respects other than those for which it is ordinarily valued and designed, the claim that the value of the machine cannot affect the value of the product is false. This printing press is a physical duplicate of that one, but it is more valuable: it is the first printing press. This book is a physical duplicate of that one, but it is more valuable: it was manufactured on the first printing press. Accordingly, when Zagzebski makes a claim about belief parallel to the one she makes about espresso, she begs the question. She writes that "[i]f the belief is true, it makes no difference if it comes from an unreliable [*or otherwise non-valuable*] belief-producing source" (13, my italics). But while it is obvious that "it makes no difference" to the value of the belief *in point of truth*, whether it makes any difference in any other respect is the issue to be addressed.

1.4. Zagzebski's hostility to the machine-product model of knowledge is made all the more puzzling by her suggestion that the value problem is best solved by identifying a *cause* of true belief – a motive – the value of which *is* transferred to its effect. What is the difference between the two kinds of cause on account of which the value of one, but not of the other, transfers to its effect? Zagzebski makes two remarks by way of answering this question. Firstly, the connection between cause and effect is said to be "external" in the case of machine and product but "internal" in the case of motive and act (14–15). Secondly, a "product" is said to be a mere "output" of the machine, whereas an act is "part" of the agent of whose motive it is an

---

⁴ Cf. Zagzebski's remark that "the espresso in a cup is not made better by the fact that it is produced by a reliable espresso maker or a properly functioning espresso maker . . . [or by an espresso maker that] gets credit for producing the espresso. That is to say, the coffee in the cup does not taste any better" (15).

effect (16). But these remarks are little more than gestures. She gives no guidance as to *how* an "internal" connection between motive and act, or a "part-whole" relationship between act and agent, can result in the value of a motive being transferred to its effect.

The idea that motive and act are connected "internally" might be construed as some such conceptual claim as: for some *G*, whether an entity *x* is describable as an act of *G*-ing is sensitive to a cause of *x* that is a motive. But a conceptual claim of this kind cannot sustain the contrast Zagzebski draws between causes that are motives and causes that are not. For whether an entity *x* is describable as (for example) "being printed on the first printing press" is likewise sensitive to a cause of *x* which is *not* a motive.[5] Alternatively, then, her idea might be construed as some such metaphysical claim as: for some (particular) act *x*, the motive of *x* is an *F*-property of *x*, whereas for no non-act *y* is the cause of *y* an *F*-property of *y*. But what might *F* be? At various junctures Zagzebski suggests that an explanation of why true belief amounting to knowledge is more valuable than mere true belief must identify a property of true belief, but that the machine-product model of knowledge fails this test.[6] Yet in one good sense of "property," being the effect of a valuable cause *is* a property of (for example) a cup of coffee brewed on a reliable espresso machine. She must, therefore, have some narrower sense of "property" in mind, one by which we should be guided when giving substance to *F*. But what sense can this be?

Intuitively, the intrinsic properties of an entity are more intimately related to it than are its extrinsic properties. Still, it won't do to interpret *F* directly as "intrinsic." It is hard to see how one of an entity's intrinsic properties can be a cause of it. That much seems like self-causation, and Zagzebski herself emphasises that motives are causes of acts. Rather, Zagzebski is better interpreted as holding that a cause that is a motive is distinguished from a cause that is not a motive by the fact that a motive can cause an act whose effect is to have an *intrinsic* property cognate with the motive: generosity causes acts that are *intrinsically* generous, courage causes acts that are intrinsically courageous, et cetera.[7] This interpretation

---

[5] Cf. my example in section 1.3 above.

[6] For example, she writes: "A properly functioning machine does not confer value on its product any more than a reliable one does. The problem is not that proper function is not a good thing but that it is not a value in the knowing state itself" (05).

[7] Although Zagzebski employs the term *intrinsic* in her subsequent discussion of the value of true belief in section 2, her so doing obscures more than clarifies the exegetical point at issue. Her concern is with the "intrinsic value" of true belief. But she does not assert that the *intrinsic* value of something must be grounded in its intrinsic *properties*, and in any case her concern is not with an intrinsic value possessed by some true beliefs – the ones amounting to knowledge – and not by others, but with the value of true belief as such. In other writings, however, she does seem to pursue the thought that a solution to the value problem must ground the additional value of knowledge in a property that is intrinsic to some true beliefs more explicitly. For example, Zagzebski remarks that "the fact that things

is promising, since there is little temptation to say as much of causes that are not motives. The effects of, for example, a reliable espresso machine do not have an intrinsic property cognate with "reliable." Although these effects are "reliably produced," the property of being reliably produced is not intrinsic to an effect that has it. The intrinsic properties of an entity are those it shares with its duplicates. But two products – two cups of espresso, two books – might be duplicates even though only one of them is the effect of a machine that is reliable.

Unfortunately, however, the idea that the properties of an act that are cognates of the act's motives are intrinsic to the act is implausible. Jones distributes alms: his motive is generosity. Smith distributes alms: his motive is sanctimoniousness. Does the difference in motive itself ensure that the two acts are not duplicates? Customary talk leads in either direction. In some circumstances it is natural to say that Jones and Smith performed the same (kind of) act, but that their motives were different. In others we might say that their acts were not the same (kind). Only theoretical considerations can warrant favouring the former alternative. But I doubt there are any. To be sure, as Zagzebski notes, we happily ascribe properties to acts that derive directly from motives, and our evaluation of acts is sensitive to such properties: we speak of an act being "generous," and we esteem it accordingly, et cetera. Yet there is nothing in this that *requires* us to postulate "acts" having *intrinsic* properties like "generous." Nor, even, are we obliged to take into account motives when evaluating acts. Of course, we esteem *something* more highly when we praise Jones's alms-giving as generous while condemning Smith's alms-giving as sanctimonious. But what we praise does not have to be the act itself. It can be Jones, via the estimableness of his motive. On this view, someone who praised Jones, and commended both his motive and his act conceived and categorised independently of his motive, would not thereby be failing to praise something – an act of which the motive is an intrinsic property – that is praiseworthy. For there is no such thing.

Moreover, there are theoretical considerations that work against the supposition that acts acquire cognate intrinsic properties from motives that cause them. Intuitively, disastrous well-intentioned acts are better dealt with if acts are conceived and categorised independently of motives. Two policemen enter what is, unbeknownst to them, a fancy-dress party, having received a complaint about the noise. A party-goer dressed as a hoodlum pulls a fake gun, thinking the policemen to be party-goers likewise in fancy dress. Protectively throwing himself in front of his partner, one of the policemen shoots the party-goer, who dies. Categorised dependently on motive, the policeman's act is quick-witted, professional, and heroic

and processes operate as designed may be a good thing, but it is a good extrinsic to the product. The product itself is neither better nor worse because it is the work of design . . . what proper functioning *consists in* is what is really valuable. *And that has to be something intrinsic* to the believer *or the belief*, not something extrinsic" (2000, 116–17, my italics).

(despite its disastrous consequences). Categorised independently of motive, it is disastrous and completely inappropriate (despite its motives). Both categorisations can yield the result that the party-goer ought not to have been shot dead. The former, however, yields it only by trading-off valuable intrinsic properties of the act against the badness of the act's consequences. And this is just the wrong way to think about such a case. There should be no trade-off. There is *nothing* to be said in favour of shooting dead a harmless party-goer in fancy dress. That he appears to threaten one's life is no more a reason to shoot him dead than is the fact that the poisoned water in the glass appears pure is a reason to drink it. These appearances might well be, respectively, the reasons the party-goer was shot and the water was drunk. But this is beside the point. As such, they are simply explanatory reasons, not normative ones. The policeman's motives were not reasons for his act *to be* performed that had to be balanced against reasons for not performing it. They were *explanatory* reasons that merely served to *mitigate* his act.

In any case, whatever the merits of Zagzebski's conception of acts, her text grates with the supposition that what allows motives to transfer their value to acts is that motive-cognate properties are intrinsic properties of acts. Under this supposition, her development of an "agent-act" model of knowledge has its origins in a requirement far removed from the value problem as originally presented. We were asked to account for the commonplace that knowledge is more valuable than true belief. But even if the knowledge-belief identity thesis is presupposed, this commonplace falls short of the requirement that we must account for a valuable *intrinsic* property that distinguishes true belief amounting to knowledge from mere true belief. A duplicate of X can be more valuable than X itself.[8] Moreover, supposing cognate properties of motives to be intrinsic properties of acts conflicts with Zagzebski's agent-act model of the knowledge-belief identity thesis. If Jones's alms-giving is not a duplicate of Smith's because it has an intrinsic property – being generous – that Smith's alms-giving lacks, and belief is analogous to, or even a species of, act, then, being motivated by intellectual virtue, Green's true belief that p, because it has an intrinsic property – being intellectually virtuous – that Brown's belief lacks is not a duplicate of Brown's differently motivated true belief that p. Similarly, if, as Zagzebski insists, Jones's alms-giving is an act different from Smith's alms-giving, Green's intellectually virtuous believing that p must be a state different from Brown's intellectually non-virtuous believing that p. But this feature is the opposite of what is required by her coupling of the agent-act version of the knowledge-belief identity thesis with virtue-theoretic episte-mology. By virtue-theoretic epistemology, Green knows that p.[9] By the

[8] See the printing press/book example in section 1.3 above.

[9] Zagzebski's account of knowledge requires more of true belief than mere intellectual virtuousness (see below, section 3). But this complication is irrelevant for the point at issue.

knowledge-belief identity thesis, the state of knowing he is in is identical to the state of believing truly that *p*. So, by the transitivity of identity, the state of knowing that *p* he is in is identical to the state *Brown* is in. For Brown too is in the state of believing truly that *p*.

1.5. If the suggestion that motives are "internally" related to acts cannot explain how, unlike causes that are not motives, motives transfer their value to their effects, what of Zagzebski's second suggestion? She says that "if we think of a belief as *part* of the agent, the belief can get evaluative properties from features of the agent in the same way that acts get evaluative properties from the agent" (15, my italics). This suggestion is obscured by the fact that her concern in the sentences that immediately follow this quotation is to illuminate not the way in which the value of a motive transfers to its effect but, rather, the way in which "an agent gets credit or discredit for an act." Indeed, this concern even takes centre stage, briefly, in her rationale for the agent-act model of knowledge. She writes that "the idea that in a state of knowing the agent gets credit for getting the truth suggests that her epistemic state is attached to her in the same way her acts are attached to her." But I think this digression is a red herring as far as the agent-act model of knowledge is concerned. After all, a coffee machine "gets credit" (so to speak) for producing coffee that tastes good. Relative to the agent-act model, it can only be heuristic to hypothesise that the distinction between true beliefs for which the agent gets credit and those for which he gets none runs parallel to the distinction between true belief amounting to knowledge and mere true belief. That hypothesis carries no independent weight in favour of the agent-act model. At best, it serves simply to suggest the model to the mind of an investigator seeking a solution to the value problem.

In effect, Zagzebski envisages a two-way transfer of value across the part-whole relation. An act, which is a "part" of an agent, can confer value on the agent, while the agent – or at any rate a "feature" of the agent – can confer value on an act that is one of his parts. However, although it is true that a part can confer value on the whole – the value of Jane's engagement ring goes up when one of its diamonds is replaced by an equally fine diamond that is larger – this fact is of no consequence to the value problem. And I don't see how the whole – or even a feature of the whole – can confer value on the part. The value of the larger diamond does not increase when the value of the ring increases because one of its garnets is replaced by a ruby.

1.6. So far, I have taken issue with the second and third morals Zagzebski draws from her discussion of the value problem. I have suggested *pace* the second moral that there is a straightforward sense in which a valuable "external" cause can confer value on its effect. And I have suggested *pace* the third moral that while there is also a sense in which a valuable "external" cause does not confer value on its effect, in the same sense a motive does not confer value on any act (or belief) it causes either. These morals concern the "location" a value must have if it is to account for the fact that knowledge is more valuable than belief. In contrast, Zagzebski's first moral concerns not the "location" of this value but its nature. Her first moral is that this value cannot be "reliability."

One reason Zagzebski gives in support of this moral is that "reliability per se has no value or disvalue" (13). Her point is that the property of reliably producing Q is valuable only in so far as Q is valuable. In particular, then, the property of reliably producing true belief is valuable only in so far as true belief is valuable. But so what? Why does Zagzebski take it for granted that this much has the consequence that reliability cannot account for the difference in value between knowledge and true belief? To be sure, it follows that the value of the property of reliably producing true belief, as such, cannot be greater than that of true belief. But it does not follow that the value of the property F in virtue of which some true belief that p is reliably produced cannot be greater than the value that that very belief has in virtue of being true. On the contrary, since the value of F derives from the value of all the true beliefs it will produce, or will potentially produce, this value will be greater than the value of any true belief it produces on some occasion. It follows that a "reliable source of truth" could explain a difference in value between *token* knowings that p, and token true believings that p. Of course, a difference in value between different tokens is not explicitly embodied in the presupposition with which we began: that knowledge is more valuable than true belief. But while the attractiveness of that presupposition is undeniable, its exact content is obscure. For all we know at the outset, it amounts to no more than the claim that, by and large, for all rational agents x and propositions p, x prefers his knowing that p to his merely believing that p truly. And this much reliabilism can accommodate in the manner shown.

1.7. To conclude this discussion of Zagzebski's treatment of the value problem, pursuit and examination of her strategy requires that much more attention be paid to the notion of "state" than she pays to it, or than I can pay to it here. But let me sketch an overview. To my mind, "states" are abstract entities akin to universals or natural kinds. As such, although states can have intrinsic properties, they cannot have them contingently. There is only one state of believing that grass is green, and one state of knowing that grass is green. Thus conceived, the state of knowing that p is no more identical to a state of believing truly that p than is the kind "animal" identical to the kind "mammal." Rather, the strongest connection that could exist between the two states is that knowledge is a "sub-state" of the state of believing truly. Interpreted in terms of "states" in this sense, then, the knowledge-belief identity thesis is trivially false.

This interpretation of the knowledge-belief identity thesis would be uncharitable, however. There are two interpretations that make this thesis more interesting. The first interprets it as being concerned with *token* states. The second, which I suspect is closer to what Zagzebski has in mind, interprets the thesis as being not about states *as such* but about states *of mind*. Clearly, the question as to whether the state of mind that is part of the state of knowing is identical to the state of mind that is part of the state of believing truly is not settled by the trite observation that the state of knowledge is no more identical to the state of believing truly than is the kind "mammal" identical to the kind "animal." This question has been answered, traditionally, in the affirmative: the state of mind involved in the state of knowing that *p* is identical to the state of mind that is involved in the state of believing truly that *p*. It is *this* part of the epistemological tradition that Timothy Williamson (2000, chapters 1–3) is concerned to reject.

It should be emphasised that it *is* charitable to read the knowledge-belief identity thesis Zagzebski presupposes as a thesis to the effect that the state of mind that is involved in knowledge that *p* is identical to the state of mind that is involved in (mere) believing truly that *p*. For whereas she is preoccupied exclusively with the relation between the "state" of knowing and the "state" of (mere) believing truly, it is obvious that believing truly is *not* a state of mind. Believing truly is a state only one component of which – believing – is a mental state.

2. The "Deeper" Value Problem

2.1. Zagzebski heralds the second section of her paper with the remark: "This brings us to the deeper value problem of knowledge: In what sense, if any, is true belief good? If true believing is not good, we have a much more serious problem than that of finding the value that makes knowing better than true believing" (19–20). But "more serious" for whom? This "deeper" value problem certainly engages reliabilism. If true believing has no value, true beliefs reliably produced can have neither more value than true believings not reliably produced nor the great absolute value knowledge possesses. But the implication of Zagzebski's evocation of the deeper value problem is that she deems it to threaten her own non-reliabilist epistemology too.[10] And yet, although the reliabilist is obliged by the absolute value of knowledge to explain the value of true belief, Zagzebski is not. A non-reliabilist virtue epistemology has the resources to explain the absolute value of knowledge irrespective of the value of true belief. Since

---

[10] This implication is strengthened when, concluding her reflections on the deeper value problem, she writes: "Consider also what happens to my proposal that knowledge is better than true belief because it is a case in which the truth is reached by intellectually virtuous motives and acts, the value of which can be traced back to the value of valuing truth. But if the truth in some cases is not valuable on balance, why should we be motivated to value it? ... *[I]f we are looking for a value that has the potential to be a significant good, we still have not found it*" (23, my italics).

such an epistemology holds that knowledge is true belief where "truth is reached by intellectually virtuous motives and acts" (23), knowledge is as valuable as is (the exercise of) intellectual virtue. And according to the non-reliabilist account of intellectual virtue Zagzebski insists on, the value of this virtue is not to be (entirely) explained in terms of the value of the true beliefs the virtue generates. It follows that the problem the absolute value of knowledge poses her non-reliabilist epistemology is not the problem of the absolute value of true belief but, rather, the problem of the absolute value of intellectual virtue. In focusing on the former at the expense of the latter, she is in danger of slipping into those reliabilist modes of thought she is concerned to repudiate.

Why then is Zagzebski preoccupied with the value of true belief? The answer lies in the re-emergence of a "knowledge-as-credit" thesis on the back of which her virtue epistemology was initially introduced. According to the knowledge-as-credit thesis, "knowledge is something the knower earns. It is a state in which the prize of truth is credited to her" (20). Virtue epistemology is introduced as an explanation of why this thesis is true: an agent who knows that p gets credit for having a true belief that p because of the admirability of the intellectual virtue which, in being a knower, he exercises in believing truly.[11] However, when, at the beginning of section 2, the knowledge-as-credit thesis once more displaces virtue epistemology on centre stage, the question "Why are some agents *credited* with true belief?" is approached from a different angle. It is addressed not by considering what it is that distinguishes those agents from true believers who are not credited but by considering what it is about true belief that makes *any* true believer worthy of credit. There is more than a switch of emphasis in the two approaches. They address the question under different interpretations. The first approach addresses the question under the interpretation "Why are *these* believers of truths credited, while *those* believers of truths are not credited?" The second approach addresses the question under the interpretation "Why are believers *of truths* credited, while those who do not believe truths are not credited?" In asking for a relevant difference among believers of truths to explain why some agents are credited with believing the truth, the first approach points (Zagzebski at least) in the direction of a non-reliabilist epistemology. But asking what it is about *true belief* that makes it appropriate to credit some agents with getting it suggests that the value of any intellectual virtue those agents exercise in pursuit of true belief is instrumental: it promotes valuable true beliefs. The second approach, therefore, points in the direction of a reliabilist epistemology.

2.3. Of course, while non-reliabilist virtue epistemology must give an account of the value of intellectual virtue that is independent of the value

[11] Cf. pp. 15–16.

of true belief, the fact remains that, at least in so far as it subscribes to the knowledge-belief identity thesis, it must also hold that knowledge is more valuable the more true belief is valuable. So whether or not a worry that true belief has no value is a problem for Zagzebski, it is in any case an issue in its own right. I think everything Zagzebski says on this score is neutral with respect to first-order epistemological theories. In particular, reliabilist non-virtue theorists can agree that true belief has some "intrinsic value," that some true beliefs are especially desirable in being "good for us," and that morally successful action requires true belief. Thereby, they are half-way to accepting Zagzebski's thesis that the most highly valued knowledge is both especially admirable and especially desirable. This thesis is attractive and, construed as an account of what the traditional view that knowledge is especially valuable is getting at, has the added attraction of reconciling this view with the fact that, often, knowledge is too easily acquired to be admirable, or is undesirable. Opponents of Zagzebski's epistemology who have already gone half-way to accepting this thesis might therefore wish to go the whole way. To do so, having already bought Zagzebski's view that some beliefs are especially desirable, they need only ground a distinction among true beliefs between those that are admirable and those that are not. But this distinction is easily drawn in the absence of any or all of virtue-theoretic epistemology, non-reliabilism, and the agent-act model of knowledge. An agent who develops some worthwhile physical skill as a result of years of practice is admirable in a way that someone to whom the skill is more innate is not. But this is so even if the skill is an "output" of the agent('s efforts), and it is the skill itself, rather than the agent who developed it, that is said, *when speaking loosely*, to be admirable.

2.4. An especially interesting idea that emerges from Zagzebski's reflection on the distinction between true beliefs that are desirable and those that are not is her thought that the reason that knowledge is *so* valuable is that "in some cases of knowing, not only is the truth of the belief credited to the agent but the desirability of the true belief is also credited to the agent" (23). In these cases, knowledge/true belief is said to be both "good as admirable" and "good as desirable," and two features are present that are both lacking in other cases: that the proposition known should be truly believed is especially desirable, and the agent gets credit not just for believing truly but for believing truly *an especially desirable proposition*. Zagzebski's idea is that cases in which an agent knows that *p* and meets the first condition without meeting the second run "parallel" to Gettier cases.

Unfortunately, Zagzebski does not give an example of the kind of case she has in mind. We are to envisage cases in which the truth of a true belief is credited to the agent, but not its desirability. How might such cases come about? One way in which they might do so would be for the agent's "love" of truth to be indifferent to *which* truths he believes. However, a case of this kind is disanalogous to Gettier cases. In a Gettier case the agent is beyond (reasonable) reproach. But an agent who is concerned to know truths while being indifferent to which truths he knows is not beyond reproach: his motivational structure leaves something to be desired. Accordingly, I think Zagzebski must have in mind a different sort of case. This is the case of an agent who, though concerned to have all and only desirable true beliefs, somehow acquires a desirable true belief, rather than an undesirable true belief, by accident.

How might such an accident come about? Consider an agent motivated beyond reproach, who chooses among the investigative procedures available the one that seems most likely to him to yield the most desirable true beliefs. It might happen that although the procedure he chooses does yield desirable true beliefs, it does not yield them for the reason he thinks. Here is an example of such a case. Suppose Jones discovers that there is a history of gene G in his family, and that there is a one-in-three chance that G has been passed to him. Having read all the right journals, it seems to Jones that G is debilitating in old age, but that the debilitating effects of G can be offset by a weekly injection. In these circumstances, Jones prefers suffering the weekly injection if the gene G has been passed on to him, but not suffering the injection if the gene has not been passed on. Jones therefore comes to believe that true belief as to whether or not he has gene G is desirable (for him). So he chooses an investigative procedure designed to establish whether he has the gene G, knowing that this procedure will establish some other facts about his genetic make-up he considers trifling. The procedure establishes that he has gene G, but it also establishes that he has the very rare gene G^*. Now, contemporary science is in fact about to show that gene G^* is not trifling but life threatening, although the threat can be averted by simple means. So procedure P has resulted in a true belief that is desirable to Jones – that he has gene G^*. But it has not resulted in the desirable true belief that Jones had wished for. It is undesirable to Jones that he truly believes that he has gene G. For while he is now obliged to suffer the weekly injection, the contemporary science is actually wrong: gene G is in fact harmless.

While this example might illustrate the sort of case Zagzebski has in mind, it has a feature that jars with things Zagzebski says and disrupts the analogy with Gettier cases. To the extent that belief that he has gene G^* is desirable to Jones, although it is accidental that he acquired *a* desirable true belief, there seems nothing accidental about the desirability to him of the belief *itself* that he has gene G^*. Yet Zagzebski speaks about "clos[ing] the gap between the admirability of a true belief and *its* desirability" (23, my italics). And in Gettier cases, a belief has a certain property: it is the result of an exemplary procedure relative to which the truth of the belief is accidental. But in my example no true belief has the property of being the result of an exemplary procedure relative to which the desirability of the belief is accidental. In it, rather, an exemplary procedure has a certain property: that it results in a true belief is not accidental, but that it results in a true belief that is desirable is accidental.

Perhaps, then, the sort of case Zagzebski has in mind is one in which Jones thinks that it is desirable for him to have a true belief as to whether p, and he selects a procedure that non-accidentally yields a true belief that p is desirable, although true belief that p is desirable is not desirable for the reason Jones thinks. A case of this kind can be illustrated by modifying the example just considered. As before, thinking that people with gene G should have a weekly injection, Jones acquires the belief that he has gene G. As before, Jones (and contemporary science) is mistaken: G is harmless. Nevertheless, this time round it is desirable (to Jones) that he should have the true belief that he has inherited gene G. Unbeknownst to anyone, among those who have gene G, true belief that one has G protects one against Alzheimer's disease.

2.5. It is natural to focus upon true beliefs that are desirable, or prerequisites of morally successful action, in the context of inquiring into the absolute value of (some) true belief(s), and hence, if the assumption that the knowledge-belief identity thesis is correct, of (some) knowledge. This focus, however, is dangerous in the context of a virtue-theoretic analysis of knowledge per se. Indeed, where, like virtue reliabilism, this analysis takes an overtly consequentialist form, doing so threatens catastrophe. An analysis of this form conceives of an intellectual virtue as a character trait, or motive, or whatever, that promotes valuable cognitions. But once this value is conceived of as Zagzebski conceives of it, and especially if one follows her in admitting the possibility of desirable false belief (22), such an analysis is bound to give the wrong result. If *intellectual* virtue is analysable in terms of the consequences it promotes, these consequences must be *intellectually* valuable. And however desirable false belief that p might be on occasion, false belief is not that. The point is especially clear when the virtue-theoretic approach is extended from the analysis of knowledge to that of epistemic justification. A character trait that promotes beliefs that are desirable is, obviously, altogether the wrong sort of trait in terms of which to analyse *epistemic* justification if desirable beliefs include false beliefs.[12]

Admittedly, in the context of a non-reliabilist virtue theory, the danger of invoking such non-epistemic values as "desirability" and moral value is less immediate. Such a theory declines to analyse intellectual virtue consequentially (that is, in terms of its promotion of valuable cognitions). Nevertheless, it is hard to see how an account of intellectual virtuousness that makes no appeal to valuable belief could be correct. So, as before, evoking non-cognitive ways in which belief can be valuable threatens to distort the account of what makes some trait or whatever *intellectually*

[12] See Percival 2002 for further discussion of the concept of epistemic consequentialism.

virtuous. Whether someone knows that *p*, or is epistemically justified in believing that *p*, are matters that are independent of whether he has an especial concern for truths that are desirable, or for truths that are prerequisites of morally successful action. When we say, for example, that Jones knows this is a red barn, but Smith does not, or that Brown is epistemically justified in believing this is a red barn, but Green is not, we draw distinctions with respect to which differences in the strength of the agents' concerns for desirable or morally important truths are irrelevant.

3. Virtue Epistemology and Cognitive Decision Theory

3.1. Zagzebski's virtue-theoretic epistemology is not given in much detail. Her sketch of it, however, evokes cognitive decision theory. On her view, "acts of believing are generally in the category of acts that are voluntary but non-intentional . . . beliefs can be and perhaps typically are motivated . . . a motive is an affective state that initiates and directs action . . . [the] motives of the agent [that] . . . make believing better . . . [include] forms of the basic motive of . . . love or valuing of truth or a disvaluing of falsehood" (17–18). This much is all cognitive decision theory needs (and more). Cognitive decision theory approaches the question "What, given his evidence, should *A* believe?" in the manner in which classical decision theory approaches the question "What, given his limited knowledge of the relevant contingencies, should *A* do?" Like its practical counterpart, it sees the problem as one of pursuing some valued quantity under uncertainty. It will therefore embrace Zagzebski's cognitive voluntarism with gratitude. And it will capture (and refine!) her talk of an agent's "valuing of truth and disvaluing of falsehood" by means of a cognitive utility function for that agent. Just as classical decision theory postulates a utility function for the agent defined over such outcomes as "taking the umbrella, and it doesn't rain," and "not taking the umbrella, and it rains," cognitive decision theory postulates a cognitive utility function for the agent defined over such outcomes as "believing *p*, and *p*," and "not believing *p*, and not-*p*," et cetera.

In some respects, then, the cognitive decision theoretic tradition appears as a friend to Zagzebski's project. It offers sophisticated measures of sophisticated cognitive values. Whereas Zagzebski speaks somewhat vaguely of love of truth, and disvaluing and hating falsehood, cognitive decision theory enables one, for example, to accommodate different ways of hating falsehood: an agent might disvalue all falsehoods the same, or he might disvalue false beliefs more the further they are from the truth, et cetera.

3.2. In other respects, however, cognitive decision theory seems less friendly to Zagzebski's epistemology. In happily accommodating agents who value truth and disvalue falsehood very differently from one another,

© Metaphilosophy LLC and Blackwell Publishing Ltd. 2003

cognitive decision theory illustrates starkly the implausibility of any suggestion that there are restrictive objective constraints on the extent to which or respects in which a rational or virtuous agent values truth and disvalues falsehood. Moreover, at first glance at least, its central result seems positively hostile. When faced with a decision as to whether to believe p, or not p, cognitive decision theory tells you that you should sometimes believe p even though you are certain that not p (in the sense that the evidence in your possession for not p is overwhelming). This is the analogue of the commonplace in practical decision making that you should sometimes embark on a course of action in which you are almost certain to incur loss – such as paying £1 for a bet that yields £1,000,000 if a random draw from the integers between 1 and 100 results in the number 1, £0 if it yields any other number. The cognitive analogue to this arises as soon as truth is construed as a valuable *quantity* pursued under uncertainty. Once this viewpoint is adopted, beliefs that are "bold" in Popper's sense, in guaranteeing *a lot* of truth if they are true, but "risky," in being unlikely to be true, become much more attractive. On occasion, they are maximisers of (subjective) cognitive utility, just as, for example, extremely risky investments can be maximisers of utility for venture capitalists.[13]

This consequence invalidates the idea that what converts intellectually virtuous belief into knowledge is truth. Cognitive decision theory tells me to believe that p – and so I do believe that p – even though the evidence in my possession is overwhelmingly in favour of not p. In these circumstances, my belief is as virtuous as it can be. (So to speak, I love truth *so much* that I am prepared to run a very high risk of falsehood in order to have an opportunity of getting a whole load of it.) But the truth of my belief in these circumstances would hardly turn it into knowledge. I cannot know that p when I am certain that not p (or at any rate, when the evidence in my possession is overwhelmingly in favour of not p). For example, suppose Einstein believed in general relativity because his so doing maximised his expected cognitive utility, even though he was certain that general relativity is false (because, say, the evidence against it provided by meta-induction on the falsity of past theories, and by some anomalous data yet to be accounted for, was overwhelming). Though his belief in general relativity be ever so virtuous, this is not to say that, if his belief was true, it amounted to knowledge. Believing truly in the face of the evidence for falsity cannot amount to knowledge. Where belief is adopted in the face of stark evidence for the falsity of the proposition believed, the truth of that belief has an element of luck that precludes knowledge.

Still, while this consideration directly undermines the suggestion that truth converts virtuous belief into knowledge, it does not directly threaten

---

[13] For discussion of cognitive decision theory and its connections with the idea of a "consequentialist" account of such epistemic evaluations of belief as "rational" and "justified," etc., see Percival 2002 and Stalnaker 2002.

Zagzebski's own virtue-theoretic epistemology. For her epistemology is developed in the light of Gettier cases that she takes to have the same moral. She takes such cases to show that what converts virtuous belief into knowledge is not truth as such but truth that is suitably non-accidentally related to the virtuousness of the belief. Of course, she is thereby obliged to give an explanation of what it is for the truth of a virtuous belief to stem non-accidentally from the belief's virtuousness, and the sort of accidental truth involved in the cognitive utility maximising case just described is different from the sort of accidental truth involved in Gettier cases. But this is of no consequence. Explaining the former is easy in comparison to explaining the latter. True belief in the cognitive decision theoretic cases described is accidental because belief is virtuous despite being entertained in the face of evidence that the proposition believed is false. In contrast, the believings in Gettier cases are virtuous in part because they are conducted in accordance with strong evidence for truth.[14]

3.3. Whether cognitive decision theory is friend or foe, it should be engaged when a virtue-theoretic epistemology of the kind Zagzebski favours is worked out in detail. Is belief credence (something that comes in degrees) or acceptance (something that does not)? And is respect for cognitive decision theoretic principles a part of intellectual virtue? If not, why not? In any case, the devil *is* in the detail, and Williamson discerns an aspect of the deeper value problem that Zagzebski neglects:

> Even if some sufficiently complex analysis [of knowledge] never succumbed to counterexamples, that would not entail the identity of the analysing concept with the concept *knows*. Indeed, the equation of the concepts might well lead to more puzzlement rather than less. For knowing matters; the difference between knowing and not knowing is very important to us. Even unsophisticated curiosity is a desire to *know*. This importance would be hard to understand if the concept *knows* were the more or less ad hoc sprawl that analyses have had to become; why should we care so much about *that*? (Williamson 2000, 31)

This amounts to the insight that the value of knowledge imposes an additional constraint to the constraint Zagzebski identifies. It requires that the

---

[14] I have laboured this negative point because while the conference talk on which this essay is based misunderstood the relationship between cognitive decision theory and Zagzebski's virtue epistemology, the misunderstanding was not cleared up at the conference. Moreover, some questioners shared my misunderstanding. Giving undue weight to such remarks as "[W]hat is added to virtuous believing to make it knowledge . . . the answer is obvious: It must be true" (25), I identified Zagzebski's position with the view that knowledge is true virtuous belief, and I argued that cognitive decision theoretic virtuous belief is not converted to knowledge by truth, and that Zagzebski will be hard put to resist admitting respect for cognitive decision theoretic principles into her conception of intellectual virtue. However, that her virtue-theoretic theory of knowledge takes the different form described in the main text above is more prominent, and clear, in other writings by her. (See in particular Zagzebski 1996, part 3, §3.2.)

analysis of knowledge be *simple*. Perhaps the prospects of a fully worked-out non-reliabilist virtue-theoretic epistemology being *that* are no worse than are those of alternative approaches to the analysis of knowledge. But this is not to say that they are good.[15]

Department of Philosophy
University of Glasgow
Glasgow G12 8QQ
United Kingdom
P.Percival@philosophy.arts.gla.ac.uk

References

Axtell, G., editor. 2000. *Knowledge, Belief and Character*. Lanham, Md.: Rowman and Littlefield.
Dancy, J. 1995. "Supervenience, Virtues, and Consequences." *Philosophical Studies* 78: 189–235.
Percival, P. 2002. "Epistemic Consequentialism I." *Proceedings of the Aristotelian Society* (supplementary volume) 76: 122–51.
Stalnaker, R. 2002. "Epistemic Consequentialism II." *Proceedings of the Aristotelian Society* (supplementary volume) 76: 153–68.
Williamson, T. 2000. *Knowledge and Its Limits*. Oxford: Oxford University Press.
Zagzebski, L. 1996. *Virtues of the Mind: An Inquiry into the Nature of Virtue and the Ethical Foundations of Knowledge*. Cambridge: Cambridge University Press.
———. 2000. "From Reliabilism to Virtue Epistemology." In *Knowledge, Belief and Character*, edited by G. Axtell, 113–22. Lanham, Md.: Rowman and Littlefield.

[15] I would like to thank Linda Zagzebski for stimulating conversation and comment. I am also grateful to Jim Edwards, who helped improve an earlier draft of this essay.

© Metaphilosophy LLC and Blackwell Publishing Ltd. 2003.
Published by Blackwell Publishing, 9600 Garsington Road, Oxford OX4 2DQ, UK and
350 Main Street, Malden, MA 02148, USA
METAPHILOSOPHY
Vol. 34, Nos. 1/2, January 2003
0026–1068

EPISTEMIC PRESUPPOSITIONS AND THEIR CONSEQUENCES

JULI EFLIN

ABSTRACT: Traditional epistemology has, in the main, presupposed that the primary task is to give a complete account of the concept *knowledge* and to state under what conditions it is possible to have it. In so doing, most accounts have been hierarchical, and all assume an idealized knower. The assumption of an idealized knower is essential for the traditional goal of generating an unassailable account of knowledge acquisition. Yet we, as individuals, fail to reach the ideal. Perhaps more important, we have epistemic goals not addressed in the traditional approach – among them, the ability to reach understanding in areas we deem important for our lives. Understanding is an epistemic concept. But how we obtain it has not traditionally been a focus. Developing an epistemic account that starts from a set of assumptions that differ from the traditional starting points will allow a different sort of epistemic theory, one on which generating understanding is a central goal and the idealized knower is replaced with an inquirer who is not merely fallible but working from a particular context with particular goals. Insight into how an epistemic account can include the particular concerns of an embedded inquirer can be found by examining the parallels between ethics and epistemology and, in particular, by examining the structure and starting points of virtue accounts. Here I develop several interrelated issues that contrast the goals and evaluative concepts that form the structure of both standard, traditional epistemological and ethical theories and virtue-centered theories. In the end, I sketch a virtue-centered epistemology that accords with who we are and how we gain understanding.

Keywords: virtue epistemology, knowledge, understanding, skepticism, askepticism, intellectual virtues, epistemic virtues, Zagzebski.

Traditional epistemology has, in the main, presupposed that the primary task is to give a complete account of the concept *knowledge* and to state under what conditions it is possible to have it. Many significant results have been developed. There are, however, assumptions that underlie the traditional account, one of the most important of which is that of the idealized knower. Assumptions, though they enable some solutions, preclude others. The assumption of an idealized knower precludes the development of an epistemic theory that accords with who we are. An epistemic theory is needed that can be lived by a human being who is not merely fallible but also works from particular desires, particular skills, and particular goals.

These local and particular concerns have no place in standard, traditional epistemological accounts.[1]

In our articulating the problems of epistemology, delineating epistemic concepts has been conceived of as establishing only the nature of knowledge. Yet we need also to attend to the nature and production of understanding. For this latter project, we need to attend to epistemic virtues. A theory based on epistemic virtues will not only give us an insight into the nature and production of understanding but will also enable us to understand the function and authority of rules.[2]

Insight into how a virtue account can include local concerns can be found by examining the parallel between ethics and epistemology. There are many parallels, including those between virtue ethics and the emerging accounts of virtue epistemology. Here I wish to develop several interrelated issues that focus on the goals and evaluative concepts that form the structure of both standard, traditional epistemological and ethical theories and virtue-centered theories. In the end, I develop a virtue-centered epistemology that accords with who we are and how we gain understanding.

The Starting Point of Reflection

Starting points set the scope and structure of both ethical and epistemic theories. Nonvirtue accounts in both domains start with hard cases. In ethics, the demand is that a moral theory help us resolve difficult moral dilemmas. The results are rule-based accounts, such as consequentialism and Kantianism. The concern is not merely right action but rather right action on principle. This prompts the development of a system of rules as the starting point that structures the theory. Hard cases are the starting point for traditional epistemology as well, and we usually think of hard cases as versions of skepticism, with Descartes's evil genius as the prime example. The epistemic parallel to right action on principle is not merely true belief, but true justified belief.

To meet the challenge of hard cases, epistemic foundationalism in general attempts to begin from either an epistemic given or a nonepistemic point and stipulates rules for moving to true beliefs. Epistemic coherentism, on the other hand, rests empirical knowledge on rules that are justified a priori.[3] The focus is then on what constraints a belief set must meet

---

[1] For traditional epistemic accounts, I have in mind foundationalism, coherentism, and naturalism. I shall discuss only the first two, however.

[2] This way of stating the problem is inspired by Alasdair MacIntyre: "Suppose however that in articulating the problems of morality the ordering of evaluative concepts has been misconceived by the spokesman of modernity and more particularly of liberalism; suppose that we need to attend to *virtues* in the first place in order to understand the function and authority of rules" (1981, 112).

[3] I shall use Laurence BonJour's 1985 account. Even though BonJour has now recanted coherentism, the view he presents in *The Structure of Empirical Knowledge* is sophisticated and clearly presented. My discussing other views, such as Lehrer's (1997), would add

for it to be knowledge. Once this structure is established, critical analysis for either approach involves finding the right hard case that will challenge the account and developing responses that fine-tune it. The goal of these epistemic accounts, then, is establishing the nature and limits of knowledge in a way that overcomes skepticism.

Skepticism exerts the hold that it does because of the value of being certain. The only way to meet a skeptical challenge, especially a global skepticism like Descartes's, is with an idealized knower. Any information about the context of a particular individual is stripped out of the account. Details about a person's context only sully the account of knowledge-producing rules. The scope of traditional epistemology, then, is limited to overcoming skepticism with an idealized knower.

Hard cases are not the only starting point. In ancient ethics, the starting point is the recognition that humans have a final end, or an overall goal. Reflection on one's life and on how ends and priorities fit together enables the agent to unify and clarify immediate goals. Given this starting point, rules and principles are not the focus. How they combine with an agent-centered account are details to be filled in once the structure of the theory has been established. What is of prime interest is an account of who and what I am and how I want to be. Overall well-being is my final end. The kind of person I should be in order to achieve that end requires an account of the skills and virtues needed to reach it.

Recently, accounts of virtue epistemology have been developed by theorists who reject the teleological underpinnings of the ancients. Linda Zagzebski (1996) takes epistemic, or intellectual, virtues as the starting point. She rejects the idealized knower in favor of an agent who is motivated to be epistemically virtuous. Like other virtue theories, her theory utilizes components internal to the agent, such as motivation, self-control, and the deliberate exercise and development of the virtues.

In contrast, the virtue-centered epistemology I develop here is teleological. We start from the fact that we implicitly or explicitly adopt understanding as an overall goal.[4] When I think about my epistemic life and the goals I have for it, I realize that it is not individual, unrelated facts that I want to pile up, especially not trivial facts – even if they do meet the necessary and sufficient conditions for knowledge. Rather, I want important, interrelated facts; I want skills that enable me to learn more; I want a coherent framework into which new information can fit and cohere. In short, I want understanding and the ability to increase my understanding in the areas I deem important for my life.

This starting point is incomplete without an inquirer who realizes that

complexity to the discussion but would not alter the view I present here. For BonJour's current foundational view, see his 1999 and 2001.

[4] Alternatively, we adopt understanding as a major goal needed for the overall goal of human flourishing.

all of her various epistemic goals fit together with her habits of mind, that is, her epistemic virtues. Her epistemic life is given direction by what it is she seeks to understand. What is needed, then, is an account of the epistemic virtues that enable an inquirer to reach understanding from within a network of goals generated from that inquirer's context.

Because understanding is the goal, what understanding an inquirer has and what further understanding she hopes to gain is within the particularized scope of virtue-centered epistemology. Yet what understanding should be sought cannot be answered in the abstract, independently of a particular inquirer's context and goals. What can be discussed are the epistemic virtues an inquirer has or can develop that enable him to work toward his sought-for understanding and the structure of an epistemic theory into which epistemic virtues fit. The purpose of an account of virtue-centered epistemology, given that understanding is the goal and that it is possible to obtain the goal, is to state how we become the kind of inquirer capable of reaching powerful, insightful, applicable understanding.

Virtue-centered epistemology has a broad scope compared to the traditional approach, just as virtue ethics has a broad scope. But the parallel between ethics and epistemology is not exact. It could be claimed that traditional epistemology does have an overall goal: truth. And after all, truth and understanding are related notions. Furthermore, there are many aspects of BonJourian coherentism that are agent-centered, the doxastic presumption and the observation requirement among them. Finally, most internalist accounts in traditional epistemology make use of the notion of coherence at some point, including the epistemic obligations that go with it.

These claims on behalf of the traditional approach are correct, and yet the two approaches differ substantially. Skepticism is what motivates traditional accounts. Truth is a goal because a justified belief of a true proposition meets the challenge of skepticism. The goal is the possession of beliefs of the right sort. When we turn to virtue-centered epistemology, the motivation is the highly practical concern of how I should be, that is, what epistemic character I should develop, rather than what propositions I should possess.

This highlights another possible response on behalf of the traditional approach. It could be maintained that traditional epistemology does give advice on how to be: specifically, be as close to an idealized knower as possible. When asked how one is to accomplish this, the response is to list such character traits as "develop the ability to avoid bias." In this way, the gap between traditional epistemology and virtue-centered epistemology seems not to be very wide. This advice, however, is not essentially part of traditional epistemology. The essence is to state under what conditions a belief is justified, and for that highly abstract task no discussion of the nature of those who hope to know is needed. But the question does arise, indicating that there is more to our epistemic lives than fulfilling the necessary and sufficient conditions for "S knows that p." There is more to our epistemic lives than reaching certainty.

Theory Structure

As we have seen, the starting point of reflection sets the scope of an epistemic account. It also sets the structure of the resulting theory. Theories are structured according to whether they are hierarchical or complete.[5] For a theory to be hierarchical, some set of notions is taken as basic and other elements in the theory are derived from or reduced to these basic elements. Even taking some notions as basic in the sense that they are used to explain and justify without they themselves being justified is hierarchical thinking. For a theory to be complete, on the other hand, everything in the theory's domain is accounted for in terms of the basic concepts.

The bulk of traditional epistemology has aimed to be both hierarchical and complete. Giving a foundational account of knowledge is the most developed approach, and foundationalism is clearly hierarchical and aims at completeness. Foundational accounts, whether internalist or externalist, begin the route to knowledge with basic beliefs. These basic beliefs are not inferentially justified and so are immune to skeptical attack. Accounts differ on how we come to have basic beliefs, and on how they come to be justified. But the goal is always the same: to show how knowledge is possible given basic beliefs as starting points. If the scope is no more than knowledge as true, justified beliefs, then these theories also aim at completeness. To give an account is to give a truth-preserving method of inferring from basic starting points, which are given, so that the necessary and sufficient conditions for knowledge are met. This is easily seen for empirical knowledge, but even a priori knowledge is frequently reduced to analytic propositions that pose no threat to the theory's hierarchical structure or to its completeness.

Coherentism, the other major view within traditional epistemology that I shall consider, may seem to be hierarchical as well. BonJour even helps generate this interpretation:

> The alternative [to linear justification] is a holistic or systematic conception of inferential justification . . . : beliefs are justified by being inferentially related to other beliefs in the overall context of a coherent system. . . . Thus the issue at hand may be merely the justification of a particular belief, or a small set of beliefs, in the context of a cognitive system whose overall justification is taken for granted; or it may be the global issue of the justification of the cognitive system itself. According to the [coherence theory of empirical knowledge] it is the latter, global issue which is fundamental for the determination of epistemic justification. (1976, 286)

[5] Much of this discussion was motivated by Julia Annas (1993).

Justification is at the level of whole conceptual systems, so it may seem that the entire conceptual system is taken as the foundation. Propositions, then, are justified derivatively as members of a justified, coherent framework of beliefs. Most important, this is true for spontaneously generated beliefs about the external world.[6]

But the coherent framework of beliefs is not basic in the sense of being able to justify without itself being justified. The justification of the entire framework, and its ability to justify derivatively any proposition within the framework, depends on its coherence. The coherent conceptual framework, the spontaneously generated beliefs, and even a priori propositions are all primary. They are all equally important to the search for knowledge, but none is taken as given. None is an unjustified or nonepistemic starting point. Nonetheless, a coherentist does aim at completeness. As in foundationalism, knowledge is defined as justified true belief. Coherentism just provides an alternative route for meeting these necessary and sufficient conditions by shifting the level of justification up to whole conceptual systems.

Contemporary Virtue Ethics

But what of virtue ethics and virtue epistemology? Can virtue ethics provide clues for an epistemology of wider scope than seeking ways to fill the necessary and sufficient conditions for knowing a proposition? Must theories be hierarchical and complete?

When we turn to virtue ethics and virtue epistemology, the story is split. Modern virtue ethics differs in important ways from ancient virtue ethics. It is contemporary virtue ethics that has had the greatest impact on the virtue epistemology that has been developed recently, and it is here that we shall start. In the main, modern virtue ethics has shared with deontic and consequentialist views a hierarchical structure and the goal of completeness.[7] Robert Louden assesses modern virtue ethics in the following way:

> Just as its utilitarian and deontological competitors begin with primitive concepts of the good state of affairs and the intrinsically right action respectively and then derive secondary concepts out of their starting points, so virtue ethics, beginning with a root conception of the morally good person, proceeds to introduce a different set of secondary concepts which are derived in terms of their relationship to the primitive element. Though the ordering of primitive and derivatives differs in each case, the overall strategy remains the same. Viewed from this perspective, virtue ethics is not unique at all. It has adopted the traditional mononomic strategy of normative ethics. What sets it apart from other approaches, again, is its strong agent orientation. (1984, 228)[8]

[6] Here again I am relying on early BonJour (1985).
[7] There are exceptions. For example, see Robert Louden (1990; 1984), and Kurt Baier (1988).
[8] Louden (1990) has begun to pull away from this opinion.

The basic notions in modern virtue ethics are worth, admirability, or some similar notion. Even though the demands of duty or obligation are not basic, some sort of imperative will be derived from the basic notions. Virtues have to do with what kind of person one is, but the hope is that from what kind of person one should be we can derive what one should do. In this way, modern virtue ethics has a hierarchical structure. Frequently, there is also a claim for completeness, a claim that a pure virtue ethics can encompass all the traditional issues important to deontic and consequentialist ethics.

No contemporary virtue ethics is more fully developed as hierarchical and complete than is Michael Slote's in *From Morality to Virtue*: "In order to show the superiority of virtue ethics to both common-sense and Kantian morality, we in effect must consider virtue ethics in an unaccustomed foundational light, and in the present part of this book, therefore, I will attempt a foundational approach to virtue ethics" (1992, 88). The basic, foundational concepts for Slote are such notions as admirable, deplorable, virtue, and personal good. These he labels "ethical" notions. They are evaluative concepts, but excluded are notions of right and wrong. Any concepts concerning duty, obligation, right or wrong Slote labels "moral" concepts: Our common-sense ethics of virtue is going to avoid specifically moral notions and make use – not of the notions of moral excellence and moral goodness – but of the broader aretaic notions of a good or admirable character trait, and excellence of character, or more briefly, a virtue" (1992, 90). For understanding Slote, we can think of ethics as a subclass of evaluative concepts. Excluded are such evaluations as "It's amazing" and "That is an unlikely event."[9] But notions of moral rightness and moral wrongness too are excluded. This gives Slote a starting point for a hierarchical account.

In the end, Slote even reduces 'virtue' to admirability. This leaves him with two foundational concepts: admirability and personal good. "Contrast the approach of virtue ethics [which] eliminates the specifically moral and [the] evaluations of the goodness, badness, betterness, etc. of states of affairs. [We are left] with two ultimate ethical categories of admirability and personal good" (1992, 200). Personal well-being or a good, desirable life is the 'personal good' and cannot be reduced to admirability. Yet most evaluative notions, Slote maintains, can be reduced with the aid of nonevaluative concepts, such as 'rationality' and 'prudence'.

Clearly, Slote's virtue ethics is hierarchical. He also means for it to be complete. An explicit goal is to derive virtue-ethics analogues to the deontic notions of wrongness and of obligation. For example, Slote uses 'deplorable' as the negative counterpart to admirable. Further, he claims that we can say of people, actions, and events that they are either

[9] See Slote 1992, 198.

© Metaphilosophy LLC and Blackwell Publishing Ltd. 2003

deplorable or admirable. This gives him the ability to say that an impera-tive is easily derived: if an action is deplorable, do not do it.[10]

Slote's overall goal is to provide a virtue ethics that addresses all the issues that nonvirtue accounts address while avoiding all the problems and inconsistencies of these views. Although in hierarchical epistemological accounts, what is taken as basic is either a nonepistemic starting point or is known better than the derivative knowledge, ethical accounts in general do not make this sort of demand. Slote, however, does. He wants a "non-moral" starting point from which, eventually, to derive moral imperatives. Thus, Slote's view is strongly hierarchical, and as we have seen, he hopes to make it complete.

Contemporary Virtue Epistemology

Traditionally, virtues are character traits over which we have some degree of control. A virtue is not a transitory disposition; rather, it requires char-acter stability and is developed through attention and habit. It includes a constant readiness to act in a virtuous manner when the situation calls for it. Epistemic virtues fit this general characterization but are somewhat narrower, usually characterized as cognitive dispositions exercised in the formation of beliefs.[11]

One claim about moral virtues that is nearly univocal is that they are deep, important traits that individuals consciously develop over time. We think of ourselves in terms of the virtues we exemplify, such as honesty, integrity, humility, and fairness. Over time and with practice, we develop some virtues. In this way, virtues that any person takes care to develop are part of his or her identity. We try to develop our virtues (and control our vices) by emulating those whom we admire. All this can be said of epistemic virtues as well. We think of ourselves as thinkers who are conscientious and impar-tial, and actively seek to develop these and other traits by emulating teach-ers and mentors who exemplify the ability to gain understanding.

Ernest Sosa (1985; 1991) coined the term *virtue epistemology*. What is virtuous, he and other reliabilists claim, are human capacities. These can include being open-minded as well as capacities like sight and smell. This reliabilist approach grafts an expanded notion of 'virtue' onto a standard approach in traditional epistemology in an attempt to meet skeptical chal-lenges. Such an approach is still concerned with finding knowledge that is certain, and hence immune to skeptical attack. Because it is generic capac-ities rather than persons that are virtuous, the reliabilist approach is of no help in knowing how we should be if we are to gain understanding.

---

[10] There is much to disagree with in Slote's view. I find his distinction between ethics and morality difficult to justify. Also, rationality and prudence seem to be evaluative concepts. Slote's view, however, is complex. I offer this partial summary only to illustrate the common structure of contemporary virtue ethics.

[11] This is Guy Axtell's formulation (1996; 1997).

Contrasting with Sosa is the work of Linda Zagzebski (1996) and James Montmarquet (1993). These authors both use the notion of virtue in a standard way. They develop "responsibilist" accounts of virtue epistemology in which what is virtuous is a person, that is, the one who consciously develops the appropriate virtues. Montmarquet's interest is not epistemology but ethics. His concern is to justify the claim that to be responsible for our actions we must be responsible for the beliefs from which they stem. Hence, he does not develop a full epistemological account. Zagzebski, on the other hand, has a strong interest in epistemology. She attempts to produce an epistemological account in which virtues are basic. All else is derived from them.

Zagzebski's view is worthy of a full discussion in itself. Here, however, we can only show that the scope and structure of her view force her into attempting to make her account both hierarchical and complete. The epistemology she develops quite closely parallels modern virtue ethics. Indeed, she has built a complex and comprehensive epistemological view around the claim that epistemic virtues parallel moral virtues. On her view, epistemic virtues are *forms* of moral virtue. She thinks of this not as reducing epistemology to ethics but as expanding ethics to cover epistemology.[12] Her account, then, is hierarchical in a couple of senses. First, virtue is the fundamental concept in both domains. "The justifiedness of beliefs is related to intellectual virtue as the rightness of acts is related to moral virtue in a pure virtue ethics" (1996, xv). Yet, and second, she frequently describes ethics as most fundamental. Even the title of her book indicates this status: *Virtues of the Mind: An Inquiry into the Nature of Virtue and the Ethical Foundations of Knowledge.*

Part of her project is to answer the question, When is a person in a state of knowledge? Having justified beliefs is part of what is needed for right action. What is of most interest here is the epistemic account Zagzebski embeds in her virtue ethics. We can examine the hierarchical nature of her epistemology while overlooking her intent to reduce its fundamental aspects to even more fundamental ethical concepts.

To begin, Zagzebski takes the term *knowledge* quite broadly. Knowledge is "used to cover a multitude of states, from the simplest case of ordinary perceptual contact with the physical world, requiring no cognitive effort or skill whatever, to the most impressive cognitive achievements" (1996, 262). She does have two straightforward definitions of knowledge:

1. Knowledge is a state of cognitive contact with reality arising out of acts of intellectual virtue.
2. Knowledge is a state of belief arising out of acts of intellectual virtue. (1996, 270)

[12] Zagzebski states: "Intellectual virtues are in fact, forms of moral virtue" (1996, xiv); "Intellectual virtues ought to be treated as subsets of the moral virtues,'' and "intellectual virtues are best viewed as forms of moral virtues" (1996, 139).

Zagzebski prefers the first formulation, because it allows, she claims, for knowledge other than propositional knowledge.[13]

There are two points to note. First, Zagzebski is assuming a correspondence theory of truth. "Cognitive contact with reality" means, roughly, an accurate description of reality or a "conception of reality which does not misperceive so that the right action is taken." Second, if 'justification' is substituted for 'acts of intellectual virtue', the result is the standard claim from any traditional theory of knowledge. Thus, it would seem that her purpose is to show that intellectual virtues produce truths or justified beliefs. Zagzebski even claims: "My aim in defining knowledge is to give necessary and sufficient conditions for knowledge that are both theoretically illuminating and practically useful" (1996, 264). In other words, from her account she wants an explanation of how we come to know, and practical advice for anyone who hopes to know. Becoming virtuous, then, is an alternative method for reaching justified beliefs.

Nonetheless, Zagzebski's view has many nontraditional aspects. One of the most important of these is that hers is a motivation-based theory: "The concept of motivation will be treated as ethically fundamental and the concept of a virtue will be constructed out of good motivation" (1996, 82). This illustrates the fundamentality of her ethics, but it also illustrates that her view is agent based. The virtues and their foundation are within the agent. There is no teleological component as in the happiness-based virtue accounts of the ancients. A motivation-based theory has no teleological explanation for the worth of the virtues. Rather, each virtue is justified independently by appeal to experience; we tell stories of people whose "goodness shines through." We see certain people as good, and good because of their virtues, so the virtues are themselves good.

Having virtues, then, is the route to finding truth, or at least justified beliefs. Zagzebski defines a 'justified belief' as "what a person who is motivated by intellectual virtue, and who has the understanding of his cognitive situation a virtuous person would have, might believe in like circumstance" (1996, 241). If knowledge is "cognitive contact with reality" and justification is the route to knowledge, then we get the following tripartite definition:

'S has a justified belief that p' ≡
S is motivated by intellectual virtues,
S knows the relevant information that a virtuous person would know, and a virtuous person would believe p in circumstance c.

These are the necessary and sufficient conditions for an agent to be justified in holding a belief. At this point Zagzebski draws from virtue ethics.

---

[13] The possibility of an account of nonpropositional knowledge is intriguing. But Zagzebski leaves the idea undeveloped.

Frequently, in a pure virtue ethical theory, act evaluation is derived from the character of an agent. Roughly, an act is right because it is what a virtuous person might do. Zagzebski wants a pure virtue epistemic theory as well; the parallel is that a justified belief is one that an intellectually virtuous person might hold.

Since her epistemic project is showing that virtues lead to justified belief, and she has given necessary and sufficient conditions for a belief to be justified, Zagzebski is still trying to meet skeptical challenges. She also takes great pains to argue that her account can meet Gettier-style counterexamples. Both of these are efforts at completeness. She hopes to cover all the standard issues in traditional epistemology.

Zagzebski attempts completeness in other respects as well. This is to address all the typical issues raised in virtue accounts. Since hers is a pure virtue account, rules and principles must be derivable from virtues. For Zagzebski, this means that both the moral rules that are a part of deontic and consequentialist ethical views as well as the rules of reasoning and principles for gaining true beliefs that are a part of foundationalist and coherentist epistemological views must be derivable from virtues.

> By a pure virtue theory I mean a theory that makes the concept of a right act derivative from the concept of a virtue or some inner state of a person that is a component of virtue. This is a point both about conceptual priority and about moral ontology. In a pure virtue theory the concept of a right act is *defined* in terms of the concept of a virtue or a component of virtue such as a motivation. Furthermore, the property of rightness is something that emerges from the inner traits of persons. So according to a pure virtue theory an act would not have been right or wrong if it were not for its relation to certain inner personal traits. (1996, 79)

What parallels rightness of act in her epistemological account is rightness of belief, as is illustrated in her tripartite condition for a justified belief. What counts as a justified belief, according to Zagzebski, is *defined* in terms of virtues and the motivation to be intellectually virtuous. Thus, at bottom, we arrive at knowledge by being intellectually virtuous, and the knowledge gained is of reality.[14]

The question arises whether or not Zagzebski's account requires a metajustification. It seems that she needs to show why being intellectually virtuous is a reliable method for reaching truth. It is analogous to asking why seeking and maintaining a coherent system of beliefs and using coherence as the criterion for when a belief is justified will result in beliefs that accurately describe reality. If being motivated by virtues and being intellectually virtuous are the criteria for when a belief is justified,

---

[14] Zagzebski's view faces all the standard objections that a pure virtue account in ethics does. The questions about grounding virtues are not easily overcome. See Amelie Rorty (1988).

what guarantee is there that the resulting beliefs will be in "cognitive contact with reality"?

This issue is further developed by considering another way in which Zagzebski aims at completeness. It is standard in virtue theories to have components both internal and external to the agent. Internal components are motivation, self-control, and the deliberate exercise and development of the virtues; the external component is success. We have seen the internal components in Zagzebski's view, and like other virtue theories, Zagzebski's theory has the external component of success as well.

> It is clear that virtuous persons acting out of virtue have certain aims, and we generally think it is not sufficient to *have* those aims in order to be virtuous, but that a virtuous person reliably produces the ends of the virtue in question. So compassionate persons are reliably successful in alleviating suffering; fair persons are reliably successful in producing fair states of affairs. (1996, 99)

The ends of the epistemic virtues are, of course, justified beliefs and knowledge. 'Virtue' is a success term. If one is epistemically virtuous, then one is successful in gaining knowledge.

If 'virtue' is a success term, it would seem that any virtue epistemology would be askeptical. Zagzebski does make the claim that her view is returning to the askeptical epistemology of the Middle Ages.[15] If a view is askeptical, then it should be built within the presupposition that cognizers do gain knowledge. The goal, then, would be to say how one should be if one is to gain knowledge, presupposing that one can. Yet, giving the necessary and sufficient conditions for a belief to be justified violates this presupposition.

Even with these concerns, there is much to be learned from studying Zagzebski's account. First, a virtue approach has much to offer where traditional epistemology must be silent. An agent-centered view makes room for motivation and intellectual habits. Second, 'virtue' is a success term. One who is epistemically virtuous does not merely have the *ability* to gain knowledge and reach understanding. To be virtuous one habitually gains knowledge and habitually deepens her understanding. This means that virtue epistemology must be askeptical.

Pluralistic Virtue-Centered Epistemology

The foregoing has allowed us to examine two distinct approaches in epistemology. The first approach parallels standard deontic or consequentialist views in ethics, in which rules are the essence and the focus is on discrete acts and the formulating of decision procedures. The epistemological

---

[15] Zagzebski explicitly makes this claim (1995). It is also discussed to some extent in her 1996 book (42, 229, 238, and especially 278–80 and 331–32).

parallel is the whole of traditional epistemology that focuses on discrete beliefs and decision procedures for knowledge. On these accounts, epistemic virtues are either entirely excluded from the structure, as in most forms of foundationalism, or they are an assumed but undeveloped part of the theory, as in coherentism.[16]

The second approach is agent centered and takes as central an inquirer's epistemic character. We have examined Zagzebski's pure aretaic view that shares with traditional epistemology a hierarchical structure and the aim of completeness. There is, however, a second type of view to be built within the virtue approach, one that is not structured hierarchically and does not aim to be a complete epistemology.

This second view more closely parallels ancient virtue ethics in which the agent's final ends are primary; they set the framework for the theory so that we understand how other notions fit together and fit with final ends. For example, a virtue may be a disposition to act morally, but what actions are moral is not justified in terms of "what will sustain or produce the virtue" (Annas 1993, 9). Rather, we realize the relationship between a disposition to act morally and our final end.

Orienting by final end for epistemology is to say that what is given is the goal, understanding, and the possibility to attain the goal. Virtues like epistemic consciousness are dispositions to reach understanding, but understanding is neither defined nor justified nor reduced to epistemic virtues. The characteristics a virtuous inquirer has are those that will fulfill the goal of understanding. Attaining the goal is part of normal human activity; it does not happen without an inquirer's active interest in pursuing the goal, but understanding is within the grasp of full-blooded, situated humans.

The result is that pluralistic virtue-centered epistemology is askeptical. If the presuppositions of the impartial, idealized subject are given up, then a shift can be made away from attempting to determine the kind of evidence needed to justify a claim "to know." Giving up the goal of overcoming skepticism and the search for certainty allows for the presupposition that we do have knowledge and understanding. In a pluralistic, virtue approach, global skepticism is not denied; rather, it is set aside. What distinguishes the askeptical approach is deliberately operating within the presupposition that it is possible for any normal person to meet the requirements to gain understanding. One result is that understanding can be gained through a multiple of paths. Once the shift is made, what becomes central is the inquirer – his or her interests, context, and circumstance. Focusing on aspects of the inquirer, rather than exclusively focusing on the nature of justification, is an askeptical move.

[16] Keith Lehrer is beginning to develop the connections between epistemic virtues, coherence and truth. See Lehrer 2000.

In setting aside global skepticism, we are not likewise setting aside the ability to be skeptical about the truth of a particular claim, hypothesis, or theory. Askeptical epistemology does not mean the abandonment of the use of reason. There are still appropriate ways to reason, and appropriate ways to use evidence. Thus, it is not part of askepticism to remove the ability to evaluate how well justified a belief is. Hypotheses and assertions, guided by what knowledge one already has and what further knowledge is sought, are subject to critical scrutiny. The issue here is not the epistemic worthiness of our rules for using evidence and our rules for making inferences; rather, what can be subject to criticism is a particular use of the rules and evidence.

Finally, in setting aside skepticism, we are free to shift away from the isolated subject seeking pure truths to a community of inquirers, all of whom are seeking knowledge and understanding. Pooling talents gives us a greater likelihood of arriving at valuable knowledge. Any understanding I may then reach is dependent on others from whom I have learned. It is also dependent on my contributions to the community, for it is the critical scrutiny my ideas receive from the community that hones my ideas and hypotheses into knowledge, and builds systems for understanding our world and ourselves.

The starting points for pluralistic, virtue-centered epistemology, then, are these: (1) Understanding is the goal, and it is possible for normal inquirers to gain understanding. Thus, we have understanding, though not complete and not perfect. (2) The understanding an inquirer generates depends on her context. This context includes what knowledge she has, what further knowledge she seeks, and the community in which she seeks knowledge. (3) We are not isolated subjects but contributors in a community of inquirers who seek understanding. All of these points make pluralistic, virtue-centered epistemology askeptical.

From the foregoing, we can see that the achievements of traditional epistemology cannot simply be abandoned. Instead, we see the place of our rules of reasoning and knowledge generating procedures in our search for understanding. Since the virtue-centered epistemology developed here is pluralistic, both the rules and procedures that are the focus of traditional epistemology and the epistemic virtues that are developed here are primary. Both have intrinsic worth; neither is basic.

Traditional epistemology has fully developed accounts of the rules as basic. The work to be done is in developing epistemic virtues as primary in a way that can be coupled with other primary elements, including a conception of epistemic rules and justificatory strategies as also primary. In pluralistic virtue-centered epistemology, as with other agent-centered views, atomic beliefs are intentionally downplayed, as are the developments of particular solution strategies; the focus is on long-term characteristic patterns of actions.

© Metaphilosophy LLC and Blackwell Publishing Ltd. 2003

The Nature of Virtues (Again)

It is important to emphasize that epistemic virtues are not mere habits; they have a cognitive aspect that mere habits lack. In virtue ethics this cognitive aspect is usually seen as connected to choice.[17] Choice is a part of cognition for epistemology as well. For example, I am epistemically responsible for being open-minded, an epistemic virtue, because that is how I have chosen to be and continue to choose to be. When I encounter a new idea or view, especially a criticism of my own view, I choose to consider it. I check to see if it can help me refine my view or locate an unarticulated assumption. It may be rare that a new idea leads me to reject my view wholesale, but if I am open-minded, that must be a possibility. My present choice is an endorsement of my disposition, which in this case is the willingness to reconsider my beliefs. In choosing once again to be open-minded, "I endorse the way I have become" (Annas 1993, 51).

For knowing how I should become, I must be aware of the range of epistemic virtues. Of the epistemologists developing virtue accounts, James Montmarquet has a condensed yet comprehensive list of such virtues. He considers four epistemic virtues. First is "epistemic conscientiousness," which he describes as a desire for finding truths and avoiding errors. Second is "impartiality." One who is impartial is willing to exchange ideas and learn from others without a bias toward one's own ideas. This virtue includes a "lively sense of one's own fallibility (Montmarquet 1993, 23ff.). Third is "intellectual sobriety." The sober-minded inquirer is cautious to the right degree. Such a person avoids intellectual fads and does not let the excitement of new and unfamiliar ideas overshadow the desire for truth. Fourth is "intellectual courage," which is a willingness to conceive and examine alternatives to popularly held beliefs. It includes a willingness to persevere in the face of opposition.[18]

Montmarquet's list of virtues assumes motivation to be central to a virtue-centered account. To be epistemically conscientious, an inquirer must have a passion for understanding. This is correct, but not a passion for understanding *simpliciter*. The inquirer must have a passion for *something* other than passion itself. That "something" is what he desires to understand.

Aristotle's list of "prized intellectual traits" overlaps to some extent with Montmarquet's list of epistemic virtues. Traditional epistemology left behind Aristotle's concern for practical wisdom, which in part is an account of how wisdom is gained by the right exercise of the right intellectual virtues. The central epistemic virtues Aristotle considers are ingenuity

---

[17] This is true for ancient virtue ethics, but many modern virtue ethics are "anti-theory." These views deny that there is any theory structure to moral virtues, including any cognitive aspect to exercising them. Clearly, this cannot be the model for virtue epistemology.

[18] Montmarquet's account is far more complex than I have represented here. Nonetheless, the very brief gloss I have given is sufficient for the present context.

(which includes intellectual creativity), perceptual sensitivity, acuity of inference, a sound sense of relevance, and an active ability to determine the relative importance of heterogeneous and sometimes incommensurable ends.[19] These are important additions, for exercising epistemic virtues enables an inquirer to focus attention and define what is salient. These are skills needed to gain context-dependent, goal-driven understanding.[20]

These lists can be condensed into the cluster of epistemic virtues I list below. They are not all and only the virtues that could be singled out as valuable, but they are some of the central virtues:

1. Having a synoptic grasp of disparate domains. This results from three other skills or virtues: having backgrounds of domain-specific knowledge, focusing at the right level, and making unusual associations. Included in a synoptic grasp is the ability to abstract the presuppositions that are particular to a domain and the presuppositions that domains share. Thus, Aristotle's "acuity of inference" is important here as well as in the following virtue.
2. Being able to represent alternative points of view, both perceptually and theoretically. This is the flexible, imaginative ability that is frequently cited as a creative trait. One proof of the ability to represent alternative points of view is the ability to reason hypothetically about the outcomes of possible alternatives. Another is the ability to transfer solution schemas to new contexts.
3. Being motivated by epistemic conscientiousness. This includes drive and courage, tempered by intellectual sobriety, in an effort to reach understanding.
4. The ability to focus at the right level and define what is salient.
5. The ability to exercise the right epistemic virtue at the right time. Aristotle would consider this part of practical wisdom.

These virtues are highly interactive. For example, being able to represent alternative points of view requires hypothetically adopting an alternative set of presuppositions. But that requires knowing currently held presuppositions and their degree of fundamentality. Developing and using the virtues is not a linear process. Frequent reevaluation is needed both of the hypotheses generated and of the process of their generation. Both of these steps require the recursive use of the epistemic virtues.

Virtues can be listed separately for discussion, but none actually acts in isolation. For not one of the virtues can it be said that one should act on it in an unqualified manner. Epistemic virtue arises only when these traits are clustered and balanced in someone who desires understanding. An epistemically virtuous person is someone with a well-constructed character

---

[19] See Aristotle, *Politics* i 1260a17, iii 1277a25; *Nicomachean Ethics* 1095a.
[20] Aristotle stimulated my thinking, but I do not claim that my approach is Aristotelian.

who acts appropriately to gain understanding. An unqualified exhortation, "Be intellectually courageous!" is foolhardy advice. To gain understanding, one must be intellectually courageous *when one should*. Yet knowing when one should requires a balancing of courage against other appropriate epistemic virtues.

On many virtue accounts, the intellectual virtues are all of the same order. Yet a sound sense of relevance seems to require inferential acuity and perceptual sensitivity. The ability to determine the relative importance of heterogeneous and sometimes incommensurable ends seems to require impartiality and intellectual sobriety. The resolution of this difficulty will be to see some virtues as first order and some as second order. This is anticipated in the short list of virtues above. Having a synoptic grasp of disparate domains, for example, is a second-order virtue, with other related skills as first-order virtues. Clearly, the ability to exercise the right epistemic virtue at the right time is a second-order virtue. Second-order virtues are not the guiding goals, yet they result *from* the first-order traits. Furthermore, they result *in* understanding.

For analysis, we can separate producing alternatives from evaluating and justifying them. In practice, we flow between the two. The greater an inquirer's ability to move fluidly between producing alternatives and evaluating them and to operate at both levels simultaneously, the better she will be at finding valuable discoveries. Just as the use of scientific methodology is a self-regulating activity, the right exercise of epistemic virtues is self-regulating to develop deep understanding. Even though a creative person may generate many possible options that are rejected, given the nature of the epistemic virtues, the results will, prima facie, meet epistemic criteria. This is what ties the exercising of epistemic virtues to understanding.

As I noted above, 'virtue' is a success term. In virtue ethics, someone who is virtuous does not merely have the capacity to be moral. Such a person *is* moral. He or she acts in a way that meets ethical criteria. So, too, can it be said that an inquirer who is epistemically virtuous arrives at hypotheses and theories that meet epistemic criteria. We can also speak of inquirers being epistemically virtuous in varying degrees analogous to the case with ethical virtues. The more epistemically virtuous an inquirer is, the deeper and broader her understanding. This is especially true if higher-order virtues are developed. These higher-order virtues are metacognitive, and they must be cultivated and practiced if deep insights are to be generated.

Concluding Remarks

As we have seen, a pluralistic, virtue-centered approach is not hierarchical, because there are no basic elements from which all else is derived. It is also not complete. In ethics, nonprimary elements are frequently added

© Metaphilosophy LLC and Blackwell Publishing Ltd. 2003

in an attempt at completeness. I shall take the lack of completeness in a much more radical way than this. A virtue approach that incorporates nonprimary elements may explain and justify those elements of epistemology within its scope, but it will not, and cannot, be a complete epistemology. There will still be epistemic questions not addressed, which virtue epistemology will not have the resources to answer. This is because some legitimate epistemic questions do not arise within the assumptions made by a virtue approach. But so, too, are there legitimate epistemic questions that do not arise within the assumptions of the traditional approach. Epistemology is not complete without addressing skepticism; but it is also not complete without addressing epistemic virtues. Both are primary.

An agent-centered, virtue epistemology will face the same objection virtue ethics faces when a critic asks how to know what the right action is for a particular kind of case. As with virtue ethics, there can be no straightforward, unambiguous answer, because there is no direct connection between *how* I should be and *what* I should do or believe. This leaves large areas of epistemic decision making ambiguous.[21] Ambiguity can only be resolved by considering the decision in context. Context includes the specific epistemic goals of an inquirer along with her background, including her knowledge base and the level and kind of virtues she has developed. Only by filling in the details of a particular inquirer can any normative claim be reached. For some cases, it may be that ambiguity can be reduced but may never result in an epistemic duty to take one and only one particular knowledge-producing action, or result in one and only one unique belief. Furthermore, different actions may produce different bits of knowledge. It may be that there are two equally good routes, or better or worse routes, to the same bit of knowledge.

Because the details about an inquirer's goals and context are needed if there is any hope to reduce the ambiguity of belief and action, pluralistic virtue-centered epistemology avoids "context stripping." This is one of Helen Longino's (1990) criteria that any theory in epistemology should meet. No account must allow for context stripping, which produces an idealized subject by removing his or her circumstances from part of the picture. We can say "understanding" in the abstract, and we can discuss the various virtues on which an inquirer needs to draw to produce it, but "understanding" *simpliciter* cannot be given an account, nor can an inquirer have it. I can only achieve particular understanding from where I am, that is, from my context. It has to be an understanding needed by an individual, achievable from her present understanding and through her epistemic virtues, or from ones she can develop.

Pluralistic virtue-centered epistemology has not been fully developed. Many issues still need to be addressed. One important issue is the role of emotion. Virtues cannot be "correctives" for our emotions. For example,

---

[21] For the parallel in ethics, see Annas 1993, 10.

on Kant's view, virtues give us strength of will to overcome feelings that might lead us astray. This is the wrong model for virtue epistemology. Rather, thinking of virtues as correctives is similar to traditional episte-mology in which "being rational," or following the rules of reason, is what we use to overcome feelings that might lead us to a false or unwar-ranted conclusion. Many fallacies, for example, "appeal to pity," even name the emotion that leads us away from knowledge. This makes us realize that not all emotions are appropriate for motivating the epistemi-cally virtuous inquirer. Yet reason without emotion has no practical result.

Another important discussion concerns the traditional distinction between duty and self-interest. In traditional ethics, these are sharply distinct. But on virtue accounts, whether ethical or epistemological, they cannot be distinct. If there is a sharp distinction between epistemic consciousness and self-interest, then the only way to motivate following epistemic rules is via a sense of duty. This is a problem for foundational-ism in particular, for there is no duty to be epistemically responsible. We may abhor epistemic sloth, but traditional epistemology does not have the resources to answer the question, Why be rational?

Traditional epistemology can only give a question-begging answer to someone who asks why he should not be satisfied with his semicoherent, inconsistent belief set. Why should I choose to make the effort to recon-sider my beliefs in the light of new evidence, or even recognize that there is evidence that has an impact on my beliefs? Rules and procedures for gaining knowledge have no normative force on their own. One might be able to say that we follow rules for self-interested reasons, hoping that others are not quite as quick, so that our own interests are satisfied over theirs. There may be domains where this fits, for example, trading stocks, but in the main this gives us a false picture of why we use rules of reason-ing. The deeper reason is that the ability to know not only how but when to use them brings us greater understanding.

For the ancients, someone who feels a sharp distinction between duty and self-interest is not virtuous. A person who follows duty is self-controlled. The self-controlled individual is not a unified person, for he battles feelings, namely, his desires to act against duty. For some, becom-ing self-controlled is a needed step on the way to becoming virtuous. Being self-controlled, however, is a lower state than being virtuous. In contrast, one whose feelings align with what one should do is unified, and as such what one wants to do is the same as what one should do. Thus, any distinction between duty and self-interest collapses. The epistemically virtuous inquirer, then, is motivated by epistemic conscientiousness and willingly endorses all the prescriptions that follow.

The above issues need further discussion, and others will doubtless arise. Nonetheless, a pluralistic virtue-centered epistemology accords with who we are, yet it is clearly normative. It leaves room for the further development of traditional epistemology and the articulation of the rules and procedures of reasoning, and at the same time shows us why they are important yet not the whole of epistemology. Pluralistic virtue-centered epistemology provides guidance for becoming epistemically virtuous and, through the exercise of virtues, guidance for gaining understanding. Finally, and most fully, it is an epistemic theory that can be lived by humans situated in life with its demands and limits.

Department of Philosophy and Religious Studies
Ball State University
Muncie, IN 47306–0500 USA
jeflin2@bsu.edu

References

Annas, J. 1993. *The Morality of Happiness*. Oxford: Oxford University Press.

Aristotle. 1941. *The Basic Works of Aristotle*, edited by Richard McKeon. New York: Random House.

Axtell, G. 1996. "Epistemic-virtue Talk: The Reemergence of American Axiology?" *Journal of Speculative Philosophy* 10: 172–98.

————. 1997. "Recent Work on Virtue Epistemology." *American Philosophical Quarterly* 34: 1–26.

Baier, K. 1988. "Radical Virtue Ethics." *Midwest Studies in Philosophy* 13: 126–35.

BonJour, L. 1976. "The Coherence Theory of Empirical Knowledge." *Philosophical Studies* 30: 281–312.

————. 1985. *The Structure of Empirical Knowledge*. Cambridge, Mass.: Harvard University Press.

————. 1999. "Foundationalism and the External World." *Philosophical Perspectives* 13: 229–49.

————. 2001. "Toward a Defense of Empirical Foundationalism." In *Resurrecting Old-Fashioned Foundationalism*, edited by Michael DePaul, 21–38. Lanham, Md.: Rowman and Littlefield.

Greco, John. 1993. "Virtues and Vices of Virtue Epistemology." *Canadian Journal of Philosophy* 23: 413–32.

Kvanvig, J. 1992. *The Intellectual Virtues and the Life of the Mind: On the Place of the Virtues in Epistemology*. Savage, Md.: Rowman and Littlefield.

Lehrer, K. 1997. *Self-trust: A Study of Reason, Knowledge, and Autonomy*. Oxford: Oxford University Press.

————. 2000. "Discursive Knowledge." *Philosophy and Phenomenological Research* 60: 637–53.

Longino, H. E. 1990. *Science as Social Knowledge: Values and Objectivity in Scientific Inquiry*. Princeton: Princeton University Press.

Louden, R. 1984. "On Some Vices of Virtue Ethics." *American Philosophical Quarterly* 21: 227–36.

———. 1990. "Virtue Ethics and Anti-theory." *Philosophia* 20: 93–114.

MacIntyre, A. 1981. *After Virtue*. Notre Dame: University of Notre Dame Press.

Montmarquet, James A. 1993. *Epistemic Virtue and Doxastic Responsibility*. Lanham, Md.: Rowman and Littlefield.

Rorty, Amelie O. 1988. "Virtues and Their Vicissitudes." *Midwest Studies in Philosophy* 13: 136–48.

Slote, M. 1992. *From Morality to Virtue*. New York: Oxford University Press.

Sosa, E. 1985. "Knowledge and Intellectual Virtue." *Monist* 68: 226–45.

———. 1991. *Knowledge in Perspective: Selected Essays in Epistemology*. Cambridge: Cambridge University Press.

Zagzebski, Linda. 1995. "Recovering Understanding: From Epistemology to Cognitive Virtue Ethics." Wheaton College Epistemology Conference, November 1995, Wheaton, Illinois.

———. 1996. *Virtues of the Mind: An Inquiry into the Nature of Virtue and the Ethical Foundations of Knowledge*. Cambridge: Cambridge University Press.

© Metaphilosophy LLC and Blackwell Publishing Ltd. 2003

© Metaphilosophy LLC and Blackwell Publishing Ltd. 2003.
Published by Blackwell Publishing, 9600 Garsington Road, Oxford OX4 2DQ, UK and
350 Main Street, Malden, MA 02148, USA
METAPHILOSOPHY
Vol. 34, Nos. 1/2, January 2003
0026–1068

TRADITIONAL EPISTEMOLOGY RECONSIDERED
A REPLY TO EFLIN

ANDREW McGONIGAL

ABSTRACT: In this article, I reply to Juli Eflin's "Epistemic Presuppositions and Their Consequences." I query Eflin's construal of the aims, scope and method of traditional epistemology, and go on to evaluate several of the central characteristics of Eflin's positive account – pluralistic virtue epistemology.

Keywords: coherentism, epistemology, foundationalism, scepticism.

Introduction

In her article, Juli Eflin is engaged in the wholly admirable exercise of attempting to identify particular assumptions shared by a philosophical tradition, and to trace the philosophical consequences of holding such assumptions. There are three interesting, and interrelated, projects that such an exercise might contribute to. Firstly, we might be concerned with the *genealogical* goal of outlining and explaining the way that intellectual history *actually* went, how we got to where we are as a result of that history, and why we came to see the philosophical landscape as we do. Secondly, we might be interested in a *demarcatory* project, identifying classical or canonical positions and commitments within a traditional debate, aiming less for a well-supported historical account than ease of oversight, categorisation and comparison. Finally, we might be interested in carrying out a *substantive* philosophical project, aiming to show, perhaps, that the presuppositions of a particular tradition have led us into trouble, and that we should take a new turn or retreat to an earlier path, or perhaps that a particular commitment of the theory is groundless, or a function of irrational forces of one kind or another, and thus that the theory ought to be amended or discarded. Such an aim, of course, requires more in the way of philosophical argument than the two previous projects do. In the normal case one will have to show not just that a philosophical position *P did* historically presuppose *X* or cause *Y*, nor that it can, for a particular classificatory purpose, be stipulated that a *P*-theorist is committed to certain canonical assumptions, but rather that such presuppositions, assumptions, methods or consequences are in some sense genuinely intrinsic or essential to the position.

For the purposes of this article, I shall treat Eflin as engaged primarily in such a *substantive* project. In particular, I shall take it that (1) her metaphilosophical claim that "starting points set the scope and structure of both ethical and epistemic theories" (49) comprises part of an argument leading to the conclusion that intrinsic features of traditional epistemology *as she construes it* (henceforth, TE) leads us to ignore or downplay crucial features of our epistemic life, and (2) she wishes to argue that 'pluralistic virtue epistemology' offers a more promising approach. I want to focus on several of the claims she makes in the course of developing this position.

1. Eflin's Description of Traditional Epistemology

Eflin, stating that by 'traditional epistemology' she has in mind primarily foundationalism and coherentism, includes the following claims in her representation of its underlying assumptions:

(a) TE makes essential appeal to the "idealized knower" (48).
(b) Such an appeal precludes "the development of an epistemological theory that accords with who we are," namely, one that can be "lived by" fallible human beings with particular concerns, desires and projects (48).
(c) "Hard cases are the starting point for traditional epistemology, and we often think of hard cases as versions of skepticism" (49).
(d) "Skepticism has the hold that it does because of the value of being certain" (50).
(e) "The only way to meet a skeptical challenge such as Descartes's is with an idealized knower. Any information about the context of a particular individual is stripped out of the account. Details about a person's context only sully the account of knowledge-producing rules" (50).
(f) "The scope of traditional epistemology . . . is limited to overcoming skepticism with an idealized knower" (50).
(g) "Truth is a goal because a justified true belief of a true proposition meets the challenge of skepticism" (51).

Constraints of space mean that I cannot hope to offer a detailed discussion of all these assertions. Rather, I shall give a brief (but I hope plausible) sketch of how I understand the aims, scope and method of traditional epistemology, contrasting as I proceed the elements in my account with those in Eflin's TE.

2. Epistemology: Aims, Scope and Method

I agree with Linda Zagzebski's claim that "the nature of knowledge is arguably the central concern of epistemology, and unarguably one of the major interests of philosophy from its beginning" (Zagzebski 1996, 1). I shall assume that the goal of epistemology has traditionally been to say something enlightening about the nature of knowledge, and the nature of the relations in which it stands to, for example, justification, evidence, rationality, truth, cognitive motivation, knowing subjects, reliability and so on. Moreover, it has tended to be the case, in the modern period, that the fundamental concepts in terms of which a theory of knowledge is to be given have been taken to relate, in the first instance, to properties of belief states. If contemporary virtue theorists are right to claim that epistemological theories that have as their 'locus of evaluation' (individual) beliefs are directly analogous to ethical theories that address themselves in the primary case to ethical qualities of acts, we can say that traditional epistemology involves presuppositions that favour a consequentialist/deontological stance towards epistemic value (Zagzebski 1996, 6–15).

It is worth noting that this seems to locate the 'starting point' for epistemology a stage *before* Eflin's TE. Eflin has in mind, remember, foundationalism and coherentism. But these are best thought of as differing accounts of the *structure* of a rationally held or justified belief set and need not be primarily concerned with, for example, substantive responses to scepticism.[1] For the foundationalist, as is familiar, certain beliefs are justified in a special way, while others are justified via 'warrant transfer' from such beliefs. (See, for example, Haack 1995, 14.) For the coherentist, on the other hand, at least on one plausible view, beliefs need not be justified via warrant transfer, since the obtaining of suitable coherence relations alone can be a source of warrant (Plantinga 1993, 178). Both accounts of the structure of belief sets seem to me to be best seen, at least in the traditional case, as attempts to flesh out a *prior* analysis of knowledge as justified true belief, or as justified true belief plus Gettier blocker. But neither foundationalism nor coherentism would in that case itself be a point of departure for epistemological theory which competes with that of the virtue theorist; rather, they both seem to be part of a debate that only becomes pressing once we are already part of the way down a deontological or consequentialist path (Zagzebski 1996, 7).

It is one of the puzzling aspects of Eflin's account that she neglects this point, since one of the most interesting and attractive aspects of virtue epistemology seems to be the manner in which it can bypass, rather than rival, debates like the one between foundationalism and coherentism. For theories that take belief states as conceptually prior, a natural place to look for justification is in the actual obtaining of the appropriate relations between beliefs, whether warrant transference or coherence. Theories that take properties of agents, rather than beliefs, as conceptually fundamental

---

[1] Historically, of course, philosophers who endorsed foundationalist or coherentist positions were often engaged in justificatory, anti-sceptical projects. This should not distract us, however, from acknowledging that judgements concerning the utility and viability of the structural projects are logically distinct from those relating to the justificatory enterprise.

seem to have wider scope for manoeuvre. For example, Zagzebski's account of the justification of belief avoids defining justification in terms of obtaining *actual* relations holding between *beliefs* and looks rather at the *counterfactual* relations between the beliefs and virtuous agents – roughly, that a belief is justified iff a virtuously motivated person, suitably aware of her cognitive situation, might believe it in like circumstances (not *would* believe it, contra Eflin; see Zagzebski 1996, 233).[2]

3. Epistemology, Scepticism and Idealisation

Eflin partially endorses Zagzebski's account but worries that it shares the fundamental concern of TE, that of endeavouring to refute scepticism. Interpreting, in the interests of charity, Eflin's concern as primarily with the underlying belief-based presuppositions of foundationalism and coherentism, rather than those theories themselves, let us turn to her claims concerning scepticism, context, idealisation and certainty.

I have described the traditional goal of epistemology as aiming to say something enlightening about the nature of knowledge, and the nature of the relations in which it stands to related concepts. How do 'hard cases' and, in particular, sceptical challenges fit with this account? Eflin clearly thinks that the project of giving necessary and sufficient conditions for central epistemological concepts is intrinsically linked to scepticism, as she reveals in her comments on Zagzebski:

> Since her epistemic project is showing that virtues lead to justified belief, and she has given necessary and sufficient conditions for a belief to be justified, Zagzebski is still trying to meet skeptical challenges. (58)

While I agree that much of traditional epistemology has been concerned with scepticism, I do not accept Eflin's claim that proposing an analysis or definition of knowledge reveals a primary concern with refuting sceptical claims. The relationship between scepticism and the attempt to say something enlightening about knowledge seems, rather, to be as follows.

In appraising any account of a concept, we wish to be able to tell whether such an analysis is correct. One way to achieve this is to look for counterexamples or counterintuitive consequences that a particular analysis

---

[2] To be clear, my claim is not that belief-centred theories *cannot* give counterfactual accounts of justificatory relations but rather that such accounts traditionally have not seemed most natural. Nor do I have unqualified sympathy for the details of Zagzebski's account. In particular, it seems to me to run into serious problems in explaining how we might be justified in holding such beliefs as: there are no suitably informed, virtuously motivated people in circumstances similar to ours. Clearly, were it the case that a virtuously motivated person was in like circumstances, she should not believe this. Yet, prima facie, there seems to be no reason why we might not be justified in holding such a belief in certain circumstances. See Plantinga (1982, 47–70), Wright (1999, 204), and Peacocke (1999, 69) for relevant discussion of the structure of this type of point.

entails. Clearly, this is not the only relevant strategy, nor is it completely free of problems.[3] Nevertheless, it is an established and relatively effective method of appraising philosophical theories, and certainly is not peculiar to the proponents of TE. Given such a methodology, and the fact that global or widespread scepticism (the view that it is metaphysically and epistemically possible that we know or have reason to believe almost nothing) has seemed to many philosophers to be extremely counterintuitive, it seems perfectly reasonable to hold it to be a disadvantage of a philosophical account that it does not rule out scepticism. Moreover, given that certain central aspects of our concepts of knowledge and justified belief seem to combine to allow for such a possibility, even on the most plausible accounts of the nature of knowledge, and even (contra Eflin) when we abandon hopes of Cartesian certainty,[4] we seem to be in the uncomfortable position of having to accept that not one of our best accounts of knowledge is problem free. As Crispin Wright puts it, in a discussion concerned to emphasise that the sceptic is essentially *our* conceptual tool,

> That generations of philosophers have felt impelled to grapple with sceptical arguments is not attributable to a courtesy due to an historically distinguished sponsorship but to the fact that these arguments are *paradoxes*: seemingly valid derivations from seemingly well-supported premises of utterly unacceptable consequences. . . . Consider the mythical glass-chinned sceptic who claims that there is no reason to believe anything at all. Nothing easier than to confound such an opponent in debate. But if you yourself are led, in camera as it were, to that absurd conclusion by a seemingly well-motivated route, it is no intellectual comfort to reflect that the position is self-defeating; on the contrary, that simply intensifies the embarrassment. (Wright 1991, 89)

Acknowledging Wright's point is, of course, consistent with holding that productive work in epistemology need not wait upon a suitable dissolution of the sceptical paradoxes. My purpose here is merely to emphasise that, contra Eflin, epistemology does not begin with 'hard cases' as an end in themselves, as it were, to the exclusion of a more everyday concern with

---

[3] Zagzebski (1996, 264–67) provides an interesting discussion of some of the disadvantages of relying too heavily on counterexamples, although she signals her support for the method as a means of making theories more precise. Appeal to counterintuitive consequences seems also to be dialectically constrained by the extent to which proponents of the analysis are prepared to bite the bullet on particular matters. See Jackson (1998) for a contemporary defence of the view that theories of our concepts are best tested by a range of reflective practices, including the method of counterexamples.

[4] Historically, Cartesian scepticism seems to play a role different from that identified here, namely, a foundationalist means of identifying the genuinely basic beliefs. See, for example, Williams (1978, 56). Since I have already argued that foundationalism comes a stage later than the original position for epistemology, and since the failure of the Cartesian project led to scepticism coming to play a quite separate role, I intend to ignore the details of Descartes's account here.

knowledge and knowing subjects.[5] Rather, it is the fact that wholly counterintuitive consequences follow from seemingly innocuous conceptual
claims about such knowledge and knowers that makes, for example, scepticism, deserving of attention.[6]

Eflin does not tell us much about what she means by an 'idealized
knower', why she thinks that TE's reply to scepticism makes essential
appeal to such a subject or how such an appeal might actually speak to
sceptical worries. It seems to me, however, that she thinks traditional
epistemology is essentially *generalist* rather than *particularist* in character – primarily concerned with what she calls "knowledge-producing
rules," at the expense of a concern with "information about the context of
a particular individual," and their "particular desires, particular skills and
particular goals" (48, 50). If this is what she has in mind, then it is clear
that this form of particularism is one of the less interesting varieties. We
might draw here on a distinction we are urged to make in the ethical case
by Roger Crisp:[7]

> There are two issues in ethics [epistemology] that must be kept apart. First,
> what is the truth about how we should live or act [be cognitively, or believe]?
> The virtue theorist will claim that we should live [believe] virtuously, the util-
> itarian that we should so live [believe] so as to maximise the overall balance of
> happiness over unhappiness [truth over falsity]. Secondly, how should we
> think, morally [cognitively]? Here, a virtue theorist is likely to put weight on
> the importance of virtuous dispositions, grounded in a solid moral [cognitive]
> education, and on a sensitivity to the morally [epistemologically] salient
> features of situations. And something like this will probably be recommended
> by the utilitarian, and by any plausible moral [epistemological] theorist. (Crisp
> 2000, 28)

Attention to Crisp's distinction allows us to be clear that there is no inconsistency in giving a general account of *what knowledge consists in*, while
stressing the particularity of *how and why we come to be knowers and gain
knowledge*. Eflin[8] seems to me to blur over or ignore such a distinction; her
TE seems to be primarily concerned with giving generalised decision
procedures that can be employed even in difficult epistemic cases.[9] But
this seems to me to be a quite separate project from the attempt to say

---

    [5] See quotations (c), (d) and (f), above.
    [6] In any case, Zagzebski (1999) attempts to offer necessary and sufficient conditions for
knowledge, and here the focus is explicitly *not* on sceptical concerns.
    [7] My additions within square brackets.
    [8] See quotations (a), (b) and (e) above.
    [9] Note Eflin's claim that "in ethics, the demand is that a moral theory help us resolve
difficult moral dilemmas. . . . The concern is not merely right action but rather right
action on principle. . . . Hard cases are the starting point for traditional epistemology as
well" (49).

something enlightening about what knowledge is, and it is the latter that is the starting point for epistemology as I recognise it.

4. Pluralistic Virtue epistemology

I have raised some problems for the way that Eflin construes the founding aims of traditional epistemology. In this final section, I wish to turn briefly to her more positive account.

Eflin outlines various characteristics and claims various merits for pluralistic epistemology. In particular, it is (1) non-hierarchical; (2) non-complete;[10] (3) not primarily concerned with sceptical worries; (4) avoids "context stripping, which produces an idealized subject by removing his or her circumstances from part of the picture" (65); (5) aims at understanding, rather than knowledge; and (6) takes both "rules and procedures" and epistemic virtues as primary.

I have already argued that Eflin's account of the relationships among traditional epistemology, scepticism and idealisation is questionable, and thus shall not address elements (3) and (4) here, since if my earlier discussion was correct they do not favour Eflin's theory over traditional epistemology. Element (6) seems to me to place pluralistic virtue epistemology at a prima facie disadvantage with regard to both traditional epistemology and 'monistic' virtue epistemology, since both of these theories aim to explain the relevant data using simpler and sparser conceptual and ontological resources. In addition, given that Eflin seems to hold that a combination of rules and procedures and virtue theory can provide the relevant explanations, it is difficult to see why her own theory is not both hierarchical and complete, contrary to advertisement – it looks to me as if she just takes a broader range of conceptually basic elements as necessary to provide complete explanations of problems within the epistemological domain.

Moreover, taking both rules and virtues as primary seems to vitiate Eflin's earlier claim that "a theory based on epistemic virtues will not only give us an insight into the nature and production of understanding but will also enable us to understand the function and authority of rules" (49). I therefore take it that (6) does not give us reason to favour pluralistic virtue epistemology over its rivals, at least not until we are presented with a convincing argument that neither of the other two theories Eflin considers can do the requisite explanatory work alone.

Eflin does offer an argument to the effect that neither standard virtue theory nor traditional epistemology can give us wholly satisfactory

---

[10] Eflin defines these terms as follows: "For a theory to be hierarchical, some set of notions is taken as basic and other elements in the theory are derived from or reduced to these basic elements. . . . For a theory to be complete, . . . everything in the theory's domain is accounted for in terms of these basic concepts" (52).

explanations of the full range of epistemological data. She suggests, roughly, that since (1) virtue theory has to presuppose that virtuous agents are epistemically successful and (2) traditional epistemology is over-concerned with formulating exceptionless decision procedures, neither offers a fully satisfactory account. I have already, I hope, done something to undermine the second horn of her proposed dilemma. But it is perhaps worth noting that there are reasons to be concerned with her presentation of the first horn as well. Eflin, noting that Zagzebski makes non-accidental epistemic success a conceptual truth about the virtuous agent, claims that "if 'virtue' is a success term, it would seem that any virtue epistemology would be askeptical" (12). But this is surely a non-sequitur. Epistemic success is a *conceptual* truth about virtuous agents, so if there are any such subjects, they are epistemically successful. But nothing about this claim entails or supports the view that there *are* any virtuous agents, or presupposes that such and such a sceptical hypothesis does not obtain. Standard virtue theory is committed to the claim that, if we have any knowledge, the nature of that knowledge is best specified in terms that refer to virtues, or to other enduring properties of agents. But this is a claim about the nature of knowledge; scepticism is a side issue.

School of Philosophy
University of Leeds
Leeds LS2 9JT
United Kingdom
a.mcgonigal@leeds.ac.uk

References

Crisp, Roger. 2000. "Particularizing Particularism." In *Moral Particularism*, edited by Brad Hooker and Margaret Olivia Little, 23–47. Oxford: Oxford University Press.

Haack, Susan. 1995. *Evidence and Enquiry.* Oxford: Basil Blackwell.

Jackson, Frank. 1998. *From Metaphysics to Ethics: A Defence of Conceptual Analysis.* Oxford: Oxford University Press.

Peacocke, Christopher. 1999. *Being Known.* Oxford: Oxford University Press.

Plantinga, Alvin. 1982. "How to Be an Anti-Realist." *Proceedings and Addresses of the American Philosophical Association* 56: 47–70.

————. 1993. *Warrant and Proper Function.* New York: Oxford University Press.

Williams, Bernard. 1978. *Descartes: The Project of Pure Enquiry.* Harmondsworth: Penguin.

Wright, Crispin. 1991. "Scepticism and Dreaming: Imploding the Demon." *Mind* 100: 87–116.

————. 1999. "Truth: A Traditional Debate Reviewed." In *Truth*, edited by Simon Blackburn and Keith Simmons, 203–38. New York: Oxford University Press.

Zagzebski, Linda. 1996. *Virtues of the Mind: An Inquiry into the Nature of Virtue and the Ethical Foundations of Knowledge*. Cambridge: Cambridge University Press.

————. 1999. "What Is Knowledge?" In *Epistemology*, edited by J. Greco and E. Sosa, 92–116. Oxford: Basil Blackwell.

© Metaphilosophy LLC and Blackwell Publishing Ltd. 2003.
Published by Blackwell Publishing, 9600 Garsington Road, Oxford OX4 2DQ, UK and
350 Main Street, Malden, MA 02148, USA
METAPHILOSOPHY
Vol. 34, Nos. 1/2, January 2003
0026-1068

AFFECTIVE STATES AND EPISTEMIC IMMEDIACY

CHRISTOPHER HOOKWAY

ABSTRACT: This article defends the view that an adequate response to some central epistemological problems requires us to find a role for emotions and other affective states in epistemic evaluation and also to invoke virtuous traits of character in order to explain how these affective evaluations are regulated. The argument is based on the need for some epistemic evaluations to possess a kind of immediacy, if we are not to face a worrying regress. The closing sections support the claim that epistemic evaluation depends upon appropriate character traits though a discussion of what is involved in being *observant*.

Keywords: emotions, epistemology, immediacy, reasons, virtues.

1. Introduction

Ethics and epistemology are both concerned with aspects of our evaluative practice. Ethics studies the evaluation of actions and agents, and their mental states and characters, from a distinctive viewpoint or employing a distinctive vocabulary. And epistemology examines the evaluation of actions (inquiries and assertions), agents (believers and inquirers), and agents' states (belief and attitudes) from a different viewpoint. Given this common concern with evaluation, we should surely expect there to be considerable similarities between the issues examined and the ideas employed in the two areas. When, however, we examine most textbooks in ethics and epistemology, this expectation is not fulfilled. Of course, the vocabularies of evaluation are different: in ethics, we are concerned with issues of right and wrong, virtue and vice, moral obligation, and so on; and in epistemology, it is most commonly assumed that we are interested in whether states count as knowledge or as justified beliefs, whether beliefs and strategies of belief formation are rational. But this should not prevent the common concern with evaluation ensuring that similar underlying issues arise in both areas, and that attending to these parallels can be a source of philosophical illumination.

This article examines some ways in which epistemology can benefit from attending to such parallels. I shall concentrate upon two ideas which have had a central role in much work in ethics, but which have received little attention in epistemology. First, most ethical theories attach importance to affective states, such as emotions. Some theorists view moral opinions themselves as affective attitudes, or as grounded in such attitudes. Others give a role to emotions in the explanation of moral motivation, not merely as states that can cause us to act badly but also as aids to acting well. Thus, even if the content of morality is not grounded in sentiments or emotions, our ability to act well may depend upon reverence for the moral law, sympathy, and so on. While everyone would agree that anger or envy can have a role in explaining our epistemic failings, few theorists insist that appropriate patterns of affective response may be *required* for inquiring or believing well. And even fewer would insist that taking the role of emotions, or other affective states, seriously is necessary if we are to deal in a satisfactory way with what we can think of as the *central* problems of epistemology – for example, the defusing of scepticism or the study of how 'internalist' and 'externalist' demands in the theory of justification can be integrated. It is rare to find the argument that affective states or emotions can have a role in explaining how epistemic evaluation is possible.

Second, there is little emphasis on the role of traits of character – habits and virtues – in ensuring our epistemic well being, although, once again, such states have a central role in most moral theories, not only in those that can be described as 'virtue ethics'. The message of this essay is that in both of these respects epistemology has failed to make use of ideas that should be central to our understanding of epistemic evaluation. Moreover, these failures are connected. Recognising the role of emotional responses in epistemic evaluation will help us to see why states of character are important for epistemology; and taking seriously the role of states of character can help us to understand how the involvement of the emotions can be an aid, rather than an impediment, to our epistemic evaluations.[1]

My focus is on the role of 'affective' evaluations in accounting for a kind of 'immediacy' that is characteristic of many of our most important epistemic evaluations. After introducing this form of 'unreflective' immediacy in section 2 through a discussion of some of Quine's views on induction, I try to clarify it and explain its interest in section 3. Section 4 makes a case for its importance by showing how it enables us to block some worrying regresses and helps with integrating internalist and externalist themes in epistemic evaluation. The final section explores the epistemic virtue of 'being observant' in order to explain how such traits may be necessary for our epistemic evaluations to succeed. The discussion complements some other recent work of mine on *doubt* and on the role of emotional evaluations in scientific inquiry.[2]

---

[1] This overstates the position, of course. The literature on virtue epistemology has grown rapidly over recent years. See Axtell 2000, Fairweather and Zagzebski 2001, Sosa 1991, Zagzebski 1996, and DePaul and Zagzebski 2003. A number of authors have begun to emphasise the role of affective states in epistemic evaluation. See, for example, Thagard (2002) and Elgin (1996).

[2] See Hookway (2000a, chaps. 9 and 10; 2001; 2002).

2. Emotions and Epistemic Evaluation

As we have noted, emotions can be invoked to explain people's epistemic *failings*: anger leads to irrationality by making us fail to take note of significant information or leading us to make flawed judgements of relevance. Anger can explain why we sometimes fail to reflect sufficiently on our grounds for our beliefs or on the ways in which have formed them. It might also explain how, even if we reflect at great length, we do so poorly, obsessively focusing on the objects of our anger or irritation and failing to notice other relevant considerations. This suggests that states like anger can impair our epistemic position by distorting our reflections on our beliefs and inquiries: we fail to notice, or to give sufficient weight to, relevant considerations. Emotions or traits of character may also have a positive role, explaining how we *can* be motivated to reflect more carefully or to be more attentive to what is most relevant: perhaps we are *anxious* about the consequences of our inquiries going wrong, or perhaps we are *proud* of our fastidious intellectual standards.

These possibilities suggest that emotions can have a role in regulating the paths taken by our reflection and deliberation, and thus can influence the ways in which our standards inform our beliefs and inquiries. From an epistemological point of view, however, such possibilities do not yet point towards a role for emotions in resolving fundamental epistemological problems. They provide no reason for supposing that taking emotions seriously is required if we are to engage in responsible epistemic evaluation at all. Perhaps they are aids to inquiring efficiently, speeding things up and providing valuable short cuts. But this is compatible with their being in principle dispensable. A role for emotions or character traits in epistemic evaluation could play a part in our strategies for resisting scepticism, or could enable us to make sense of the phenomenon of recognising something as a reason for belief or of our ability to arrive at beliefs we can take to be justified, only if this role could be seen to be indispensable and not just a heuristic aid.

We may feel that it is unsurprising that affective states have a lesser role in epistemology than in ethics: this can be explained by reference to a significant lack of parallel between the central problems we confront in the two areas. The goals of our epistemic evaluations, we might suppose, are uncontroversial: we seek true beliefs or we seek knowledge. And these goals – in spite of the failures of many attempts to provide one – can receive an uncontroversial clarification. If that is right, then the fundamental role for emotions in accounting for epistemic evaluation lies in explaining how we can be efficient in pursuing these goals: they guide the choice of means to epistemic ends. Perhaps the fundamentals of ethics and action, the goals of our evaluations, are more controversial. In that case, it may be suggested, the problems of epistemology concern the selection of means to uncontroversial ends, while those of ethics also concern the identification of ends for action and ideas about the good life. Questions of motivation and integrity – questions to which discussion of emotion and virtue may be relevant – may have a role in debates about the nature of moral worth, but they are less obviously relevant to the question of whether a belief is true or counts as knowledge.

There is much to discuss in this suggestion, in particular its assumptions about the role of *truth* and *knowledge* in setting our cognitive goals, but I shall not pursue all those questions here. Instead, I want to urge that a satisfactory response to central problems of epistemology *can* and *should* make use of facts about emotions and traits of character or habits. Their role is not simply one of making our deliberations and evaluations more efficient; they may have a role in showing how such evaluations are possible at all. I shall begin with emotions and affective states, and I shall consider a passage from chapter 1 of Quine's *Word and Object* in which he discusses how we evaluate beliefs (the acceptance of sentences) in the light of evidence:

> The sifting of evidence would seem . . . to be a strangely passive affair, apart from the effort to intercept helpful stimuli: we just try to be as responsive as possible to the ensuing interplay of chain stimulations. What conscious policy does one follow, then, when not simply passive towards this inter-animation of sentences? Consciously the quest seems to be for the simplest story. Yet this supposed quality of simplicity is more easily sensed than described. Perhaps our vaunted sense of simplicity, or of likeliest explanation, is in many cases just a feeling of conviction attaching to the blind resultant of the interplay of chain stimulations in their various strengths. (Quine 1960, 19)

Although the topic is not mentioned, we can read this passage as an acknowledgment of the challenge to the Carnapian project of inductive logic found in Goodman's 'new riddle' of induction. That all observed emeralds are green (and are thus also grue) gives us a reason to believe that all emeralds are green but does not provide us with a reason to believe that all emeralds are grue. We sense ('feel') that the 'green' hypothesis is simpler than the 'grue' one, and this reflects facts about the structure of our 'web of belief': but reflection does not make transparent to us just what factors we are sensitive to, and, according to Quine, we cannot identify the formal principles of inductive reasoning that we are following. And the claim that the green hypothesis is 'simpler' is best seen as an expression of the fact that we find it more plausible, and not as the identification of the deep fact that explains its plausibility. In view of our background knowledge and the evidence we have collected, the inference is plausible and compelling: we find it compelling, and we are right to do so. But how and why this is the case is not something that is transparent to us, it is not something that we can bring to full reflective consciousness. If we want to describe the phenomenology of such an inference, of the sense that it is compelling, we might say that it possesses a kind of 'immediacy'.

82   CHRISTOPHER HOOKWAY

It is not my aim to defend any of the details of Quine's theory of knowledge here. But the passage suggests a number of conjectures about beliefs that are based upon evidence and inductive reasoning:

1. Forming beliefs on the basis of evidence does not depend upon rules that we can formulate and appeal to in defending our conclusions. We should not expect to be able to construct a system of inductive logic that parallels familiar systems of formal logic for deductive arguments.
2. Reflection is shallow: we are right not to ask too many questions, not to carry reflection into the grounds of our beliefs to excess; we should trust our responses to evidence without being able to understand how they work or to control their operation. The conclusion may possess a kind of immediacy.
3. The goodness of the inference is something that is felt. This I take to be a phenomenological point and to suggest that the vehicle of our confidence in the inference is *affective*.
4. We say we look for a *simple* account of our evidence. But we have no independent account of simplicity; the inference feels simple because it is inductively good. Thus a theory of simplicity does not provide the basis of a system of inductive logic. Talk of simplicity is, simply, an acknowledgment of the felt 'immediate' attractiveness of the inference. Thus simplicity "is implicit in unconscious steps (of inference) as well as half explicit in deliberate ones" (Quine 1960, 20). It is unlikely to be 'fully explicit'.
5. Belief formation has a largely holistic character. This is implicit in most of the earlier points: when we acquire beliefs on the basis of evidence, there is not a definite body of premises on which we depend, all our other beliefs and opinions having no role in the formation of the belief.

These claims concern what we may describe as the 'internal' dimension of justification. Perhaps the relations between our beliefs and their evidence can receive some sort of theoretical explanation, but, if it can, this is not available to reflection, and it is not something that can guide us in thinking about our beliefs and ensuring that they are well supported. In normal circumstances, we trust our 'passive' habitual responses, recognising (or hoping) that they manifest a better understanding of our epistemic position than we can articulate. The evidential relations on which we depend are not available to reflection. We might express this by saying that the goodness of the inference has a sort of *immediacy*: we may be able to point to the evidence on which we depend and say *something* about how it supports our conclusions, but the adequacy of this evidence to its purpose is not determined by other beliefs and principles that are available to us. These views reflect supposed facts about the structure of the support of our beliefs (it reflects what Quine calls 'moderate holism') and about the degree to which such facts are available to reflection. This makes it plausible that, if we were not equipped with a reasonably reliable faculty for making 'immediate' judgements of plausibility, we would not able to make sound judgements of the support of our beliefs and theories at all. We can be confident of the rationality of our beliefs only if we can be confident of our habits of 'immediate evaluation'.

I shall develop some ideas suggested by the passage from Quine, but, in doing so, I am not undertaking Quinean exegesis or working within a Quinean approach to epistemology. The passage is supposed to illustrate four themes. First, the goodness of an inference, even a complex one, often has a kind of *immediacy*. I can point to reasons that are claimed to support the conclusion, but I may not be able to articulate why they are sufficient to establish its truth or even explain how they support it. The second is a kind of 'anti-intellectualism'. That my reasons are good ones depends upon, supervenes on, a mass of background knowledge. But to represent what I am doing as making a formal inference, perhaps one that depends on many unstated premises, distorts what is going on. We should not model this kind of cognitive activity upon the deliberate carrying out of inferences that can receive a formal representation.

The third theme is that our standards of evidence and of rational belief are manifested in our inferential practice, in the inferences we find compelling, rather than in principles that we can state and defend. We can leave it open whether there are principles that could be formulated by theorists: the point is that such principles have little role in our reflective evaluative practice. As Quine suggests, which inferences feel simple to us provides evidence of which inferences we take to be good. It is a matter for empirical study how our practice can be systematised and explained.

The quotation from Quine suggests that 'deliberate' reasoning is only 'half explicit'. We might appeal to considerations as providing reasons for our beliefs. But they can serve as good reasons only against the background of a mass of unstated views and habits. We may also appeal to standards or principles that justify us in reasoning as we do. But these often serve as rules of thumb that are reliable, once again, only because of a largely non-explicit background. Reasons and the rules we invoke possess a kind of salience, standing out from the background and receiving explicit formulation or recognition. This does not suffice to make our reasoning fully explicit: the portion that is explicit functions against this non-explicit background.

These remarks are offered as a description of our practice of reasoning about theoretical matters. Although the description is abstract, I hope it captures something of the phenomenology of such reasoning. Its interest lies in the way it can be used to make plausible the thesis that affective states can have an important role in epistemic evaluation.

If this Quinean description is right, then, when we accept a proposition on the basis of evidence, we possess:

1. A feeling towards a belief or proposition
2. that reveals standards of epistemic evaluation
3. which we cannot necessarily articulate
4. but with which we can confidently identify ourselves, which we trust.

The conjecture to be explored is that this is an affective evaluation, and that the fact that it is affective explains a number of puzzling features of our evaluative practice.

These features are of two kinds. The first I shall call 'motivational': these evaluations are involved in the ways in which we are motivated to terminate and initiate inquiries and deliberations. For example, our positive evaluation of our inductive inference explains why we feel no need to inquire further into the matter under consideration, at least for the time being. We rest content with the proposition unless further evidence or reflection disturbs it, producing a doubt of the merits of the earlier inference. Once we acknowledge the inductive inference as a good one, our inquiries are suspended; and our account of how such reasoning works must explain how this happens.

A second 'motivational' issue relates to doubt (cf. Hookway 2000a, chap. 10): why do we feel doubt of (experience anxiety about) other beliefs that are in tension with this one? The production of doubt in one proposition once we feel confident of another is similar to the ways in which our emotional economy regulates our conduct. Once I feel confident that there are storm clouds on the horizon, fear leads me to seek the quickest route home. Once I feel confident that I made an error in my proof, if I am rational I anxiously reflect on whether this was my sole reason for accepting its conclusion, and consider whether it should be abandoned. So, in addition to explaining why inquiries come to an end, these evaluations can explain how they are initiated.

How does the appeal to emotions and the affective explain these features? As well as embodying evaluations that appeal to standards that we do not, and perhaps cannot, articulate, and as well as motivating us to inquire and reflect in distinctive ways, these evaluations 'spread' through our cognitive systems. When I come to doubt a method of inquiry, this produces anxiety about beliefs that are known to result from the application of this method; when I evaluate a proposition positively, I am disposed to evaluate positively propositions that follow from it and to feel anxiety about beliefs that conflict with it. Thus, it is suggested, the way in which paradigmatic emotional evaluations spread through our concerns and actions provides a model for understanding how epistemic evaluations spread as well. It also casts light on how tensions can emerge within our system of epistemic evaluations, making sense, for example, of epistemic akrasia (Fairweather and Zagzebski 2001, chap. 11).

Thus, the conjecture is that, in these sorts of immediate epistemic evaluation, we are concerned with:

1. An affectively characterised judgement about an inference or proposition
2. that expresses my values,
3. which cannot be replaced by a full intellectual defence of the inference or proposition,
4. which has a *motivational* force,
5. and whose impact depends upon the way its influence is spread through my affective economy.

3. Immediacy

The important point is that the range of phenomena I have been describing introduce a kind of epistemic/evaluative *immediacy*. This notion has a number of uses in epistemology, so I should try to clarify what I have in mind. One notion of immediacy is metaphysical: for an inference to be immediately compelling, there are no other facts upon which its being compelling depends (or, perhaps, there are no other facts in virtue of which it is compelling). This is not the notion that concerns me here. An inference would be immediately compelling if my finding it compelling is not *grounded* in knowledge of other facts that, it is recognised, render it compelling. If asked why the inference is compelling, I can offer no reasons that justify my acceptance of it. Although I cannot justify my belief, it may be possible to construct an explanation of why it is compelling. For example, a cognitive psychologist may explain why our sensory apparatus is reliable, and this might enable us to understand the complex causal processes that mediate between us and the objects of our perceptions. It is compatible with our having such an explanation that perceptual judgements might be immediate in the sense that interests me. Ordinary reflection on such judgements as we form them does not treat them as inferential. They are phenomenologically immediate. Such immediacy involves possession of a kind of salience: inferences and propositions stand out as possessing particular epistemic values, as being relevant, in different ways, to our epistemic practice. Even if the goodness of a piece of inductive reasoning may supervene on the membership and structure of my web of belief, the judgement that it is a good inference may possess this kind of immediacy: I cannot provide an argument which establishes that it is good. Even if I can point to some of the features of my environment on which this inference depends, their being relevant (or salient) for the evaluation of my argument may possess this kind of immediacy.

My aim is to argue that the solution to some central epistemological problems requires us to make sense of just this kind of immediacy. We shall then move on to virtues or character traits. I shall argue that these can be invoked to make sense of the stable patterns of immediate (emotional) response that are required to make sense of epistemic evaluation.

What sorts of things, which may have epistemological relevance, can have the sort of immediacy that I have been describing? As I noted, we can think of propositions, et cetera, that have this kind of immediacy as possessing a sort of (emotional or affective) *salience*. And the possibility we are concerned with is that the possession of such salience by things may be necessary for our epistemic well-being. The kinds of things that can possess such salience can differ, as can the particular (epistemic) evaluations that this salience can record. Before indicating some of this variety, let us introduce a (somewhat crude) way of thinking about epistemic evaluation.

We can begin by thinking about the activity of *inquiry*: this is an attempt to answer a question or solve a problem. When we carry out such an inquiry reflectively, we raise and consider further questions or problems concerning how it is carried out, how it has progressed, the appropriateness of methods employed and so on. Our inquiries may fail if we fail to raise relevant questions; they may be inefficient or even falter if we ask too many. Hence, if we think that our practice of epistemic evaluation regulates such activities of inquiry, we can begin to identify the different forms of (emotional) salience and immediacy by reference to their role in regulating this activity.

So here are some objects of epistemic salience:

1. Inferences can be immediately compelling. Notice that what this means is that distinctive questions do *not* arise concerning them. If the inference is immediately compelling, then the question of why that inference is to be accepted is lacking in salience – the question simply does not arise.
2. Some doubts are immediately forceful (real or felt doubts). If, as I suggested above and have argued at length elsewhere, real felt doubt should be viewed as a kind of anxiety, we can take it that the need to address a question, or to solve a problem, can possess an immediate kind of salience. (See Hookway 2000a, chap. 10.)
3. In general, inquiring well typically involves the right questions becoming salient to us. We succeed so long as the questions that occur to us as needing answers are relevant to the success of our project.

When Quine emphasises the shallowness of reflection, the claim is that many of the questions that philosophers have assumed should be salient to us in regulating our inquiries quite correctly lack salience. There are two claims here: in general, these questions *are* not salient for us; and, if they were to become salient, this would be a bad thing and would impair our capacity for responsible reflective inquiry.

I suggested that it is important for our practice of responsible inquiry that some questions simply do not arise. Such claims can be of different kinds. One sort of example concerns cases where questions simply do not occur to me. Normally, when I judge the colour of something by casual observation, it does not occur to me to ask whether lighting conditions are normal. I *could* ask this and, if I were to do so, I would probably be able to answer my question. But since abnormal lighting conditions are rare and, when they occur, they would normally force themselves upon my attention, it is good strategy not to waste time and energy thinking about the matter – except in very special cases. Trusting to the immediate salience (lack of salience) of such questions is a good time-saving strategy, but it is dispensable (in principle if not in practice) and thus probably does not touch deep issues of epistemic evaluation. (It could still touch such issues if the task of raising and responding to every such question would impose burdens of reflection and investigation that would prevent our ever finishing our inquiries. But perhaps it would be enough that we could address *any* such question even if we could not address *every* such question.)

The Quinean example suggests a more complex kind of case. If Quine is right about the structure of inductive reasoning, there are questions that I would not be able to answer if I did raise them. In such cases it is more plausible that the ability to avoid raising some such questions is essential to epistemic well-being. The explanation of why this question should not be raised is a different one, but it is not obvious that such differences are reflected in the 'phenomenology of deliberation'. Perhaps it is, perhaps not: either way, it is important that education and training equip us to avoid questions that should not be addressed. In other cases ("Might I be a brain in a vat?") the explanation of why it is good not to address such questions may be different again. But the difficulty philosophers have in explaining just what is wrong with such questions serves further to underline the importance of their having no immediate appeal outside the philosophy class. The differences in explanation do not rule out the possibility that the phenomenology does not differ, that our habits of not addressing such issues can take the form of affectively loaded immediate evaluations.

In order to make these points clearer, I want to consider two different regresses that might engage us when we think about the epistemic status of our beliefs. The first of these I shall call the regress of reasons. Suppose that when my belief in p is challenged I offer a reason in its defence – say q: my reason for believing that p is that q. We would face a worrying regress in our account of how responsible regulation of our cognitive states is possible if I could always then ask:

What reason have I to accept q?
What reason is there for thinking that q is a reason for believing p?

Responsible reflection would then have no end. But, of course, in general this does not happen, and it does not need to happen. If these questions do not arise, if they lack epistemic salience, and it is a sign of my strong epistemic position that they have no salience for me, then there is no requirement that I be able to respond to questions about the soundness of my reasons. This will occur, as we have seen, if it is immediately evident that I can accept q as a reason to believe q and it is immediately evident to me that q. And immediate evidence, here, is to be understood as a form of emotional salience. This means that this claim is consistent with it being the case that q's being a reason for me to believe that p supervenes or depends upon many other features of my web of belief. Had my overall cognitive position been different, I might indeed have found these questions salient: in appropriate circumstances, it may indeed be controversial whether q is a reason to believe that p. Thus many of my beliefs, much of my experience, and many of my habits of inference and judgement might, as we can put it, be relevant to the fact that my belief is justified without providing material that is (or should be) salient to epistemic reflection. Propositions count as my *reasons* for a belief when they stand out from the crowd, when I identify them as salient considerations that – against a background view of things – support the proposition in question.[3] There is no regress in the giving of reasons, and this is because the propositions that express my reasons and the belief that they do express satisfactory reasons can both be immediate in the way that I have described. What grounds my reasons does not have to be salient, so salient questions will not necessarily arise about the grounds of my reasons.

We are all familiar with a second regress, one that concerns justification. Suppose my belief that p depends for its justification on q. There are at least two candidate 'questions' that might arise about this claim:

What justifies my claim that q justifies p?
What reason is there for believing that q justifies p?

(There are similar candidate questions about the claim that the belief that q: What justifies it? and What reason is there for holding it?) If whenever I take a belief to be justified, or I take myself to have a reason for holding some belief, these further questions were to become salient (or ought to become salient), I would face a burden of reflection that could not be discharged. Responsible deliberation and inquiry would not be possible. But once we are careful about the features of evaluation that I have described, there is no reason to think that we do face that burden of reflection. When properly trained in the mastery of concepts and techniques of inquiry, when properly educated in the exercise of judgement, our habitual evaluations enable us to inquire well without excessive reflection.

First, however, we should look at two reasons for thinking that these things should be salient. First: if we have an excessively intellectualist

---

[3] The idea that "emotions can serve rationality by dealing with the insufficiencies of (conscious deliberative) reason by controlling salience" is found in de Sousa (1987, 201). For further discussion of de Sousa's views, see Hookway (2002, 259–61).

picture of justification, then everything that is *relevant* to the belief being justified would be identified as a reason for holding it. This may be the picture of justification that we saw Quine reacting against. It has to be possible for everything relevant to the epistemic status of my views to be 'open to view'. Then we would indeed have reasons for thinking q, and we should ask what they are. If we do not have that picture, it is harder to see how this regress can be grounded in a regress of justification.

There *may* be a second way to argue for a regress of reasons based on facts about 'justification'. Moreover, examining how this could go will help us to see why it is necessary for our evaluations to be guided by aspects of salience that are specifically *emotional* or affective. More important for present purposes, it also helps us to see why we should give an important role to such states as virtues.

The argument takes off from the fact that whether our emotional evaluations are well attuned to the efficient pursuit of correct answers to our questions is a contingent matter. Flaws in our background knowledge, reliance on simple heuristics that work only in specific kinds of circumstances, and various kinds of emotional disturbance could all ensure that our affective valuations will lead us wrong. So, we might suppose, dependence upon the immediacy provided by emotional salience, together with the contingency of any match between emotional salience and epistemic relevance, ensures that at best we obtain a conditional justification for our beliefs. Our beliefs are justified so long as our evaluative practice is attuned to what is epistemically relevant.

This looks like a familiar epistemological problem:

(a) We can investigate what can be called the subjective dimension of our practice: how far our ways of forming beliefs conform to standards that we accept. Once we acknowledge that reflection is often shallow, this can turn into a question about whether any questions occur as salient that we cannot answer, about whether reasonable reflection on our beliefs gives rise to doubts and uncertainties. If we pass these tests, we are normally confident of the beliefs we arrive at and the inquiries we conduct.

(b) We can investigate how far our strategies of epistemic evaluation meet our cognitive needs. Do they make us reliable in the pursuit of truth?

To answer scepticism, it seems, we need to combine these perspectives: we must be *properly confident* (subjective) that we are *reliable* (objective).[4]

---

[4] This is probably much too simple a formulation. In *Knowledge and Reference in Empirical Science*, Jody Azzouni defends a view according to which what is required is that we be confident that we understand the scope of our theories, the range of questions we can handle successfully, while acknowledging that we may not be reliable over the whole range of questions that form the program or goal of our concerns.

The worry we now face is that we can only be properly confident that our emotional evaluations are *conditionally* reliable. So long as emotional salience tracks epistemic relevance, our confidence may be properly grounded. But this suggests that all we can be confident of is:

If what we find epistemically salient tracks what is epistemically relevant, then we can be reliable in solving problems, answering questions, obtaining knowledge, getting justified beliefs, and so on.

Now I want to suggest that, if justification rests on feelings towards beliefs and inferences that involve 'immediate' evaluations, the problem of closing this gap fades. The "problem" has two aspects:

1. *Explanatory*: there is an interesting explanatory question of accounting for why our emotional evaluations are appropriate to our cognitive needs.

As this is an explanatory question, perhaps even a naturalistic explanation (for example, an evolutionary one) will prove adequate. The present argument does not require that this be the case. If this is the aspect of the problem we focus on, however, the problem stated above does not arise. Our confidence in our cognitive capacities will not be shaken unless we acquire strong *reasons* for thinking that such an explanation cannot be provided. Unless we acquire such reasons, it is reasonable to hope that one can be provided and that our failure to do so need not make epistemically salient any doubts that we cannot deal with.

2. *Justificatory*: What justifies our confidence in our practice? We might argue that unless we can give a justification of our trust in our emotional evaluations, we should feel anxiety about the ordinary beliefs that depend upon them. If we don't we can see that this is an epistemic failing – and we should thus feel anxiety about the fact that we feel no such anxieties.

This, however, is a mistake. So long as we identify with our emotional evaluations, this quite properly produces doubt of most considerations that question them. Our confidence is untouched, and this is fully appropriate. If we accept that our immediate evaluations are carried by judgements of *emotional* salience, then (*ceteris paribus*) these abstract doubts about unreliability lack the salience to shake our confidence. But this line of response will not be available if our epistemic evaluations are not carried by emotions or other affective states.

4. Patterns of Salience

Before turning to some examples, I want to explain why habits of salience and such character traits as virtues form an important part of this story. Let us start by asking what excellences we need to possess in order to inquire well.

First, we possess a variety of skills and capacities: we might think of good eyesight or memory, knowledge of some subject matter, and so on. Although they contribute to our success as inquirers, they do not suffice for epistemic effectiveness. We have to use these skills and excellences effectively, to manage them, regulating the inquiries and other activities in which they are employed. That I possess good eyesight says nothing about how attentive I am to the things I see. Nor does it say anything about which things I notice: I could exercise my good eyesight by dwelling obsessively on distinguishing the shades of the different bricks in the wall or constantly checking on the presence of all of my finger nails. I shall inquire well only when I notice things that are epistemically relevant – only when what is epistemically salient tracks what is epistemically relevant. We might think that traits analogous to Aristotelian virtues may have a role here: they guide the use we make of our skills and capacities in carrying out inquiries effectively.

The reason for talking about *virtues* is that they relate to *patterns* in the ways in which we use our various skills and capacities. I shall suggest that the possession of such traits explains patterns in our emotional epistemic saliences; they explain how there can be questions we find immediately pressing, conclusions and inferences we find immediately evident. In this section I shall illustrate this point by considering an example. Then I shall argue that without such patterns, our confidence in our immediate epistemic evaluations will be potentially unstable.

Earlier sections of this essay have focused on the subjective side, on what we might call the phenomenology of epistemic evaluation. The current section approaches the questions from the direction of epistemic relevance. The question is: What do we need to be able to do in order to be effective in our epistemic evaluations? And I shall assume, simply as a hypothetical basis for argument, that we accept an analysis of knowledge that appeals to 'relevant alternatives': suppose that knowledge is understood as requiring the ability to identify and defeat all relevant alternatives to the proposition we know. In order to obtain knowledge so understood, we require the following abilities:

(a) The ability to identify whether something is an alternative.
(b) The ability to recognise whether it is a *relevant* one.
(c) The ability to recognise whether a relevant alternative is still 'live'.
(d) The ability to establish what information is relevant to defeating any given relevant alternative.
(e) The ability to establish whether that information is available.
(f) The ability to judge that no relevant alternative is live.

These abilities obviously depend upon on a host of other skills, capacities, faculties, et cetera. Their exercise also depends upon a large mass of background knowledge – assumptions about prior probabilities and so on.

Unless we can do these things – and do them reliably – our epistemic position would be flawed.

It is evident that carrying out these tasks in a fully explicit way would put impossible demands on time, memory, energy, et cetera. An equally implausible view of how things work would be that, if we are well attuned, well educated, and so forth, an alternative occurs to us as relevant if, and only if, it is relevant and live. That is: considerations become salient for us if and only if they are relevant to the task of seeking knowledge. The only alternatives that occur to us are relevant; and all the alternatives that occur to us are relevant. In general, there is a role for some reflection, and also for some reflection about how much reflection is appropriate. But there are limits to the reflection that occurs, and the existence of these limits can serve our epistemic needs.

Perhaps we *normally* expect that we shall *normally* find ourselves attending to possibilities only if:

1. They are relevant to whether we possess knowledge.
2. Or they are relevant to assessing whether some alternative is relevant to the possession of knowledge.

Unless there is this sort of pattern in our habits of attending to possibilities, and unless we take ourselves to possess habits that display this sort of pattern, we cannot be confident in our 'immediate' judgements of relevance. And we shall not be able to have confidence in our ability to reflect (to the degree that we do) about these matters. So we must possess general capacities that control:

(*a*) What we attend to.
(*b*) What questions occur to us as relevant to the success of our epistemic concerns.
(*c*) What questions simply do not occur to us as relevant to the success of our epistemic concerns.

Notice that these capacities have to regulate what we notice and what we *attend* to. And unless we possess patterns of attention, patterns of immediate salience, then the sort of confident epistemic evaluation described in the early sections of this essay would be impossible. Thus: epistemic evaluation requires *emotional* or affective evaluations that present inferences, propositions and questions as immediately salient; and it requires patterns in these evaluations that enable us to inquire responsibly and effectively. It is these patterns that manifest traits of character that we can describe (loosely) as habits or virtues.

I shall consider just one example of such a trait (I have discussed others elsewhere – such as responses of *doubt* as immediate feelings of epistemic anxiety directed at beliefs that are a source of epistemic 'danger' or risk).

© Metaphilosophy LLC and Blackwell Publishing Ltd. 2003

The example I want to consider is that of being *observant*. This, I take it, is a character trait that has an epistemic focus and regulates what we notice and what we attend to. Moreover, it probably depends upon the possession of some relatively specific skills or faculties – such as having good eyesight. (I think – can you be observant if your eyesight is poor?). Furthermore, it is not reducible to any collection of such skills or to any combination of skills and beliefs about them. It is, rather, a cognitively informed disposition to use those skills and capacities in particular ways. The ways in which the capacities are used appear to be fully epistemic in their character: someone who is observant attends to things that are relevant to his or her goals and epistemic projects.

This characteristic is manifested in the objects, events and states of affairs that become *salient* to the observer in what is noticed (which is not the same as what one is, in a broad sense, aware of). One would not be observant if *everything* in one's field of view became salient. What does become salient should be a reflection of goals and interests at the time (although we do not want to rule out the value of random oddities being salient as well). It is easy to see that our cognitive goals would be impeded if matters that were relevant to our cognitive needs did not become salient. And if lots of things became salient that were not relevant to our cognitive goals, this would get in the way of our inquiries.

5. Salience and Epistemic Virtue

A number of candidate epistemic virtues can be seen as identifying ways in which information can be salient or noticeable. We have already noted the suggestion that real doubt involves some question or problem becoming salient. And virtue can require that we doubt propositions when doing so is relevant to our inquiries, and that we *feel* no doubt when attending to the question would not benefit our inquiries (*ceteris paribus*). Some kinds of epistemic rashness are vices because they encourage us to ask too few questions, to be insensitive to epistemic risks. There are also vices of meticulousness that lead us to be too risk averse, to attend to too many questions.

A supposed virtue such as open-mindedness allows a wider range of possibilities, et cetera, to be salient – or to be candidates for salience. And dogmatism restricts the range of questions, doubts and possibilities that are treated as salient or relevant. Either can be a virtue or a vice, according to the circumstances, and epistemic virtue may require us to adjust our degrees of open-mindedness and dogmatism to our information about the epistemic context. When we consider public co-operative inquiry, we can understand how one person's relative dogmatism can be a virtue so long as there are others who are more open to a wide range of views. My emphasis here is upon the need for traits of character, patterns of emotional evaluation, that provide the immediate evidences required for effective inquiry.

So the fact that someone is observant determines which of the observ-able states of affairs (and perceptual beliefs) become salient. It requires sensitivity to the information that is perceptually available to us: if there is something which, if we noticed it, we would regard it as relevant, then we notice it. In addition, it seems to require sensitivity to the sorts of consid-erations that we *ought* to regard as relevant: if something is noticed, we would normally regard it as relevant. Thus, being observant is a state that informs our habits of attention. It is normally assumed that being observant is a characteristic that is topic neutral. What I notice will, of course, depend upon my background knowledge, my knowledge of the field. But the virtue equips me to attend to the right things, in the light of the background knowledge I possess, whatever the subject matter. My patterns of attention are sensitive to the problem I am concerned with and to my background knowledge; but it is a virtue that can be applied in the service of any subject matter, so long as I possess the appropriate knowledge of the field. (It is, I suppose, an empirical question how far this is true: many people will be observant to different degrees, and someone who is colour blind will be limited in what he or she can notice by this flaw in the underlying skills and capacities upon which being observant depends.)

I have wanted to emphasise the differences between such states as *being observant* and such capacities as *having good eyesight*. And I have tried to suggest that this provides an example of a truly epistemic virtue. When philosophers discuss epistemic virtues, they generally discuss examples of virtues whose content is not wholly epistemic: epistemic courage and open-mindedness are popular examples, and these are cases of more general virtues which apply to the regulation of practical conduct and deliberation as well as matters that are the objects of epistemic evaluation. The virtue of being observant suggests that we do have such a vocabulary, albeit a limited one.[5]

I shall conclude by noting one important similarity between having good eyesight and being observant: both can be misused. If I am easily distracted, applying the capacity involved in my being observant to ends that are irrelevant to my overarching epistemic purpose, then I can fail in my epistemic pursuits. So although my being observant reflects *the use I make* of my good eyesight (et cetera), my success in obtaining knowledge or reaching the truth is sensitive to (among other things) the ways in which I *manage* the use of my trait of being observant. It requires that I be persis-tent in keeping my cognitive goals in view and avoiding distraction, for example. Thus we can understand the role of this virtue only by taking into account its relations to other habits and traits.

This essay, then, has offered considerations suggesting that there is an important role for states that are similar to ethical virtues in epistemic

---

[5] The question whether there are any specifically epistemic virtues was raised by Adam Morton.

evaluation. The first stage of the argument emphasised the role of emotions and sentiments in epistemic evaluation, arguing that they were required in order to make sense of an important kind of immediacy. The second stage urged that success in our inquiries requires us to have stable patterns of finding emotionally salient things that enabled us to use our skills and other excellences effectively. And I have suggested, through an example, that these stable patterns are very similar to the states described as virtues in ethics.

Department of Philosophy
University of Sheffield
Sheffield S10 2TN
United Kingdom
c.j.hookway@sheffield.ac.uk

Acknowledgments

I am grateful to those who contributed to the discussion of the paper on which this article is based, at the conference at Stirling, especially to Marie McGinn for her response. Thanks are also due for some very helpful discussions of papers discussing related material at UNAM, at the University of Durham and at a conference on emotions and rationality at the Center for Philosophical Education at Santa Barbara City College.

References

Axtell, G. 2000. *Knowledge, Belief, and Character*. Lanham, Md.: Rowman and Littlefield.
Carruthers, P. et al., editors. 2002. *The Cognitive Basis of Science*. Cambridge: Cambridge University Press.
Dancy, J., editor. 2000. *Normativity*. Oxford: Basil Blackwell.
DePaul, M., and L. Zagzebski, editors. 2003. *Intellectual Virtue: Perspectives from Ethics and Epistemology*. New York: Oxford University Press.
De Sousa, R. 1987. *The Rationality of Emotion*. Cambridge, Mass.: MIT Press.
Elgin, C. 1996. *Considered Judgement*. Princeton: Princeton University Press.
Fairweather, A. and L. Zagzebski, editors. 2001. *Virtue Epistemology: Essays on Epistemic Virtue and Responsibility*. New York: Oxford University Press.
Hookway, C. 2000a. *Truth, Rationality, and Pragmatism*. Oxford: Clarendon Press.
———. 2000b. "Epistemic Norms and Theoretical Deliberation." In *Normativity*, edited by J. Dancy, 60–77. Oxford: Basil Blackwell.

Hookway, C. 2001. "Epistemic *Akrasia* and Epistemic Virtue." In *Virtue Epistemology: Essays on Epistemic Virtue and Responsibility*, edited by A. Fairweather and L. Zagzebski, 178–99. New York: Oxford University Press.

———. 2002. "Emotions and Epistemic Evaluations." In *The Cognitive Basis of Science*, edited by P. Carruthers et al., 251–62. Cambridge: Cambridge University Press.

Quine, W. V. O. 1960. *Word and Object*. Cambridge, Mass.: MIT Press.

Sosa, Ernest. 1991. *Knowledge in Perspective: Selected Essays in Epistemology*. Cambridge: Cambridge University Press.

Thagard, P. 2002. "The Passionate Scientist: Emotion in Scientific Cognition." In *The Cognitive Basis of Science*, edited by P. Carruthers et al., 235–50. Cambridge: Cambridge University Press.

Zagzebski, L. 1996. *Virtues of the Mind: An Inquiry into the Nature of Virtue and the Ethical Foundations of Knowledge*. New York: Cambridge University Press.

© Metaphilosophy LLC and Blackwell Publishing Ltd. 2003.
Published by Blackwell Publishing,9600 Garsington Road, Oxford OX4 2DQ, UK and
350 Main Street, Malden, MA 02148, USA
METAPHILOSOPHY
Vol. 34, Nos. 1/2, January 2003
0026–1068

REPLY TO HOOKWAY

MARIE McGINN

ABSTRACT: Frege takes the view that "like ethics, logic can also be called a normative science." The parallel that he detects depends upon his commitment to the idea of objective constraints on thought and action, against which particular acts or particular pieces of reasoning can be judged. The point of the comparison is to get us to see that logic is not an empirical science, concerned with laws of thought in a psychological sense; rather, the laws of logic are 'prescriptions for making judgement'. Hookway also detects a parallel, but it prompts him to move in the opposite direction: the point of the parallel is to bring us to appreciate the role of human emotional responses in our ordinary cognitive assessments of the truth of propositions, the soundness of inferences, the relevance of doubts, the appropriateness of questions, and so on. He argues that appreciation of this point enables us to solve some central epistemological problems, in particular, the problem of epistemological scepticism. I argue that Hookway shows, at best, that without our emotional convictions, our ordinary practices could not get off the ground, but that this, on its own, does not amount to a satisfying reply to the sceptic.

Keywords: scepticism, virtue epistemology.

Frege once remarked that "like ethics, logic can also be called a normative science" (Frege 1997b, 228). The parallel that Frege detects here is one that depends upon his commitment to the idea of objective constraints on thought and action, against which particular acts or particular pieces of reasoning can be judged as correct or incorrect, valid or invalid. The point of the comparison is to get us to see that logic is not an empirical science, concerned with laws of thought in a psychological sense; rather, the laws of logic are "prescriptions for making judgement," in so far as "we must comply with them in our judgements if we are not to fail of the truth" (Frege 1997a, 246). Thus, the rules for our thinking are not a matter of how human beings happen to think but are prescribed by "the laws of truth" – and logic "is the science of the most general laws of truth" (Frege 1997b, 228).

The same sense of a common concern with evaluation is the starting point for Christopher Hookway's argument that epistemologists have something important to learn from the parallel between ethics and epistemology. The thrust of Hookway's argument, however, is in the opposite direction from the one that we have just seen Frege take. Hookway uses his sense of the parallel to argue that human psychological traits – emotional responses and states of character – are "central to our under-standing of epistemic evaluation" (79). Thus, the point of the parallel is to bring us to appreciate the role of human emotional responses in our ordinary cognitive assessments of the truth of propositions, the soundness of inferences, the relevance of doubts, the appropriateness of questions, and so on. It is, Hookway believes, by recognising the essential role of emotions, traits of character and habits in our epistemological practice of evaluating judgements that we can resist the idealised, or over-intellectualised, conception of rationality that lies at the root of some central epistemological problems, in particular, the problem of epistemological scepticism. The question I want to focus on here is whether the understanding of the nature of our epistemic practices that Hookway develops in the light of ideas that he draws from ethics provides an effective means of "defusing . . . scepticism" (79), or of "block[ing] some worrying regresses" (79).

Hookway's aim, then, is "to urge that a satisfactory response to central problems of epistemology *can* and *should* make use of facts about emotions and traits of character or habits" (81). It is not merely that human emotional responses play a vital pragmatic role – for example, in determining what questions we ask or what lines of enquiry we pursue, or in setting standards of evidence – but that they somehow "have a role in showing how such evaluations are possible at all" (81). Taking his inspiration from a passage from Quine, Hookway provides a characterisation of our ordinary epistemic practice that brings out how far this practice diverges from the intellectualist ideal that is associated with scepticism. He makes five main claims:

1. We do not form beliefs on the basis of formulable rules.
2. Reflection is limited; we trust our responses; our conclusions have a certain immediacy.
3. The goodness of an inference is something felt; the vehicle of our confidence is affective.
4. We have no independent criterion of simplicity; an inference feels simple because it feels good.
5. Belief formation is holistic.

Hookway argues that these features of our ordinary practice reveal the way in which our ordinary capacity for forming beliefs depends upon our ability to "make 'immediate' judgements of plausibility" (83). He goes on to claim that these immediate judgements are to be seen as a form of "affective evaluation," and thus that the emotions, or affectivity, play a central role in our practice of making, defending and questioning judgements. We are moved to make judgements not from the emotionally disengaged position of the would-be intellectualist but from a position of emotional involvement. Not only that, but the role that is played by the emotions could not be played by any purely rational procedure: the emotional element, it is argued, is necessary to the existence of our – or perhaps even any – epistemic practice. Thus, it is essential that our judgements have an affective as well as a rational aspect. This affective aspect of judgement reflects our epistemic values and lends judgement a motivating force that draws it into not just a system of belief but a practice of active enquiry.

There is a great deal in this that is compelling – in particular, the implicit suggestion that the epistemologist should prioritise our ordinary practice of judging, inquiring, questioning, doubting, et cetera, over disengaged philosophical arguments that attempt to put our ability to know about the world in doubt. Again, many would agree that our ability to see what is wrong or misconceived about philosophical scepticism depends upon our recognising the way in which our manner of inhabiting our ordinary practice is essential to our ability to frame judgements, attribute beliefs or express doubts at all. It is, therefore, entirely reasonable to suggest that a philosophically clarified view of our ordinary practice – that is, a view which shows why our everyday inquiries and judgements are immune to sceptical doubt – provides the best hope of showing exactly why the philosophical sceptic's doubts are idle or empty. The question is, however, how this promising thought is to be transformed into an effective reply to the sceptic – that is, a reply that provides us with an understanding on which we feel the challenge of scepticism to have been removed, rather than dogmatically rejected. How are these descriptive remarks concerning the nature of our ordinary epistemic practice to be made the basis of a self-understanding that deprives the sceptic's argument of its power to unsettle us, or to make us feel that he has raised a legitimate question? Hookway's idea – based on his understanding of the parallel between ethics and epistemology – is that the key to this problem of self-understanding lies in our coming to recognise the essential role of emotional responses in our practice of judgement. I shall indicate why this move seems to me mistaken.

First of all, I want to question Hookway's moving from the observation that our ordinary practice of inquiry is undertaken from a position of practical involvement to the conclusion that our practice depends not merely on our capacity to reason but also upon our emotional responses. It is, he suggests, only if we acknowledge a role for the emotions that we can understand our ability, for example, to recognise an inference as good, or a doubt as relevant, or a fact as salient, and so on. The idea is that if the process of justification comes to a halt, the power of a proposition, or an inference, to move us to assent must arise from its "possessing a sort of (emotional or affective) *salience*" (86). This salience or immediacy – which is the basis of our practice – can only be understood, or made sense of, in terms of our making an emotional as well as a rational evaluation of the judgement or inference concerned. Thus, real doubts "should be viewed as a kind of anxiety" (86), and where this anxiety is absent "we rest content with the proposition" (84).

It seems to me that all this is both philosophically and phenomenologically unpersuasive. The implicit opposition, or dualism, between reason and emotion, where the former is taken to be disengaged or practically unconstrained and the latter to be motivating and selective, concedes too much to the sceptic's intellectualist conception of reasoning. Why can't we hold that learning to reason is learning, on particular concrete occasions – not only what is good support for what, but also how to judge what is important, how to raise questions, how to follow up leads, and so on. It is one thing to say that reasoning is first and foremost a practical skill – one for which precise rules cannot be formulated – that we acquire on the hoof and in circumstances in which we are involved, and quite another to say that it needs an input from emotional responses to explain what makes a particular piece of reasoning good (or apt, or adequate, or effective, or trustworthy). Perhaps only someone who is involved in human life can learn how to reason (indeed, we might take this to be the main implication of Hookway's characterisation of our ordinary practice), but this still leaves available the idea that the practice of reasoning itself provides the standards of what constitutes correct reasoning or adequate justification. It is quite unclear why the sense of "epistemic salience" that training in the practice of theoretical enquiry depends upon is "to be understood as a form of emotional salience." For even if we recognise that the reasoning or modes of inquiry involved in the formation of beliefs about the world is a form of practical ability, there is little temptation to think that the emotional responses or needs of the agent have any role to play in it, or in what makes it correct.

The role that Hookway gives to the emotions or affectivity in our ordinary practice of forming and justifying beliefs about the world is also phenomenologically quite unpersuasive. Although we often take (the right sort of) emotional involvement in a situation to be vital in motivating appropriate actions, we generally take the direct influence of emotions on judgements about what is the case to be a bad thing. A conviction that a proposition is true, or that a justification for believing it is adequate, which is based on the appeal that the truth of a proposition has for our emotions is one we need to be wary of; far from providing a natural stopping point for inquiry, it is just the sort of case where we should feel a need to look for further evidence to back up our belief. Hookway does, of course, acknowledge this point, and he attempts to answer it by appeal to the importance of developing patterns of emotional response that reveal our ability "to inquire responsibly and effectively" (92). Thus, he uses his understanding of the central role of emotional responses in our ordinary epistemic practices to motivate the importance of the idea that epistemic habits or virtues give us the right to trust our emotional assessments. Even

© Metaphilosophy LLC and Blackwell Publishing Ltd. 2003

so, there is something prima facie perverse in trying to answer the philosophical sceptic by appeal to the essential role of emotional responses in
our epistemic evaluations, in so far as we do not normally regard the
emotions as having any special or privileged connection with veridicality.

Hookway argues that once we recognise that epistemic evaluation is
essentially regulated by a form of emotional salience, we can draw a halt
to two familiar forms of sceptical regress: the regress of reason, where my
belief that p is challenged by a third person; and the regress of justification, where I am considering my justification for my belief that p. Let us
suppose that in each case I give q as my reason for believing p. The regress
threatens if it can now be asked what reason I have for believing q or for
believing that q provides a reason for believing p. Hookway argues that we
can put a stop to both regresses in so far as q and the fact that q provides
a reason for believing p possess an immediate emotional salience which is
an expression of my background commitments and values, and which the
question raised about them altogether lacks. However, to the extent that
this implies that the emotional salience of judgements is what makes them
good, or apt, or appropriate judgements, it surely invites the following
philosophical reflection on our ordinary practice: What reason do we have
to think that the emotional convictions that form the stopping point for
epistemic evaluation of beliefs are a reliable guide to truth, or to how
things are in objective reality?

As Hookway himself acknowledges, there is no necessary connection
between emotional evaluations and truth; emotional evaluations could lead
us astray: "Whether our emotional evaluations are well attuned to the efficient pursuit of correct answers to our questions is a contingent matter"
(89). Yet once the question of reliability has been raised, we seem faced
with the problem that all our ordinary justifications depend upon an
unproved assumption. And thus we are forced to acknowledge that our
ordinary practice provides us, at best, with conditional justifications of our
beliefs: if our emotional evaluations are reliable in tracking truth, then our
beliefs are justified. In so far as putting ourselves in a position to assert the
antecedent would involve proving, for example, that we are not brains in a
vat, the sceptic once again seems set to win the philosophical argument.

It is hard not to feel that here we come up against what we can be made
to feel is an intuitive disanalogy between ethics and epistemology, which
makes us prone to epistemologically sceptical reflections. Thus, there is an
idea of objectivity which may seem inescapable when it comes to assessing our beliefs about the world, but which has very little appeal applied to
our ethical beliefs, and which is often associated with a subjectivist
conception of the latter. This is the idea that there is an objective reality,
completely independent of human beings, at which our beliefs aim and to
which we require the results of our epistemic evaluations to correspond.
Our sense that the question of the reliability of our epistemic practices is
pressing surely turns on this intuitive disanalogy. For, in so far as belief

formation is regulated by subjective criteria, it seems that I cannot reasonably take myself to have knowledge of the objective world *unless* I have reason to believe that my subjective criteria are a reliable guide to objective states of affairs. One of the problems with a philosophical account that grounds our epistemic practices in human emotional responses is that it seems to invite this reflective question in spades. Hookway acknowledges the worry as follows:

> The worry we now face is that we can only be properly confident that our emotional evaluations are *conditionally* reliable. So long as emotional salience tracks epistemic relevance, our confidence may be properly grounded. But this suggests that all we can be confident of is:
>   If what we find epistemically salient tracks what is epistemically relevant, then we can be reliable in solving problems, answering questions, obtaining knowledge, getting justified beliefs, and so on. (90)

Hookway's response to the worry is to suggest that, on his account of the role of the emotions in our practice of justification, "the problem of closing this gap fades" (90). In so far as this suggests that we call a halt to scepticism by showing that there is no further, legitimate question of justification raised by the sceptic's doubts, the idea is a compelling one. The question is whether an approach that seeks to understand our practice in terms of an essential role for the emotions in what makes a judgement, or an inference, or a question good can accomplish this task satisfactorily. Can such an approach close the gap between subjective and objective in a way that does not look as if it has simply begged the sceptic's question?

Let us look, then, at how Hookway uses his reflections on the nature of our practice of epistemic evaluation to show that the sceptic does not raise a question that calls for a response. He suggests that the problem of closing the gap has two aspects:

1. We need to *explain* why our emotional evaluations are "appropriate to our cognitive needs" (90); I shall take this to mean "lead us reliably to believe what is objectively the case."
2. We need to *justify* "our confidence in our practice (90);" I shall take this to mean "in our practice's being a reliable guide to how things objectively are."

In response to the first problem, Hookway argues that it is enough for our confidence in our cognitive practices to remain unshaken, if we have no good reason to think that such an explanation cannot be provided:

> Our confidence in our cognitive capacities will not be shaken unless we acquire strong *reasons* for thinking that such an explanation cannot be provided. Unless we acquire such reasons, it is reasonable to hope that one can be provided and

that our failure to do so need not make epistemically salient any doubts that we cannot deal with. (90)

However, once it has been allowed – as it seems to have been – that the question of reliability makes sense, and once the contingency of the relation between our practices and objective truth has been acknowledged, surely the sceptic is in a position to show that we do have good reason to think that no such explanation can be forthcoming. For the only explanation we can construct for the reliability of our epistemic practices will inevitably be one that presupposes their reliability. And in so far as we are in the business of providing a form of self-understanding that allows us to resist the sceptic's reasoning without simply begging the question, a circular explanation of the reliability of our practices is no explanation at all. Hookway's acknowledgment of the contingency of the connection between our criteria of judgement and the truth of what we believe seems to open up the very divide on which scepticism thrives: it makes the demand for an explanation of reliability look both apt and unachievable.

In response to the second problem, Hookway argues as follows. The demand for a justification of our confidence that our practices are reliable implicitly suggests that, in the absence of such a justification, we ought to feel a real doubt (that is, a real anxiety) about our ordinary beliefs. Not to feel this anxiety, and not to seek to remove it by means of a justification, is an epistemic failing. Hookway now uses the idea of emotional salience to argue that this is wrong. For if we are strongly identified with the emotional evaluations of judgements, doubts, questions, et cetera, that our ordinary practices have given rise to, then doubts that attempt to put these practices in question will not have the emotional salience for us that would require us to answer them. The argument seems to be that, as epistemic agents whose epistemic evaluations are based on emotional salience, we can justifiably reject a demand to justify the reliability of a practice based on emotional salience, in so far as this demand for justification, or the doubts on which it is based, do not possess the emotional salience required to shake our confidence in our practice. This certainly looks much more promising as an attempt to close the gap, in so far as it suggests that the question of justification, on which the sceptic's argument depends, can be rejected before it gets started. The idea is that there is no doubt or demand for justification that we, as agents operating within our epistemic practices, should feel called upon to answer.

This argument depends, to some extent, on our treating the sceptical voice as an alien intrusion upon someone who is unreflectively engaged in our ordinary practice. If we think of the sceptical voice as one that arises in us when we come to reflect on our epistemic practices, and thus as one that we need to respond to from a position of reflection, then I think we can begin to see the limits of this strategy. For all we have really been told is that sceptical questions do not arise in the context of ordinary, empirical inquiry, and this does not on its own show how they are to be resisted within the context of philosophy. Moreover, given that Hookway's account of our ordinary practice acknowledges that the relation between the emotional evaluations on which it rests and objective truth is contingent, it is hard to see how the work of resisting scepticism in a philosophical context is to be achieved. It seems, rather, that the sceptic in us will be able to show that there is a gap between our subjective criteria and objective truth that needs to be closed, and that no appeal to our ordinary epistemic convictions can possibly close it.

To make this clearer, let us focus on a particular example. It seems reasonable to suppose that the judgement "This is a hand" possesses the sort of emotional salience that Hookway believes to be the basis of our epistemic practices: it is a judgement that immediately strikes me as correct. But now I myself want to raise the question of what justification I have for believing that a practice that rests upon emotional conviction is a reliable guide to objective truth. Hookway suggests that I can now use the fact that my conviction that this is a hand has more emotional salience than the sceptic's doubt as a ground for rejecting the sceptical question as irrelevant. Given that there is no essential connection between emotional salience and objective truth, however, this looks problematic. For surely I can reflectively accept these patterns of emotional salience as a proper ground for rejecting the sceptic's question only if our emotional responses are, as a matter of fact, a reliable guide to objective truth. But this means that I can take my current emotional evaluations as a proper ground for rejecting the sceptic's question only by assuming the very thing that the sceptical voice in me doubts – that is, by arguing in a circle. By a familiar triad, the only other alternatives are dogmatic assumption that our emotional evaluations are reliable or the merely conditional claim that, if my emotional evaluations are a reliable guide to objective truth, then I have a proper ground for rejecting my sceptical doubts about my ability to have objective knowledge of the world.

All of the options clearly fall short of a philosophically satisfying answer to the sceptical question that reflection on our practice seems to invite. The only way out of the problem seems to be to abandon the question of objectivity and settle for the mere coherence of our subjective practices. In the context of the understanding of our epistemic position that Hookway has developed, however, this may be seen not as a reply to the sceptic but as the concession that a philosophical understanding of how we are able to achieve knowledge of the objective world is beyond us.

In the end, Hookway's argument shows, at best, that without our emotional convictions, our practices could not get off the ground. It does not show why we cannot, from a position of philosophical reflection, raise the question of whether our practices are reliable, or why the sceptical assessment that is made from this reflective position is not, from an epistemological point of view, superior to our ordinary convictions. It is true that in ordinary life we are entirely convinced of a lot of things, and even that, within our ordinary practice, we would be disinclined to consider the sorts of questions the sceptic raises. However, Hookway does not show either why our ordinary attitudes can reflectively be deemed to yield knowledge of the world, or how they are to be made the basis of a philosophical account on which we can see that the sceptic's doubts do not raise an intelligible question of justification – that is, an account on which those doubts can be seen to be nonsensical.

I remarked at the beginning that there is something compelling in Hookway's thought that it is through an understanding of our way of inhabiting our ordinary practice of judging that we should hope to reveal the confusion or mistake that lies at the root of the sceptic's reflections. It seems to me a mistake, however, to think that merely because sceptical doubts do not arise within our ordinary practice, we can make our ordinary attitudes a philosophical basis for rejecting the legitimacy of the philosophical sceptic's question. If we cannot say why the sceptic's question does not make sense, then we cannot make a refusal to harken to it appear philosophically satisfying; and if we can show that it does not make sense, then the questions of explanation and justification which, given his understanding of the nature of our ordinary practice, Hookway feels a need to address simply do not arise.

Department of Philosophy
University of York
York YO10 5DD
United Kingdom
mem3@york.ac.uk

References

Frege, G. 1997a. "Logic." In *The Frege Reader*, edited by Michael Beaney, 227–50. Oxford: Basil Blackwell.
Frege, G. 1997b. "The Thought." In *The Frege Reader*, edited by Michael Beaney. Oxford: Basil Blackwell.

© Metaphilosophy LLC and Blackwell Publishing Ltd. 2003.
Published by Blackwell Publishing, 9600 Garsington Road, Oxford OX4 2DQ, UK and
350 Main Street, Malden, MA 02148, USA
METAPHILOSOPHY
Vol. 34, Nos. 1/2, January 2003
0026-1068

VIRTUE EPISTEMOLOGY AND EPISTEMIC LUCK

DUNCAN PRITCHARD

ABSTRACT: The recent movement towards virtue-theoretic treatments of epistemological concepts can be understood in terms of the desire to eliminate epistemic luck. Significantly, however, it is argued that the two main varieties of virtue
epistemology are responding to *different* types of epistemic luck. In particular,
whilst proponents of reliabilism-based virtue theories have been focusing on the
problem of what I call "veritic" epistemic luck, non-reliabilism-based virtue theories have instead been concerned with a very different type of epistemic luck, what
I call "reflective" epistemic luck. It is argued that, prima facie at least, both forms
of epistemic luck need to be responded to by any adequate epistemological theory.
The problem, however, is that one can best eliminate veritic epistemic luck by
adducing a so-called safety-based epistemological theory that need not be allied to
a virtue-based account, and there is *no* fully adequate way of eliminating reflective
epistemic luck. I thus conclude that this raises a fundamental difficulty for virtue-
based epistemological theories, on either construal.

Keywords: epistemology, Gettier, luck, reliabilism, responsibilism, virtues.

Introduction

Much of the recent work in epistemology has been concerned with the
possibility of offering virtue-theoretic accounts of our key epistemic
concepts – in particular, justification and knowledge.[1] In essence, such
views mark a break with traditional epistemological analyses by defining
the key epistemic concepts in terms of the epistemic virtues and/or faculties
of the agent (rather than vice versa).[2] As we shall see, however, this basic
conception of virtue theory is open to a number of divergent interpretations,
and two interpretations in particular that seem almost diametrically

[1] For some of the recent work on virtue epistemology, see the essays in the anthologies
edited by Axtell (2000), Fairweather and Zagzebski (2001), DePaul and Zagzebski (2002),
and Steup (2001) and the articles in this collection. See also the excellent survey article by
Axtell (1997).

[2] A slightly weaker virtue-based thesis might hold that the epistemic virtues merely
present the best *criteria* for determining positive epistemic status, although it is difficult to
identify anyone who clearly endorses such a view. Since the objections that I raise against
virtue theory in this article are equally applicable on either interpretation, for ease of expression I shall focus on the stronger and more standard rendering of the position.

opposed in terms of what they are trying to achieve in advancing this type of thesis. I argue that the key to understanding this divergence is to recognise that whilst both these types of account of virtue theory regard the elimination of epistemic luck as being a fundamental adequacy condition on their theory, each is focusing upon a *different* species of epistemic luck.[3] Simply noting this fact, however, does not suffice to resolve the debate, since, as we shall see, there are further complications at issue here.

In section 1 I describe how the first renderings of virtue epistemology that appeared in the contemporary literature were primarily understood in terms of extant versions of reliabilism. In section 2 I argue that these reliabilism-based versions of virtue epistemology are responding to the problem of what I call "veritic" epistemic luck. Section 3 offers a critique of these reliabilism-based virtue theories on the grounds that there are non-virtue-based reliabilist theories which are equally adept at eliminating veritic luck and that, in any case, the best accounts of knowledge available which respond to the problem of veritic epistemic luck make no essential mention of the epistemic virtues at all. Section 4 introduces the problem of what I call "reflective" epistemic luck, and it explains how one can understand non-reliabilism-based responsibilist virtue epistemological theories in terms of the desire to eliminate this variety of epistemic luck. I also argue, however, that there is no fully satisfactory response to the problem of reflective epistemic luck, and thus that this form of virtue epistemology is in danger of defining knowledge in such a way as to make it unattainable. Section 5 offers some concluding remarks.

1. From Simple Process Reliabilism to Agent Reliabilism

For our purposes, we can take simple process reliabilism to consist, in essence, in the thesis that one has knowledge if, and only if, one forms one's true belief via a reliable process, where this is a process that ensures a high ratio of true beliefs relative to false beliefs (we shall consider later how a more elaborated version of process reliabilism might go). Such a view is, of course, usually associated with the work of Alvin Goldman.[4] In terms of rather "low-grade" knowledge, such as basic perceptual knowledge, this is a fairly plausible account. Intuitively, such beliefs count as knowledge just so long as they are formed in reliable ways, which, as the products of our perceptual faculties in normal circumstances, we would

---

[3] Although others have commented on the relationship between virtue epistemology and epistemic luck, no-one, so far as I am aware at any rate, offers anything like the account I present here. For the best discussions in this regard, see Zagzebski (1996, passim), Axtell (2002) and Greco (2002).

[4] See, for example, Goldman (1976; 1979; 1986). See also Armstrong (1973) for a contemporaneous account of a similar theory, and Talbott (1990) for a recent defence of a view of this sort.

expect them to be. Nothing more seems to be necessary to knowledge than meeting such a condition.

However the details are to be spelt out, it should be clear that simple process reliabilism is a paradigm example of an epistemologically externalist thesis, in that it identifies epistemic conditions which are necessary and sufficient for knowledge possession but does not further demand that the agent should be in a position to know, by reflection alone, that these conditions have obtained. More precisely, we can define epistemological internalism as the view that internalist justification is necessary for knowledge, and further define internalist justification as follows:

> For all agents, φ, an agent's belief in a proposition, φ, is internalistically justified if, and only if, the facts which determine that justification are knowable by the agent via reflection alone (that is, through a priori reasoning, introspection of her own mental states, or memory of knowledge gained via either of these means).[5]

I shall henceforth take epistemological externalism about knowledge to consist in the denial of epistemological internalism about knowledge, and thus in the rejection of the thesis that internalist justification is necessary for knowledge. Of course, any characterisation of so contentious a distinction is bound to be at least partly stipulative, but the advantage of this formulation is that it captures what it is about simple process reliabilism that makes it an externalist thesis without committing proponents of simple process reliabilism to an unnecessarily austere rendering of the view. On this model, simple process reliabilists are externalists in that they allow that agents might have knowledge simply by employing reliable processes. It is not further demanded that agents should possess internalist justification for their beliefs. But neither is it excluded that internalist justification might play a fundamental – albeit, perforce, *secondary* – role in such a theory, perhaps as being an important and useful (though inessential) property for one's beliefs about certain matters to have.[6]

As a representative of the externalist position, simple process reliabilism faces the usual kinds of objections levelled against epistemological theses of

---

[5] In both this characterisation of epistemological internalism and reflective access, I follow the account given by Pryor (2001) in his extremely useful survey of recent trends in epistemology.

[6] For a similar conception of the epistemological externalism/internalism distinction, see Brandom (1998). For discussion of the contrast between internalist and externalist notions of justification, see Goldman (1988). Note that a further advantage of this way of construing the externalism/internalism distinction is that it does not commit internalists to an unnecessarily strong rendering of their position either. Internalists can perfectly well allow that there should be external conditions on knowledge over and above the truth condition. The crux for them will only be that the agents in question have internalist justification for what they believe. For more on the epistemological externalism/internalism distinction, see the essays collected in the excellent anthology edited by Kornblith (2001).

this sort, and we shall consider a sample objection of this type below. Those who see in simple process reliabilism the basics for a more developed reliabilist theory understood along virtue-theoretic lines are not concerned about its association with externalism, however, since the revised reliabilist view that they envisage is also an externalist thesis. Instead, their dissatisfaction with simple process reliabilism relates to how it is prone to certain key types of counterexample. Of the main proponents of such a view, John Greco is, perhaps, the most explicit about this, arguing that his reliabilism-based version of virtue epistemology – what he calls "agent" reliabilism – can be motivated by how it is able to respond, in a reliabilist fashion, to various basic problems facing the simple process reliabilist view.[7] Accordingly, we shall here focus on his view, but the conclusions that are offered should equally apply (*mutatis mutandis*) to other views of this general sort, especially that propounded by Ernest Sosa (e.g., 1985; 1991; 1993).

The problems that Greco is primarily concerned with are those that involve what he calls "strange and fleeting processes." Different examples of such processes raise different issues. First, consider the case where a strange and fleeting process is reliable but where the reliability in question is due to the world's tracking the agent's beliefs rather than vice versa. For example, suppose that there is a benevolent demon who ensures that every time our protagonist forms a belief the world is adjusted to make it such that the belief is true. Clearly, this would be a highly reliable way of forming beliefs, since it would never fail to result in a true belief. Nevertheless, our intuition in such a case is that the agent lacks knowledge because her reliably formed true beliefs do not reflect a cognitive achievement on her part at all. Greco describes just such an example:

> René thinks he can beat the roulette tables with a system he has devised. Reasoning according to the Gambler's Fallacy, he believes that numbers which have not come up for long strings are more likely to come up next. However, unlike Descartes' demon victim, our René has a demon helper. Acting as a kind of epistemic guardian, the demon arranges reality so as to make the belief come out as true. Given the ever present interventions of the helpful demon, René's belief forming process is highly reliable. But this is because the world is made to conform to René's beliefs, rather than because René's beliefs conform to the world. (Greco 1999, 286)

In order to ensure that the reliable process at issue here is strange and fleeting, we need to stipulate further that in most near-by possible worlds the demon does not intervene in this way (perhaps because he does not exist in these worlds).[8]

---

[7] See, for example, Greco (1999; 2000, chapters 7 and 8).

[8] Strictly speaking, then, it is the *reliability* of the process, rather than the process itself, that is strange and fleeting. Greco himself is not always clear about this point. As we shall see below, however, this issue is important because it leaves open a possible response to "counterexamples" of this sort that an exponent of a more refined version of process reliabilism can make.

Second, consider the case where a strange and fleeting process is reliable, but where the reliability is due to a "malfunction" on the part of the agent. An example of this sort, offered by Alvin Plantinga (1988; 1993a), concerns a rare brain lesion that causes the victim to believe that he has a brain lesion. Greco (1999, 285; 2000, 175) quotes Plantinga, who describes this scenario as follows:

> Suppose . . . that S suffers from this sort of disorder and accordingly believes that he suffers from a brain lesion. Add that he has no evidence at all for this belief: no symptoms of which he is aware, no testimony on the part of physicians or other expert witnesses, nothing. (Add if you like, that he has much evidence *against* it; but then add also that the malfunction induced by the lesion makes it impossible for him to take appropriate account of this evidence). Then the relevant [cognitive process] will certainly be reliable; but the resulting belief – that he has a brain lesion – will have little by way of warrant for S. (Plantinga 1993a, 199)

Again, in order to ensure that the reliability of this process is strange and fleeting in the relevant respect, we need to stipulate further that in most near-by possible worlds this brain lesion would not result in the agent's forming a belief that he has the brain lesion (and thus would not result in a true belief). We have a strong intuition that there is something epistemically amiss about forming true beliefs via malfunctions in this way, even where those malfunctions happen to support a process of forming beliefs that is reliable.[9]

The basic idea behind the kind of agent reliabilism advanced by Greco – and similar such theories advanced by Sosa, the later Goldman (1993), and others[10] – is to restrict the range of reliable processes that can support knowledge in a principled way by focusing upon the stable and successful dispositions of the agent that are relevant to knowledge and justification – her intellectual *faculties*, if you will. For example (the details need not detain us here), our faculty of sight, if working properly and applied in the right conditions, is a highly reliable way of forming true beliefs about the world. In contrast, the reliability that might attach itself to a cognitive malfunction will not count as knowledge producing on this view, because

---

[9] It is significant, of course, that in neither of these examples does the agent have counterevidence which would lead him to believe that the process in question is unreliable. This is because most extant versions of process reliabilism incorporate some extra condition to the effect that if the agent has such a belief then he lacks justification for that belief (and thus knowledge of what is believed). Goldman (1986) is a prime example here. He further adds that the agent should not be in a mental state (such as being in the possession of relevant evidence) from which reliable processes would lead him to conclude that the process at issue is unreliable.

[10] Of course, there are important differences between these views, but they are not relevant to the current discussion. A related view in this respect is Plantinga's (1988; 1993b; 1993c) "proper functionalism," although Plantinga has explicitly resisted the description of his view as a virtue-based theory. For an overview of proposals of this sort, see Axtell (1997, especially §2).

such a cognitive process is not one of our natural faculties and this means that it lacks the kind of dispositional stability required. Similarly, forming beliefs in a way that is reliably successful for reasons that are independent of one's cognitive endeavours, as is the case in the "benevolent demon" example, is also ruled out, because this reliable process does not concern a faculty of the agent at all, in any sense of that term, and so is not even in the ballpark to be considered a stable and successful intellectual faculty. The shift from simple process reliabilism to some form of faculty or agent reliabilism thus enables reliabilists to meet two core objections to their view.

2. Veritic Epistemic Luck

One can regard this transition from simple process reliabilism to agent reliabilism as motivated in terms of the need to eliminate a certain form of luck regarding the truth of what one believes. We shall call this type of luck "veritic" luck, and characterise it as follows:[11]

> For all agents, φ, the truth of an agent's belief in a proposition, φ, is veritically lucky if, and only if, the agent's belief that φ is true in the actual world but false in nearly all near-by possible worlds in which the belief is formed in the same manner as in the actual world.

For example, take my entirely ungrounded guess that Lucky Lass will be the winner of today's derby. Suppose, further, that I go on to form the belief that this horse will win, and that the belief turns out to be true (that it's a "lucky guess").[12] Intuitively, to say that this is a lucky guess is to say that although it turned out to be correct, in nearly all near-by possible worlds it would have been false. The belief that results from the guess is thus veritically lucky in the sense just described. It is clearly the task of a theory of knowledge to disallow beliefs formed in this kind of fashion from enjoying the privileged status of being instances of knowledge. If one meets all the relevant epistemic conditions set down by the favoured epistemological theory and one's belief is still veritically lucky, however, then what we have here is a case of veritic *epistemic* luck and thus, prima facie at least, a counterexample to the theory of knowledge in question.[13] It is

---

[11] I borrow the term from Engel (1992), who argues for a similar characterisation of epistemic luck, although he specifically puts the point in terms of evidence. For further discussion of Engel's view, see Hall (1994), Harper (1996), Vahid (2001), Axtell (2002) and Pritchard (2003; cf. Pritchard and Smith 2002).

[12] It should be noted that a guess that *p* rarely does result in a belief that *p*, though we need not concern ourselves with this complication here.

[13] Of course, there will no doubt be a lot more involved in the notion of luck than this, though the details need not detain us here. I discuss the notion of luck at more length in Smith and Pritchard 2002, and offer a fuller analysis of veritic epistemic luck (and the "reflective" epistemic luck that I discuss below) in Pritchard 2003. For more on the notion of luck, see Rescher (1995).

this type of luck that is famously at issue in the types of counterexamples to the classical tripartite account of knowledge associated with Edmund Gettier (1963).

Consider the following example adapted from one given (though in a different regard) by Bertrand Russell (1948, 170–71). Our protagonist comes downstairs every morning about the same time and looks at the time on the old clock in her hall. The clock has been a highly reliable timepiece now for many years, and she has no reason for thinking that it is faulty this morning. The clock tells her that it is 8:22, and it is indeed usually around about 8:20 A.M. that she comes downstairs. Furthermore, the clock is right, because it *is* 8:22 A.M. Nevertheless, unbeknownst to the agent, the clock has stopped. Given that, intuitively, one cannot acquire knowledge of the time by looking at a stopped clock, the agent in this example lacks knowledge, even though she has a justified belief (and thus, seemingly, has met all the relevant epistemic conditions in this regard) and even though her belief is in fact true.

The type of epistemic luck that is at issue here is veritic in that the problem which an example like this highlights is that, on the classical tripartite model, meeting the relevant epistemic conditions does not eliminate the possibility that one's belief is only luckily true. More precisely, whilst our protagonist has met all the relevant epistemic conditions, and whilst her belief is true, it nevertheless remains that in nearly all near-by possible worlds in which she forms her belief in the same manner as in the actual world (by looking at her clock), she will form a false belief as a result.

As Linda Zagzebski (1994; 1996, §3.1; 1999) points out, what is common to all Gettier-type counterexamples is that they involve a mix of "double luck." First, there is the "bad" luck that would usually prevent the agent from forming a true belief, even despite the fact that the agent has met all the relevant epistemic conditions (that is, that the agent's normally reliable clock has stopped). Second, there is the "good" luck that cancels out the bad luck by ensuring that, even despite this epistemic misfortune, the agent forms a true belief regardless (that is, that the agent happens to look at the stopped clock when it is telling the right time). Moreover, notice that this double-luck method for constructing Gettier counterexamples is only possible because the epistemic conditions at issue allow the existence of veritic luck in the first place. That is, if these conditions excluded such luck – such that, in so far as one met all the required epistemic conditions and had a true belief then one also had a true belief in nearly all near-by possible worlds where one formed that belief in the same manner as in the actual world – then it would not be possible to be a victim of bad luck in the relevant sense in the first place (that is, bad luck that would ensure that one's belief would *normally* be false).

Like the Gettier counterexamples, the putative counterexamples to the simple process reliabilist account that we have just considered also work by highlighting how this account of knowledge is consistent with veritic luck. In the benevolent-demon example, for instance, that the agent meets the epistemic conditions of having employed a reliable process does not ensure that his true belief is not lucky. After all, in most near-by possible worlds in which he forms the same belief via the same process (the Gambler's Fallacy), his beliefs will turn out as false because in these worlds there is no demon helping him out. The same goes for the "malfunction" case. Again, although the agent meets the relevant epistemic condition because his belief is formed as a result of what is, in fact, a reliable process of being caused by the brain lesion itself, his true belief is nevertheless lucky in that in most near-by possible worlds this brain lesion would not have resulted in a true belief in this way.

Moreover, these examples are also, in the relevant sense, Gettier-type examples, in that they both involve a kind of double luck. Despite meeting the required epistemic conditions (forming his belief in a reliable fashion), the agent in the benevolent-demon example would normally have formed a false belief, and yet this bad luck is cancelled out by the good fortune of being assisted by a benevolent demon who nevertheless ensures that his belief is true. Similarly, in the malfunction case one would normally expect the agent's belief to be false, and yet this bad luck is cancelled out by the good luck that this particular brain lesion happens to generate true beliefs of the required sort.

Accordingly, one can regard the introduction of stable cognitive dispositions into the reliabilist theory as devices to limit the degree of veritic luck so as to avoid examples like these. For what makes such dispositions relevant in this regard is that they enable the agent to form true beliefs not just in the actual world but also in nearly all near-by possible worlds in which the agent forms her beliefs in the same way as in the actual world. Thus, if the agent's belief in the actual world is formed via a cognitive faculty in this way, then one would expect that the truth of the belief formed will not be a matter of veritic luck.

In responding to these examples, then, the agent reliabilist is trying to eliminate possible ways in which veritic luck can creep into the simple process reliabilist account of knowledge, and in this sense the intuitions that are being appealed to are the same anti-luck intuitions that are at work in the Gettier counterexamples. Agent reliabilism – at least as Greco understands the thesis – can thus be regarded as one way in which one can meet a particular type of species of Gettier-type counterexample that applies to simple process reliabilism by eliminating the veritic luck that is at issue in these examples.

3. Modalized Process Reliabilism and the Safety Principle

Matters are not quite as straightforward as this presentation of the development of agent reliabilism out of simple process reliabilism suggests, however. The reason for this is that there is a more nuanced version of process reliabilism available that "modalizes" the construal of what counts as a reliable process in such a way that it can deal with these two examples just as adequately as agent reliabilism can. In effect, what the modalized process reliabilist account achieves is to rule out veritic luck to roughly the same extent as agent reliabilism does.

Recall that the putative counterexamples offered against simple reliabilism only worked because it was stipulated that the reliability at issue was strange and fleeting. A crude process reliabilism that simply worked by analysing the reliability of the process at issue in terms of the actual truth-to-falsity ratio of that process is susceptible to such counterexamples because actually reliable processes can nevertheless be strange and fleeting ones, in that their reliability is unstable. For whilst it is true in the benevolent-demon world that our agent always forms true beliefs via the relevant process, in most near-by possible worlds he will (by stipulation) form false beliefs via this method, and thus the "reliability" of the process will disappear. The same goes for the brain-lesion example, at least as it was understood above. For whilst this brain lesion will in the actual world support true beliefs, in most near-by possible worlds this will not be the case. That the reliability at issue is strange and fleeting is thus a result of how it is a reliability that is not sustained in most near-by possible worlds. In contrast, the kind of stable cognitive dispositions that Greco and other agent reliabilists have in mind are defined such that they will retain their reliability in nearly all near-by possible worlds (this is what is meant by calling these dispositions "stable").

There is no essential reason why process reliabilism should restrict itself to a non-modalized account of reliability, however, and, indeed, there is every reason to think that it *should not* confine itself, given the problems just mentioned coupled with the fact that the very notion of reliability seems to be a partly modal one. Intuitively, a "reliable" thermometer, for example, is not one that just happens to tell the temperature well in the actual world but one that is similarly accurate in nearly all near-by possible worlds as well.[14] Indeed, Goldman himself has expressed the process reliabilist point in counterfactual terms, arguing for what he calls a "normal worlds" reliabilism, which demands that a belief (in any possible world) is justified just in case the process by which it is generated is reliable in normal worlds, where such worlds are in turn understood as those worlds that are consistent with our general beliefs about the actual world.[15]

---

[14] Of course, there is a respectable sense of "reliability" in which the thermometer can be reliable even if it fails to tell the temperature in the actual world or any near-by possible worlds, such as when the environment is radically different from the environment that the thermometer was designed for. In such cases, however, the reliability of the thermometer consists in the fact that, in a world for which it was designed, it tells the temperature in that world and nearly all near-by possible worlds as well.

[15] See Goldman (1986). Goldman (1976) also argues for a counterfactual understanding of the reliabilist position. In recent work, Goldman has moved away from such a position.

On this construal of what counts as a reliable process, the counterexamples at issue above are defused. The Gambler's Fallacy is not a reliable way of forming beliefs in normal worlds, and neither (by stipulation) is the malfunction-based process at issue in the brain-lesion example. Suitably modalized, therefore, process reliabilism is not subject to the critique levelled against it by the agent reliabilist.

Interestingly, what the modalized version of process reliabilism achieves is to restrict the range of processes at issue so that they do not include the ones consistent with veritic luck in the manner of our two examples. In both cases, the veritic luck at issue depends upon the fact that, normally, forming beliefs via the actual manner in which they are formed would lead to falsity rather than truth. By making the notion of reliability at issue relative to a range of normal possible worlds, this variety of process reliabilism ensures that it is not possible for the agent's true belief to meet the relevant epistemic conditions in such a way that, nevertheless, the belief would normally have been false. On this matter, then, modalized process reliabilism is on a par with agent reliabilism. So why should one prefer agent reliabilism over process reliabilism?

This problem becomes further accentuated if one considers how each of the theories fares against the examples just discussed given that we drop the stipulation that the reliability at issue is incidental (and thereby strange *and* fleeting). Consider first the benevolent-demon example. Modalized process reliabilism can accommodate a suitably adapted version of this example just as well as agent reliabilism can. Suppose, for example, that the demon in question necessarily exists and essentially has this property of being benevolent in this way. In such circumstances, it is not an incidental feature of the example that the agent in question forms the true beliefs that he does, since he would form true beliefs via this method in all near-by possible worlds as well. Modalized process reliabilism handles an example like this by claiming that although this process is in fact reliable in the actual world and in most near-by possible worlds, it is not reliable in normal worlds, and so cannot support knowledge or justification. In contrast, the agent reliabilist copes with this sort of example by arguing that the Gambler's Fallacy is just not a virtuous method by which one can gain knowledge and that, in any case, the method at issue here does not reflect a stable and reliable disposition *on the part of the agent* for acquiring true beliefs (the reliability is due to the demon, remember, rather than the agent).

It is when it comes to the brain-lesion example that the accounts come apart, or at least seem to. Suppose that this type of brain lesion *always* produces true beliefs of this sort and that, furthermore, this fact is subsequently discovered by scientific inquiry. On this construal, the brain lesion supports not just a process that mainly results in true beliefs in the actual world but also one that would support such a reliable process in most normal possible worlds in which it occurs as well. What would we then say about the agents who (lacking this scientific knowledge) believed that they had a brain lesion?

On a radical externalist view of knowledge, the temptation would be to accord them knowledge and, indeed, argue that the brain lesion does not represent a cognitive malfunction at all but rather a bona fide successful cognitive process that had erstwhile gone unnoticed. Moreover, on the supposition that the brain lesion always produces true beliefs, the response employed by the agent reliabilist loses its cogency. For what is now preventing such a process from counting as a stable cognitive faculty?

Reliabilists are used to problems like this, and although there may be qualifications that can be added to the thesis to evade this particular example, it is clear that reliabilists are going to be committed to allowing that *some* type of example of this sort will go through (though perhaps one that is not quite so controversial – we shall consider a possible scenario below). Greco's response to the problem is not so sanguine, however. Instead, he argues that what is lacking in such cases is "subjective justification," which he defines as follows:

> A belief p is subjectively justified for a person S . . . if and only if S's believing p is grounded in the cognitive dispositions that S manifests when S is thinking conscientiously. (Greco 1999, 289; cf. Greco 2000, §7.II)

On the face of it, this seems to rule out the kind of cases under consideration because the belief in question is clearly not grounded in cognitive dispositions that the subject manifests when she is thinking conscientiously. The devil, however, is in the detail concerning what counts as "thinking conscientiously." Greco characterises such thinking in terms of the good hitting of a baseball player, in that one can manifest the relevant dispositions in the appropriate conditions without thereby having beliefs (true or otherwise) about the nature and character of these dispositions (as he neatly puts it, one can be a good baseball player without thereby being a good coach). Accordingly, all that is being demanded here is a doxastic sensitivity to the reliability in question. If this is the case, however, then it seems that Greco's view *does* succumb to brain-lesion-type examples after all, since in such cases agents will, *ex hypothesi*, form their true beliefs in ways that will be sensitive to the reliability in question. At the very least, we need to be given a clearer idea of why agents in such examples are not subjectively justified in forming the beliefs that they do.

Of course, a natural response to this line of objection – one that I take it Greco wants to avoid – is simply to beef up the notion of subjective justification in such a way as to demand that agents have some degree of internalist justification for their beliefs. So understood, brain-lesion-type examples are easily avoided, because agents clearly lack grounds for their belief that would support internalist justification. But note that this move represents not merely a modification of the reliabilist position but rather a *rejection* of it, in that it involves incorporating a necessary internalist condition on knowledge and thus entails an endorsement of epistemological internalism.

So, in so far as one remains within a reliabilist framework (and we shall consider in a moment how virtue epistemology is developed when it is not constrained in this way), there is little to tell between an agent reliabilist theory and a modalized process reliabilist position. Crucially, however, neither modalized process reliabilism nor agent reliabilism can exclude all types of veritic luck. In particular, as both these theories stand they have difficulties with the kind of veritic luck at issue in Gettier counterexamples. Since the reliability in question in both cases is consistent with the production of a false belief, it is possible to formulate the kind of double-luck examples that we saw Zagzebski arguing above were characteristic of Gettier counterexamples. The "stopped-clock" example discussed earlier cannot be used here because, at the very least, modalized process reliabilism can meet this problem, since employing a stopped clock to form beliefs is not a reliable way of acquiring true beliefs in normal possible worlds. How agent reliabilism would respond to this example is not altogether clear, but for the sake of parity we shall consider a different example that has application to both agent reliabilism and modalized process reliabilism.

Here is a scenario proposed by Zagzebski that will serve our purposes:[16]

> Suppose that Mary has good eyesight, but it is not perfect. It is good enough to allow her to identify her husband sitting in his usual chair in the living room from a distance of fifteen feet in somewhat dim light. . . . Of course, her faculties may not be functioning perfectly, but they are functioning well enough that if she goes on to form the belief *My husband is sitting in the living room*, her belief has enough warrant to constitute knowledge when true and we can assume that it is almost always true. . . .
>
> Suppose Mary simply misidentifies the chair sitter, who is, we'll suppose, her husband's brother, who looks very much like him. . . . We can now easily amend the case as a Gettier example. Mary's husband could be sitting on the other side of the room, unseen by her. (Zagzebski 1996, 285–87; emphasis in the original)

As regards agent reliabilism, we have here the reliable functioning of a faculty that is producing a true belief, but there is nevertheless the kind of veritic double luck involved that prevents the true belief formed from being an instance of knowledge. Moreover, as regards modalized process reliabilism, we also have a process that is reliable in normal possible

---

[16] Zagzebski was actually directing this example against Plantinga's related proper-functionalism theory, although the differences between proper functionalism and the agent/faculty reliabilist theory are not important in this regard. Indeed, Greco himself discusses this example and notes that it is just as much a problem for his view as it is for Plantinga's. See Greco (2000, 251).

worlds and is generating a true belief in the actual world but cannot support knowledge because of the veritic double luck that is in play.

It is far from obvious how one amends the modalized process reliabilist or agent reliabilist accounts to meet veritic luck of this sort (though there have been some notable attempts).[17] Crucially, however, whatever amendment one comes up with will be tantamount to the demand that knowledge is true belief formed in a non-veritically lucky fashion, where this means not only that the belief should be true but also that it remains true in nearly all near-by possible worlds where the belief is formed on the same basis. In this way, one is left with an account of knowledge that can accommodate the example just cited. After all, there will be a number of near-by possible worlds where Mary forms her belief in the same way but where her husband is not in the room and thus where the belief formed is false.

The type of anti-veritic-luck epistemology that is at issue here is one that is based around something like the following "safety" principle for knowledge:

For all agents, φ, if an agent knows a contingent proposition, φ, then, in nearly all near-by possible worlds in which the agent forms her belief that φ in the same way as in the actual world, her belief is true.[18]

Like process and faculty reliabilism, any account of knowledge that is solely based on the safety principle will be epistemologically externalist, in that it merely specifies a set of conditions that must be met if the agent is to have knowledge, without further demanding that the agent should also have internalist justification for the target belief. What this principle ensures is that there is no gap between the agent's meeting the epistemic conditions and forming a true belief in which veritic luck can get a hold, for in so far as the agent meets the epistemic conditions – which includes meeting the safety principle – it cannot be a matter of veritic epistemic luck that her belief is true, since in nearly all near-by possible worlds where she forms her belief on the same basis she will form a true belief as a result. For example, Mary's belief that her husband is in the room is not knowledge on this view because there are a number of near-by possible worlds where she forms her belief on the same basis and yet what she believes is no longer true.

One can regard the move from a simple process reliabilist view to either a modalized or agent-based reliabilist view as a move towards something

---

[17] Goldman's (1967) "causal" theory could be construed as (broadly speaking) a process reliabilist attempt to meet the problem. See also Armstrong (1973). Sosa (1996) offers one influential rendering of the agent reliabilist position that, he claims, can meet the Gettier counterexamples. See also Plantinga (1988).

[18] Since necessary truths are true in all possible worlds, they present complications for any view of this sort. As these complications are not important to the present discussion, I focus here solely upon contingent propositions.

like a safety-based account, in that the reliability in question becomes tied not just to actual truth-to-falsity ratios but also to what those ratios would be across a range of normal possible worlds (either directly, in the case of modalized process reliabilism, or indirectly, in the case of agent reliabilism). The trick is thus to supplement the basic reliabilist account in such a way as to achieve something like that achieved by the safety principle.

The salient question to ask at this juncture, however, is just why we need a reliabilist account at all if a safety-based theory will do just as well (which will meet the Gettier-type examples, along with all the other examples that play upon the presence of veritic luck). Indeed, this issue is especially pertinent once one notes that the foremost defenders of agent reliabilism, Greco and Sosa, have each used something like a safety principle in order to meet the sceptical challenge. In both cases, the basic idea is that sceptical error possibilities can be dismissed in that they are concerned with far-off possible worlds, so that just so long as the reliability at issue is maintained in near-by possible worlds, this will suffice for knowledge. Accordingly, so long as the actual world is "normal" in the sense that we saw Goldman characterise it above, we can know such anti-sceptical truths as that we are not brains in vats, since in normal worlds our means of determining these kinds of truths are appropriately reliable and thus generate "safe" beliefs.[19]

There is no inherent reason, however, why a safety-based account of knowledge should mention the reliability of processes at all, whether those at issue in agent reliabilism or those at issue in the modalized process reliabilist story. Indeed, given the difficulty that reliabilist accounts have in meeting the Gettier counterexamples, the appropriate moral to draw (at least given that we are happy with epistemological externalism) does not seem to be that we need to keep supplementing the reliabilist thesis ad infinitum in order to try to meet the challenge posed by Gettier cases, but rather that we should simply accept that knowledge is, at root, just true belief that meets the safety principle. The job of reliabilism, of either description, would then be to tell the necessary *explanatory* story about how, as the creatures we are in the environment that we find ourselves in, we come to form true beliefs about the world in such a way as to support knowledge. Here one would expect the reliabilist story to be essential, but this project is not the project of discovering necessary and sufficient conditions for the possession of knowledge.[20]

[19] See Greco (1994; 2000, chapter 8) and Sosa (1999; 2000). Sainsbury (1997), Williamson (2000a; 2000b, chapter 8) and Pritchard (2001a; 2002a; 2002b; 2002d) have all defended versions of the safety-based response to scepticism (the so-called neo-Moorean response to scepticism). Black (2002) offers an account of Nozick's counterfactual conditions on knowledge that ends up construing them as much like the safety principle. For further discussion of this type of anti-sceptical thesis, and how it relates to the other main anti-sceptical theories in the literature, see Pritchard (2002c).
[20] This point is especially germane as regards Greco's account because his agent reliabilist theory does not entail the safety-based response to the relevant Gettier-type counterexamples that he offers. (Indeed, Greco seems to be aware of this, noting only that his safety-based

So, in so far as it is the elimination of veritic epistemic luck that is motivating the adoption of the agent reliabilist thesis over the process reliabilist thesis, the position is ill motivated as a theory of knowledge for two reasons. First, because a modalized version of process reliabilism can be just as successful in this regard. Second, because, in any case, both agent reliabilism and modalized process reliabilism are subject to a certain form of veritic epistemic luck. Accordingly, if one is to take the challenge posed by such luck seriously, one should prefer the type of safety-based account of knowledge that is specifically defined such that it eliminates veritic epistemic luck. The upshot of this is that in so far as we should advocate a version of virtue epistemology modelled on reliabilism, this should be as an explanatory thesis concerning how creatures such as ourselves come to have safe beliefs, and thus knowledge. This conclusion hits right to the heart of the view, however, since the defining characteristic of virtue epistemology was meant to be the fact that it characterised epistemic concepts in terms of epistemic virtues rather than the other way around. Hence, this conclusion is not simply a *demotion* of the status of virtue epistemology but a straightforward *rejection*.[21]

4. Responsibilist Virtue Epistemology and Reflective Epistemic Luck

Not all virtue-based epistemological theories model themselves on reliabilism in the way that agent reliabilism does, however, so this conclusion

account of relevant alternatives is "grounded" by his version of agent reliabilism.) Accordingly, his agent reliabilist theory seems to be more of an explanation of how cognitive beings come to have safe beliefs (and thus knowledge) rather than a definition of knowledge. See Greco (2000, chapter 8). Foley (1994) also raises the issue of why we need a virtue-*based* epistemology, rather than simply an epistemology that involves an account of the epistemic virtues, though his point is specifically directed at Sosa's version of virtue-based reliabilism.

[21] In a recent essay, Greco (2002) has argued that safety alone will not suffice for knowledge because it cannot handle the so-called lottery problem. Suppose I buy a ticket for a free and fair lottery with long odds and form the belief that I shall not win. Now suppose that the draw has been made and this belief has been confirmed, but that I have not been informed of the result yet. Do I *know* that I haven't won? Intuitively, I do not, but Greco argues that the safety-based theory demands an affirmative answer to this question because my belief is true not only in the actual world but in nearly all near-by possible worlds as well. Thus, safety alone cannot meet our epistemic intuitions, and Greco diagnoses this difficulty by arguing that the problem rests with the fact that safety-based views cannot capture the sense in which knowledge demands responsibility for truth. This argument does not go through, however, for the simple reason that, contrary to first impressions, there *are* near-by possible worlds in which one wins the lottery. After all, the whole attraction of a free and fair lottery is that the possible world in which I win is extremely similar to the actual world in which I do not (just a few coloured balls need to fall in a slightly different configuration). The example misleads us by talking of a low-probability event, thereby giving us the impression that the event only obtains in far-off possible worlds, but possible worlds are ordered in terms of their *similarity* to the actual world, not in terms of their *probability* (though the two notions are of course related). It follows that Greco cannot motivate his position via examples of this sort. I am grateful to John Greco for useful discussion on this point.

does not have an unrestricted application to virtue epistemology as a whole. There are a number of reasons for this schism, but one of the main sources of dissatisfaction with the agent reliabilist account of virtue epistemology has been its commitment to epistemological externalism, a thesis that some epistemologists find counterintuitive, *especially* when it comes to the epistemic virtues. As we shall see, the issue here is that merely offering an account of knowledge that is (largely) free of veritic epistemic luck does not appear to be enough – we also seem to need a theory that eliminates what I shall call "reflective" epistemic luck, at least as regards our knowledge in a wide range of cases.

We have already seen that as externalist theories modalized process reliabilism and agent reliabilism appear obliged to allow that in the "strengthened" brain-lesion case – where, we recall, it is stipulated that the process in question is stable in the relevant respects, and thereby will support true beliefs in nearly all (normal) near-by possible worlds – the agent *can* know that he has a brain lesion. Such cases are standard fare in epistemology these days. The most famous is the so-called chicken-sexer example. In this case we are asked to imagine an agent who has a natural and highly reliable ability to distinguish between male and female chicks, but who has no idea how she is doing this and is not even aware that she is reliable in this respect. (Some even supplement the example by saying that she is mistaken about how she is doing it, thinking that she is seeing or touching something distinctive, when in fact she is guided by her unusually sensitive sense of smell).[22]

Externalists are inclined to allow that such agents can indeed have knowledge in such cases, whilst internalists tend to demur. Internalists contend that this cannot be knowledge, because the agent has no reasons to support her beliefs. Externalists respond by arguing, as it were, from the third-person perspective – by looking at what we would say about the epistemic status of the agent's belief rather than at what she would say about it. This shift in perspective is important in that it distinguishes the issue of what the agent is able properly to claim regarding her epistemic situation from what her epistemic situation actually is.[23] Crucially, however, in so far as it is plausible to contend that the chicken-sexer has knowledge via the employment of her reflectively inaccessible though reliable belief-forming processes, it ought (as we noted earlier) to be plausible to contend that one can gain knowledge via brain lesions just so long as the reliability in question is stable in the relevant respects.

[22] For further discussion of the chicken-sexer example, see Foley (1987, 168–69), Lewis (1996), Zagzebski (1996, §2.1 and §4.1), and Brandom (1998). See also the exchange between Sainsbury (1996) and Wright (1996).

[23] This is a key move that the epistemological externalist needs to make if she is to offer the necessary motivation for her view, because whilst the possession conditions for knowledge will closely mirror the propriety conditions for knowledge claims on the internalist view, this will not be so on the externalist view. The externalist is thus able to use this observation in order to explain why certain cases of knowledge, whilst in fact bona fide, might nevertheless *seem* suspect. For more on this point, see Pritchard (2001b).

Expecting a consensus to emerge concerning examples like this is almost certainly expecting too much. What we *can* expect to achieve, however, is a consensus that there is *something* lacking about the epistemic status of the agent's beliefs in these examples, even if the further issue of whether or not what is missing is essential to knowledge possession is one that cannot be settled in a way that is acceptable to both externalists and internalists. For even externalists would surely agree that the knowledge possessed by the chicken sexer (if indeed it is knowledge) is knowledge of a very "brute" variety, and that it would be preferable (even if unnecessary, strictly speaking) that the agent have an internalist justification in support of her belief as well.

Notice, however, that one cannot capture the "lack" at issue here in terms of veritic epistemic luck. If the chicken sexer is exhibiting a genuine stable cognitive faculty that generates safe beliefs, then not only will her belief be true in the actual world but, in nearly all near-by possible worlds in which she forms her belief in the same way, she will also continue to form true beliefs as a result. Nevertheless, whilst it is not veritic epistemic luck that is at issue, it does seem to be a matter of luck, *in some sense*, that the agent has knowledge in this case, and this at least partly explains why we are reluctant to ascribe knowledge.

We shall call the luck that is at issue here "reflective" luck, since it concerns not simply the luck that one's belief is true but rather the luck that one's belief is true given what one is able to know by reflection alone. We can express this form of luck as follows:

For all agents, φ, the truth of an agent's belief in a proposition, φ, is reflectively lucky if, and only if, the agent's belief that φ is true in the actual world, but, in nearly all possible worlds consistent with what the agent is able to know by reflection alone, were the agent to form a belief that φ, that belief would be false.

As with veritic luck, if one meets all the relevant epistemic conditions set down by the favoured epistemological theory and one's belief is still reflectively lucky, then this is a case of reflective *epistemic* luck.[24]

The description of the relevant class of possible worlds here deserves comment. These worlds are described in this manner because we are trying to capture the sense in which, whilst it may be the case that the agent's belief is in fact safe such that it matches the truth in near-by possible worlds in which it is formed in the appropriate way, this alone does not ensure that the truth of the belief is not reflectively lucky. Consider again the example just given of the chicken sexer, but this time compare our chicken sexer with an "enlightened" counterpart who not only has this

[24] Riggs (1998) offers a distinction between two types of epistemic luck that roughly parallels (though is still importantly different from) that offered here between veritic and reflective epistemic luck. For discussion of this view, see Axtell (2002).

ability but also has the reflective knowledge to back up the beliefs that she is forming about the sex of the chicks (she has, say, true beliefs about how this ability works, and about its relative reliability in different types of environmental conditions). Clearly, neither of these agents has a belief that is veritically lucky, since the safety of their beliefs ensures that in nearly all near-by possible worlds in which they form their beliefs in the same way as in the actual world, their beliefs will be true.[25]

Nevertheless, in terms of what the agents are able to know by reflection alone, the "unenlightened" agent is lucky to have a true belief in a way that the enlightened agent is not. This is because, unlike the enlightened agent, the unenlightened agent has no knowledge reflectively available to her to indicate that her belief is safe. We can express this point by saying that whilst the enlightened chicken sexer has reflective knowledge that excludes various error possibilities from obtaining, this is not true of the unenlightened chicken sexer. So far as she is able to know in this respect, her beliefs could be radically in error. So whilst in most possible worlds consistent with what she is able to know by reflection alone the enlightened chicken sexer's belief remains true, this will not be the case for her unenlightened counterpart. Instead, there will be a wide class of worlds that are consistent with what she can know by reflection alone but where she is radically in error, such as those worlds where she simply lacks this ability. The same goes for the brain-lesion example, since here too there are many possible worlds that are consistent with what the agent is able to know by reflection alone but where the belief formed is false.

So whilst externalist epistemological theories eliminate one type of epistemic luck – veritic epistemic luck – they do not eliminate another type of epistemic luck that is reflective. Externalists may well be sanguine about this fact – in the sense that they do not think that reflective epistemic luck is a bar to knowledge possession – but this should not prevent them from being aware that reflective epistemic luck, whilst perhaps consistent with knowledge possession, is at least epistemically *undesirable*. Part of the problem here is that the reliability at issue, since it is not reflectively accessible to the agent, operates in this sense merely at the "sub-personal" level. As a result, it does not seem entirely appropriate to ascribe the cognitive achievement of knowledge possession to such an agent when, in one sense at least, the cognitive ability in question is not due to the *agent* at all.

It is a worry of this sort that has prompted some commentators attracted

---

[25] Though, of course, one would expect the agent who has the reflective knowledge to have a belief that tracks the truth in far more near-by possible worlds than her counterpart who lacks this knowledge because, unlike the unenlightened chicken sexer, she will revise her beliefs in appropriate ways in response to different circumstances. For example, given that she reflectively knows that she has evidence which strongly suggests that her ability is based on smell, she will be cautious about forming beliefs about the sex of chicks via this ability in situations where she is aware that this faculty is not functioning as normal (e.g., when she has a cold).

by the prospects of a virtue-based epistemology to make the move away from reliabilism altogether and adopt an agent-based epistemology that is, in the relevant regard, non-reliabilist. The central idea is that what is lacking from the reliabilist schema, even when modified along agent reliabilist lines, is a fundamental role for the epistemic *responsibility* of the agent. Such views are, to varying extents, approximations to an Aristotelian virtue-theoretic account of knowledge that conceives of intellectual virtues in terms of processes at the personal level – *traits of character* – that agents are, at least in some sense, responsible for (as opposed to the broader, possibly Platonic, reading of "virtue" merely in terms of an excellence [*arete*] that could just as well apply to mere cognitive faculties).[26] Zagzebski is, perhaps, the foremost exponent of a view of this sort, a view that is often referred to as "neo-Aristotelian." Accordingly, I shall focus on her theory here, though much of what I say ought to be equally applicable, *mutatis mutandis*, to any view of this sort.

Zagzebski sees the central problem with reliabilist theories as being their inability to explain what is valuable about knowledge possession. In particular, she argues that the "machine-product" analogy they work with is faulty, in the sense that no matter how reliable a machine is at producing a certain (valuable) product, the reliability of the machine alone will not explain the value of the product. The same is meant to apply to knowledge, in that she argues that if knowledge is to be solely understood in terms of reliability, it is difficult to see why knowledge is such a valuable thing to have. The chicken-sexer example provides support for this contention, in that both externalists and internalists would surely agree that there is *something* more valuable about the knowledge possessed by the enlightened chicken sexer that is missing in the case of her unenlightened counterpart. Plausibly, this difference in value is a direct result of the fact that the enlightened chicken sexer is able to take responsibility for her beliefs in a way that is impossible for the unenlightened chicken sexer.

Zagzebski argues that the way to deal with this problem is to abandon the machine-product analogy and focus instead upon the motivational states of the agent in much the same way as we are inclined to do in the moral case. Simply being able to act in such a way as to produce good consequences reliably is not sufficient for being accorded a high moral status for one's character. Rather, it is necessary that one also have the right motivational states that forge the required connection between one's inner psychological states and one's resultant actions. Similarly, in the epistemic case, it is important that the agent should be motivated by the right epistemic virtues and thus that the reliability is brought about in the right way.

---

[26] For further discussion of this contrast between reliabilism-based and responsibilism-based virtue epistemologies, see Axtell (1997; 1998), although note that Axtell allows some virtue theories to count as responsibilist even though they allow the possibility that the cognitive processes in question might operate at the sub-personal level. In particular, Axtell (1997, 13) cites Greco as being an example of a responsibilist virtue epistemologist.

Zagzebski, therefore, understands beliefs on the model of actions, and in doing so, she brings the deontic theoretical machinery to bear on the epistemic character of the agent.[27]

The problems regarding veritic luck facing process reliabilism thus lead some epistemologists to opt for an agent-centred version of reliabilism, but the further problems that remain spur others, such as Zagzebski, to go further and develop an epistemology entirely focused upon the epistemic acts of the agent. In doing so, Zagzebski moves away from epistemological externalism by arguing that it is essential to knowledge possession that the agent be able to know by reflection alone those facts that determine the justification for her belief. Consider the following passage:

> The value of knowledge is connected with the components of intellectual virtue. . . . It is in part because knowledge arises out of acts of intellectual virtue that it is an achievement in a way that mere true belief cannot be. The value of the truth obtained by a reliable process in the absence of any conscious awareness of a connection between the behaviour of the agent and the truth he thereby acquires is no better than the value of the lucky guess. (Zagzebski 1996, 303–4)

If this model of knowledge is to rule out cases like those of the chicken sexers as being genuine instances of knowledge (on the grounds that an instance of knowledge of this sort would be no better than a "lucky guess"), then we need to interpret the "conscious awareness" of the reliability at issue here in terms of the agent having evidence reflectively available to her in such a way as to support internalist justification of the target belief. In effect, then, Zagzebski is demanding that reliability alone is not enough and that what is further needed is *internalist* knowledge, knowledge that meets the internalist rubric as defined above. Moreover, it is important to note that Zagzebski is here explicitly making the point that the problem with an account of knowledge construed externalistically solely in terms of reliability (or, *a fortiori*, safety) is that it does not eliminate epistemic luck. Since, as we have seen, safety-based accounts – of which modalized process reliabilism and agent reliabilism are approximations – *do* succeed in eliminating veritic epistemic luck, and given that Zagzebski clearly believes that the type of epistemic luck she has in mind is dealt with via an appeal to reflective knowledge, we can safely assume that it is specifically *reflective* epistemic luck that is being referred to here. The problem with agent reliabilist versions of virtue epistemological theories

---

[27] See Zagzebski (1996, especially part 3) for a full account of her position. She expounds upon what she calls the "value problem" facing externalist theories of knowledge at more length in her essay in this collection. For discussion of the issues that she raises, see Greco (2002), Riggs (2002) and Percival's essay in this collection. For other versions of the virtue epistemology thesis that have more in common with Zagzebski's account than agent reliabilism, see Code (1984; 1987), Montmarquet (1987; 1993), Kvanvig (1992) and Hookway (1994).

according to Zagzebski is thus that, unlike the neo-Aristotelian responsi-bilist view that she endorses, they fail to eliminate reflective epistemic luck. One can thus understand the move from a reliabilism-based virtue theory to a responsibilist virtue theory in terms of how the latter is concerned to eliminate not just veritic epistemic luck but also reflective epistemic luck.

The problem with understanding this type of virtue epistemology as being motivated by a desire to eliminate reflective epistemic luck is that *no* epistemological theory can meet this challenge. This is highlighted for us by the radical sceptic via her use of radical sceptical error scenarios (such as that one might be a brain in a vat being "fed" one's experiences). It is part of the point of these sceptical error possibilities that they are entirely consistent with what one is able to know by reflection alone, even in the best case. Given this fact, however, this means that it is part of what we might call the "epistemic condition" that one's knowledge is always in this sense subject to reflective epistemic luck. Accordingly, if one demands that one's theory of knowledge should eliminate this type of luck, one is directly playing into the hands of the sceptic.

If the responsibilist view is to work, then, it must be willing to counte-nance at least one variety of reflective epistemic luck, despite protestations to the contrary by those who advance such a position. The difficulty facing this form of virtue theory now is to explain just what it offers over and above a mere epistemologically internalist account of knowledge that combines a safety-based view with the demand for internalist justification. Recall that the responsibilist position is meant to be a further refinement of an agent reliabilist thesis that eliminates the problem of veritic epistemic luck. Given that agent reliabilism can be regarded as an approximation to the kind of safety-based view that does fully succeed in eliminating veritic epistemic luck, any viable responsibilist theory is going to have to incor-porate a safety-type principle. We have already seen that a non-virtue safety-based account seems, prima facie at least, to present the best way of dealing with the problem of veritic epistemic luck. The challenge facing responsibilist virtue theories is thus to supplement this type of principle in such a way as to eliminate non-sceptical cases of reflective epistemic luck whilst also explaining why appeal to the epistemic virtues is essential to one's theory of knowledge. As it stands, however, there is no reason to prefer this responsibilist view over a safety-based internalist theory of knowledge that, whilst conceding that it cannot meet sceptical cases of reflective epistemic luck, nevertheless incorporates a role for responsibil-ity by demanding internalist justification and eliminates veritic epistemic luck by including a safety condition.

Note that I am not denying here that the responsibilist account of the epistemic virtues may well be an important feature of any fully fledged internalist theory of knowledge. Rather, I am simply questioning the key virtue-theoretic claim that one cannot account for knowledge and the other key epistemic concepts *without* appeal to the virtues. If veritic epistemic luck is the problem, then a safety-based account of knowledge is the answer, and this need make no essential reference to the epistemic virtues. Similarly, if reflective epistemic luck is a supplementary problem in this regard and one is entitled to set aside the radical sceptical challenge, then a safety-based account of knowledge coupled with the demand for internalist justification is the answer, and, again, this need make no essential reference to the epistemic virtues. Far from motivating the adoption of virtue-based theories, consideration of the role of epistemic luck, in both its most salient forms, actually reveals that virtue epistemology is curiously ill motivated as it stands.

5. Concluding Remarks

Not one of the considerations adduced here is meant to constitute decisive grounds for rejection of the virtue-epistemological project. Aside from anything else, the particular views that I have focused upon do not exhaust the theoretical possibilities as regards the two main types of virtue epistemology, and there may be, in any case, other types of virtue epistemology available that do not fall into either of these camps. Nevertheless, the considerations adduced here should suffice to prompt proponents of virtue epistemology to reflect further on just what it is that is motivating their adoption of this thesis. In particular, the play with epistemic luck that is common amongst defenders of this type of account of knowledge masks important distinctions concerning what is involved in epistemic luck that are substantively relevant to the plausibility of the position. Despite the pessimism that is expressed here, I am actually quietly optimistic about the prospects for virtue epistemology. Until it is clear what question virtue epistemology is an answer to, however, and that it does constitute an answer to this question, this optimism needs to remain on ice.[28]

Department of Philosophy
University of Stirling
Stirling FK9 4LA
United Kingdom
d.h.pritchard@stir.ac.uk

References

Armstrong, David M. 1973. *Belief, Truth and Knowledge*. Cambridge: Cambridge University Press.

[28] Thanks to Guy Axtell, Michael Brady and John Greco, and to the Leverhulme Trust for the award of a Special Research Fellowship to undertake work in this area.

Axtell, Guy. 1997. "Recent Work on Virtue Epistemology." *American Philosophical Quarterly* 34: 1–26.

————. 1998. "The Role of the Intellectual Virtues in the Reunification of Epistemology." *Monist* 81: 488–508.

Axtell, Guy. 2001. "Epistemic Luck in Light of the Virtues." In *Virtue Epistemology: Essays on Epistemic Virtue and Responsibility*, edited by A. Fairweather and L. Zagzebski. Oxford: Oxford University Press.

————, editor. 2000. *Knowledge, Belief and Character: Readings in Virtue Epistemology*. Lanham, Md.: Rowman and Littlefield.

Black, Tim. 2002. "A Moorean Response to Brain-in-a-Vat Scepticism." *Australasian Journal of Philosophy* 80: 148–63.

Brandom, Robert. 1998. "Insights and Blindspots of Reliabilism." *Monist* 81: 371–92.

Code, Lorraine. 1984. "Toward a "Responsibilist" Epistemology." *Philosophy and Phenomenological Research* 44: 29–50.

————. 1987. *Epistemic Responsibility*. Hanover, N.H.: University Press of New England and Brown University Press.

DePaul, Michael, and Linda Zagzebski, editors. 2002. *Intellectual Virtue: Perspectives from Ethics and Epistemology*. Oxford: Oxford University Press.

Engel, Mylan. 1992. "Is Epistemic Luck Compatible with Knowledge?" *Southern Journal of Philosophy* 30: 59–75.

Fairweather, Abrol, and Linda Zagzebski, editors. 2001. *Virtue Epistemology: Essays on Epistemic Virtue and Responsibility*. Oxford: Oxford University Press.

Foley, Richard. 1987. *A Theory of Epistemic Rationality*. Cambridge, Mass.: Harvard University Press.

————. 1994. "Sosa's Epistemology." *Philosophical Issues* 5: 42–58.

Gettier, Edmund. 1963. "Is Justified True Belief Knowledge?" *Analysis* 23: 121–23.

Goldman, Alvin. 1967. "A Causal Theory of Knowing." *Journal of Philosophy* 64: 355–72.

————. 1976. "Discrimination and Perceptual Knowledge." *Journal of Philosophy* 73: 771–91.

————. 1979. "What Is Justified Belief?" In *Justification and Knowledge*, edited by G. S. Pappas, 1–23. Dordrecht: D. Reidel.

————. 1986. *Epistemology and Cognition*. Cambridge, Mass.: Harvard University Press.

————. 1988. "Strong and Weak Justification." *Philosophical Perspectives* 2: 51–69.

————. 1993. "Epistemic Folkways and Scientific Epistemology." *Philosophical Issues* 3: 271–84.

Greco, John. 1993. "Virtues and Vices of Virtue Epistemology." *Canadian Journal of Philosophy* 23: 413–32.

————. 1994. "Virtue Epistemology and the Relevant Sense of Relevant Possibility." *Southern Journal of Philosophy* 32: 61–77.

————. 1999. "Agent Reliabilism." *Philosophical Perspectives* 13: 273–96.

————. 2000. *Putting Skeptics in Their Place: The Nature of Skeptical Arguments and Their Role in Philosophical Inquiry.* Cambridge: Cambridge University Press.

————. 2002. "Knowledge as Credit for True Belief." In *Intellectual Virtue: Perspectives from Ethics and Epistemology*, edited by Michael DePaul and Linda Zagzebski. Oxford: Oxford University Press.

Hall, Barbara J. 1994. "On Epistemic Luck." *Southern Journal of Philosophy* 32: 79–84.

Harper, William. 1996. "Knowledge and Luck." *Southern Journal of Philosophy* 34: 273–83.

Hookway, Christopher. 1994. "Cognitive Virtues and Epistemic Evaluations." *International Journal of Philosophical Studies* 2: 211–27.

Kornblith, Hilary, editor. 2001. *Epistemology: Internalism and Externalism.* Oxford: Basil Blackwell.

Kvanvig, John. 1992. *The Intellectual Virtues and the Life of the Mind: On the Place of Virtues in Epistemology.* Savage, Md.: Rowman and Littlefield.

Lewis, David. 1996. "Elusive Knowledge." *Australasian Journal of Philosophy* 74: 549–67.

Montmarquet, James. 1987. "Epistemic Virtue." *Mind* 96: 487–97.

————. 1993. *Epistemic Virtue and Doxastic Responsibility.* Lanham, Md.: Rowman and Littlefield.

Plantinga, Alvin. 1988. "Positive Epistemic Status and Proper Function." *Philosophical Perspectives* 2: 1–50.

————. 1993a. *Warrant and Proper Function.* New York: Oxford University Press.

————. 1993b. "Why We Need Proper Function." *Noûs* 27: 66–82.

Pritchard, Duncan H. 2001a. "Contextualism, Scepticism, and the Problem of Epistemic Descent." *Dialectica* 55: 327–49.

————. 2001b. "Radical Scepticism, Epistemological Externalism, and 'Hinge' Propositions." *Wittgenstein-Studien*: 81–105.

————. 2002a. "McKinsey Paradoxes, Radical Scepticism, and the Transmission of Knowledge across Known Entailments." *Synthese* 130: 279–302.

————. 2002b. "Radical Scepticism, Epistemological Externalism and Closure." *Theoria* 69: 129–61.

————. 2002c. "Recent Work on Radical Skepticism." *American Philosophical Quarterly* 39: 215–57.

————. 2002d. "Resurrecting the Moorean Response to Scepticism." *International Journal of Philosophical Studies* 10: 283–307.

————. 2003. "Epistemic Luck." *Journal of Philosophical Research* 28.

Pritchard, Duncan H., and Matthew Smith. 2002. "The Philosophy and Psychology of Luck." Typescript.

Pryor, James. 2001. "Highlights of Recent Epistemology." *British Journal for the Philosophy of Science* 52: 95–124.

Rescher, Nicholas. 1995. *Luck: The Brilliant Randomness of Everyday Life*. New York: Farrar, Straus, and Giroux.

Riggs, Wayne. 1998. "What Are the 'Chances' of Being Justified?" *Monist* 81: 452–72.

————. 2002. "Reliability and the Value of Knowledge." *Philosophy and Phenomenological Research* 64: 79–96.

Russell, Bertrand. 1948. *Human Knowledge: Its Scope and Its Limits*, London: George Allen and Unwin.

Sainsbury, Mark. 1996. "Crispin Wright: *Truth and Objectivity*." *Philosophy and Phenomenological Research* 56: 899–904.

Sosa, Ernest. 1985. "Knowledge and Intellectual Virtue." *Monist* 68: 224–45.

————. 1991. *Knowledge in Perspective: Selected Essays in Epistemology*. Cambridge: Cambridge University Press.

————. 1993. "Proper Functionalism and Virtue Epistemology." *Noûs* 27: 51–65.

————. 1999. "How to Defeat Opposition to Moore." *Philosophical Perspectives* 13: 141–54.

————. 2000. "Skepticism and Contextualism." *Philosophical Issues* 10: 1–18.

Steup, Mathias, editor. 2002. *Knowledge, Truth, and Duty: Essays on Epistemic Justification, Responsibility, and Virtue*. Oxford: Oxford University Press.

Talbott, William J. 1990. *The Reliability of the Cognitive Mechanism*. New York: Garland Publishing.

Vahid, Hamid. 2001. "Knowledge and Varieties of Epistemic Luck." *Dialectica* 55: 351–62.

Williamson, Timothy. 2000a. "Scepticism and Evidence." *Philosophy and Phenomenological Research* 60: 613–28.

————. 2000b. *Knowledge and Its Limits*. Oxford: Oxford University Press.

Wright, Crispin. 1996. "Response to Commentators." *Philosophy and Phenomenological Research* 56: 911–41.

Zagzebski, Linda. 1994. "The Inescapability of Gettier Problems." *Philosophical Quarterly* 44: 65–73.

————. 1996. *Virtues of the Mind: An Inquiry into the Nature of Virtue and the Ethical Foundations of Knowledge*. Cambridge: Cambridge University Press.

————. 1999. "What Is Knowledge?" In *Epistemology*, edited by J. Greco and E. Sosa, 92–116. Oxford: Basil Blackwell.

© Metaphilosophy LLC and Blackwell Publishing Ltd. 2003.
Published by Blackwell Publishing, 9600 Garsington Road, Oxford OX4 2DQ, UK and
350 Main Street, Malden, MA 02148, USA
METAPHILOSOPHY
Vol. 34, Nos. 1/2, January 2003
0026–1068

SENTIMENTALIST VIRTUE AND MORAL JUDGEMENT OUTLINE OF A PROJECT

MICHAEL SLOTE

ABSTRACT: Ethical rationalism has recently dominated the philosophical land-scape, but sentimentalist forms of normative ethics (such as the ethics of caring) and of metaethics (such as Blackburn's projectivism and various ideal-observer and response-dependent views) have also been prominent. But none of this has been systematic in the manner of Hume and Hutcheson. Hume based both ethics and metaethics in his notion of sympathy, but the project sketched here focuses rather on the (related) notion of empathy. I argue that empathy is essential to the development of morally required caring about others and also to deontological limits or restrictions on self-concern and other-concern. But empathy also plays a grounding role in moral judgement. Moral approval and disapproval can be non-circularly understood as empathic reflections of the concern or lack of concern that agents show towards other people; and moral utterances can plausibly be seen not as projections, expressions, or descriptions of sentiment but as "objective" and "non-relative" judgements whose reference and content are fixed by sentiments of approval and disapproval.

Keywords: care, empathy, ethics, Hume, metaethics, sentimentalism, virtues.

The eighteenth-century moral sentimentalists, most notably Hume and Hutcheson, sought to give an account of both normative ethics and metaethics in sentimentalist terms. But in recent years and decades, Kantian, Rawlsian, and Aristotelian forms of rationalism have dominated the moral-philosophical landscape. That is not, however, to say that senti-mentalism has been anything like lifeless. The metaethical sentimentalism of Blackburn, Mackie, Wiggins, and others picks up on theories of the meaning of moral utterances that one can find (inconsistently vying with one another) in Hume. Likewise, on the normative ethical front the recent ethics of caring is sentimentalist and has recognised its similarity, if not indebtedness, to Hume.

But none of this has been as systematic as Hume and Hutcheson were, and from a contemporary standpoint the most distinctive feature of the sentimentalist project I am currently engaged in is that it *does* attempt to offer an integrated account of normative ethics and metaethics along senti-mentalist lines. My *Morals from Motives* (2001) presented and defended a virtue ethics of caring, but this was a work of normative ethics, not of metaethics, and since then I (believe I) have seen a way to defend sentimentalism more broadly. The notion of empathy and of empathic caring can enrich our (virtue-ethical) picture of what is virtuous and obligatory beyond anything the notion of caring by itself can accomplish (or did accomplish in my 2001). But perhaps more interestingly, I believe that the notion of empathy can show us how to frame a reasonable and attractive sentimentalist metaethics of moral terms and utterances.

Instead of relying on a Hutchesonian moral sense, Hume held that both moral virtue and moral judgements or utterances involved processes of sympathy. But Hume does not distinguish sympathy from empathy: the word *empathy* did not even exist until the twentieth century. It is important to distinguish these two notions, however, and we can say, very roughly, that the difference corresponds to that between feeling *for* someone's pain and feeling their pain. One needs to say more, but I believe what I want to say about empathy will be intuitively clear enough for the limited purposes of this outline, and I would like to begin by saying something, in normative ethical terms, about the role of empathy in the moral life (in being virtuous). I shall then offer a brief metaethical account of the role of empathy in moral judgement.

The idea that empathy might be important to our understanding of morality first occurred to me when a colleague of mine mentioned an article on abortion by conservative Catholic thinker (and U.S. Court of Appeals judge) John Noonan (1973) that focused not on the rights of the foetus but on the moral implications of *empathy* with foetuses. I was told that Noonan appealed to such empathy in support of a general prohibition on aborting foetuses, but before I had even seen the article, it hit me that an appeal to empathy might be taken in just the opposite direction. It is arguably more difficult to empathise with a foetus (much less an embryo) than with a born human being, and I thought that might help us to explain why most of us think it is morally not as bad to abort a foetus as to kill a born baby. Reading the article made me even more hopeful about the potential significance of empathy. Given the notion of caring taken on its own, there might be no moral reason to care more about born babies than about foetuses, but adding in an appeal to the empathic tendencies of human beings does enable us to explain this, and at the time it occurred to me that it might also help us with other moral issues (like our differential obligations to animals as opposed to fellow human beings).

I was also helped by reading some recent work by psychologists on the importance of empathy to moral development, most notably C. D. Batson's *The Altruism Question* (1991) and Martin Hoffman's *Empathy and Moral Development* (2000). These books summarise recent experimental studies of empathy and argue that the development of empathy plays a crucial role in the development of long-term genuinely altruistic caring motivation. But rather than try to say more about this here, I would like now to consider how empathy can help us make some intuitive moral distinctions we have not yet mentioned.

Consider the well-known example of miners trapped in a coalmine as a result of a cave-in. We typically feel morally impelled to help the miners rather than (at that point) expend an equivalent amount of money or effort to install safety devices in the mines that will save a greater number of lives in the long run. But some have disagreed. Charles Fried (1970, especially 207–27) discusses this example in his *Anatomy of Values* and claims that we should prefer to install the safety devices and let the miners die. In fact, he gives his argument a rather barbaric twist by saying that we should even be willing to convey the decision to the ill-fated miners face-to-face, if that is somehow possible.

By why is his suggestion barbaric? Why does it show what most of us would call a lack of compassion? Why would most of us have a different reaction from Fried's and (without perhaps even thinking in terms of right and wrong) be strongly moved to help the trapped miners rather than do some greater expectable good for future miners? The answer to these questions, I believe, has to do with the natural flow or evocation of human empathy. A clear and present danger engages or arouses our empathy more readily or thoroughly than a danger or disaster that lies in the future, and we can mark the difference by saying that the present danger and threatened disaster are more empathetically *immediate* for us than any (equally probable or predictable) danger or disaster lying in the future.

Normally developed human empathy reacts more strongly to clear and present danger, and a caring concern for others that is based in developed empathy will therefore be contoured to prefer to save those who are in clear and present, or (temporally) immediate, danger. In that case, we might claim that the distinction between right and wrong is not given by the simple distinction between what expresses or reflects a caring attitude versus what expresses or reflects an uncaring attitude toward others. Rather, it can (to a first approximation) be understood in richer virtue-ethical terms as the distinction between what reflects fully developed human empathic concern for others and what reflects less than fully developed empathic concern for other people. And this would enable us to explain why Fried's "solution" to the problem of the miners is (intuitively) unacceptable.

Nor does it make sense at this point to object to this argument on the grounds that sentimentalism is thereby moving illicitly from facts about human psychology to value judgements about certain motives or actions. For *anyone* who asserts a basic ethical principle (like "lying is wrong" or "pleasure is the only good") moves from a certain fact to a certain value. Now a virtue ethics of (empathic) caring ties a certain factually described motive to the moral value of that motive and of actions exhibiting it, but aside from the fact that what is involved here is *virtue ethics*, the move from fact to value as such is no more suspect here than anywhere else.

Having now seen how temporal immediacy bears, in sentimentalist terms, on certain moral distinctions and intuitions, I would like us to consider another kind of empathic immediacy and its relevance to recent debates about the nature and extent of our obligations to help other people.

The immediacy at issue in the miners' case involved our greater empathic reaction to clear and present dangers. Given the present approach, we have in effect argued for a certain kind of *partiality* in our response to such cases (as opposed to the impartiality recommended by Fried). But there is another kind of empathic immediacy that also, I think, cuts a great deal of moral ice: the immediacy of what we (directly) perceive as opposed to what we merely know about, what we can call *perceptual* immediacy. I think that dangers we perceive arouse our empathy more easily and thoroughly than those we merely know about ("by description"), but the example of the miners does not or need not illustrate this point, because that example works in the terms previously discussed even if we don't perceive the miners and merely learn about them through the media. That is because the main issue in such cases is temporal immediacy.

To illustrate how empathy engages the distinction between what we perceive and what we merely know about, it is best, therefore, to use examples where the danger or disaster is present, not future, and where there is a distinction to which we as empathic beings are sensitive between what we perceive and what we do not. And in fact such a distinction is implicit in the kinds of cases that have been made familiar to us by Peter Singer. In "Famine, Altruism, and Morality," Singer (1972) points out that (everyone would agree that) it is wrong not to save a child drowning right in front of one if one can easily do so. But most people think we are not similarly, or as strongly, obligated to save the life of a distant child by making, say, a small contribution to Oxfam. Singer, however, argues that sheer distance cannot reasonably make a difference to our obligations to people and concludes that it is as wrong for us not to make a child-saving contribution to Oxfam as to let a child drown in a fountain right in front of us. But the same point iterates with respect to the many (other) children we could save through Oxfam, and, according to Singer, we end up with a cumulative obligation to give away most of our money to help those who are and remain more needy than we are.

Many have objected to Singer's rather iconoclastic conclusion, and one argument has been that distance may well make a difference to our obligations of beneficence. But what has not been seen is that Singer's arguments can also be blocked by an appeal to considerations of empathy, and this sort of objection is perhaps more effective than an appeal merely to spatial distance, because of all the other areas or topics where empathy appears to make an intuitive moral difference. We have stronger empathy for those whose plight is perceptually immediate for us than for those we only know about, and if such differences make a moral difference, then we have reason to hold, contra Singer, that it is morally worse not to save the drowning child than not to save some (or a) child by making a contribution to Oxfam. This, then, in effect justifies a(nother) kind of partiality in the area of human beneficence.

At this point, however, a very large objection to what I am proposing needs to be considered. We have been speaking about ways in which natural human empathic reactions may be thought to give shape to our obligations to help others. But all such obligations fall within the sphere of beneficence, and it is not surprising that our obligations in that area should turn out to be a matter of proper human feeling or sentiment. What we should give to others can more or less easily be seen as a matter of what proper feelings or motives would lead us to do for others, and this remains true, I think, whether or not one thinks of proper beneficence as reflecting impartial concern for overall human or sentient welfare or as reflecting the more contoured sensitivities that are built into human empathy.

But there is arguably more to morality than obligations (and supererogations) of beneficence. Those who believe in deontology suppose that there are times when human beneficence – whether conceived of in partial or impartial terms – has to be limited or restricted. And if (proper) beneficence seems a matter of human feeling, then the deontological considerations that such beneficence sometimes has to yield to are naturally regarded as limiting or restricting the play or expression of such feelings. Our desire to help people, then, is easily regarded as reflecting certain cultivatable feelings, but any deontological prohibition on (say) killing forbids us to kill even if doing so would on the whole be more helpful than not doing so. Here the desire to help, the sentiment of human concern for others, seems to be restricted in the name of *something other* than sentiment. In that case, a greater sentimentalism that seeks to account for deontology would seem to face an uphill battle.

Of course, Francis Hutcheson anticipated utilitarianism in *denying* the ultimate validity of deontology, but it would be unfortunate for moral sentimentalism (as it seems unfortunate for act-utilitarianism) to have to deny the validity of all our intuitions concerning deontological prohibitions, and I believe sentimentalism needs to look for some alternative. Hume did in fact seek such an alternative, and his account of the artificial virtues certainly attempts to deal with a major part of deontology in sentimentalist terms. But given all the worries there are about "Hume's circle" and other features of his account of deontology, I think the contemporary sentimentalist would do well to look elsewhere for an account of deontology. What I want to suggest here is that sentimentalism can have a "second chance" with deontology by appealing to "natural" (as opposed to Humean, artificial) facts about human empathy and to a notion of immediacy different from, but allied to, the forms of immediacy we have already (too briefly) discussed. Given limitations of space, the issue of deontology

I want to focus on is the (arguably) central one of doing versus allowing – for example, killing versus letting die.

We saw earlier that empathy works though certain modalities or aspects of an agent's interaction with the world. Agents are more empathic and more empathetically concerned with what they *perceive* than with what they do not; and they are also empathetically more sensitive to what *they know to be going on at the same time* as their decision making and choices. And these differences of empathy correspond to what we naturally think of as the greater immediacy of dangers that we perceive or that are contemporaneous with our concern. But there are other facts about, or factors in, our interactions with the world to which empathy is also sensitive, and which give rise to a form of immediacy we have not yet mentioned.

When we cause a death, kill someone, we are in causal terms more strongly connected to a death than if we merely allow someone to die, and I believe we are empathetically sensitive to this distinction in a way that allows us to make sense of (certain crucial issues of) deontology. If we are more empathetically sensitive to perceived or contemporaneous (potential) pain, so too do we seem to be more empathetically sensitive to (potentially) causing pain (or death) than to (potentially) allowing it. We *flinch* from the former in a way or to an extent that we do not with respect to the latter, and I would like to say that pain or harm that we (may) cause has, therefore, a greater *causal* immediacy for us than pain or harm that we (may) merely allow. In that case, and given the weight I have argued we should give to human empathic concern for others, we have some reason to conclude that it is worse to kill or harm than (other things being equal) to allow these actions to happen, and this gives a sentimental basis to a core element of deontology.

Most attempts to ground deontology appeal to some form of (practical or theoretical) reason or rationality and to reason-based rules, principles, or intuitions that can oppose sentiment. But if an empathy-based sentimentalist account is on the right track, it is our empathic sensitivity to situational factors of immediacy rather than a conscientious adherence to rules or explicit moral beliefs that can lead one not to kill or steal even if doing so would have better overall results. In that case, deontology may not need to be conceived of as different from and opposed to all human feeling and sentiment but may actually have its roots in certain very particular sentiments. The familiar moral opposition between (partial or impartial) beneficence and deontology may occur *within* the realm of sentiment rather than reflect any (limited) conflict between feeling or sentiment and something else of moral importance. But what I have said here is just a sketch or (perhaps even less than that) the promise of a new sentimentalist conception of deontology. I haven't at all mentioned issues of social justice and human rights and fidelity to promises that are typically regarded as important to deontology, and these topics would have to be adequately dealt with if the project of a new or revived sentimentalism is ever to succeed. For

© Metaphilosophy LLC and Blackwell Publishing Ltd. 2003

reasons of space, however, I must leave these matters for another occasion and focus in what remains of this essay on what I earlier spoke of as the other side or aspect of a full-scale moral sentimentalism – that is, on questions of metaethics.

Sentimentalism has sought, historically at least, to base moral claims or utterances in sentiments or feelings of approval or disapproval on the part of those making the claims or giving vent to the utterances. But this creates problems for sentimentalism because (as Thomas Reid was perhaps the first to note) it threatens sentimentalist metaethics with circularity. The sentimentalist seeks to analyse moral utterances or judgements in terms of feelings like approval and disapproval, but what if, in fact, approval and disapproval are not (just) feelings (even "corrected" ones) *but themselves contain or involve, respectively, the belief or judgement that something is right and the belief or judgement that something is wrong*? The threat of such a circle and the sheer plausibility of the idea that approval and disapproval have conceptual or cognitive content have made many ethicists very wary of sentimentalist accounts of moral judgement, and they are right to be wary.

What I would like to propose, however, is that sentimentalism is in fact in a position to make good on its essential assumption that approval and disapproval are feelings, and that it can on that basis then offer an account of what moral judgements or moral utterances are. To that end, it will be useful, I think, to say a bit more about eighteenth-century sentimentalist theories of approval and disapproval. Some of their shortcomings may help point the way to some more promising contemporary possibilities.

Hutcheson sees moral approval and disapproval as operating via a distinct moral sense (analogous to the five senses), whereas Hume bases these moral feelings in mechanisms of (what he calls) sympathy. I assume (with Hume) that a psychological mechanism is preferable to an unanalysed new form of perception or sensing, but there is a problem with Hume's account, his specification of the mechanisms of approval, because of its emphasis on the effects or consequences of what we approve or disapprove of. For Hume (and leaving aside what he says about a how our sentiments have to be corrected), we approve of traits or motives that tend to have beneficial effects and disapprove of those with the opposite tendency because of our sympathetic (or what we might today call empathic) pleasure or displeasure at those (likely) effects.

Adam Smith criticised Hume's theory for its inability to explain why we do not morally approve and disapprove of inanimate objects for *their* predictable effects on human happiness and unhappiness, and although Hume tries to answer this objection in his *Enquiry Concerning the Principles of Morals*, what he says is neither clear nor convincing. In my view, the problem with Hume's approach to approval is that it involves the approver or disapprover in sentimental identification or "sympathy" with those affected by actions *rather than* with those one is actually approving

138MICHAEL SLOTE

or disapproving of, that is, moral agents. And (not surprisingly) Adam Smith in *The Theory of Moral Sentiments* offers an account of approval and disapproval in terms relating more to agents. Smith says that we approve of someone's motives, if, when we put ourselves in their position, we find that we would have the same sort of motivation. Now this involves or comes close to involving what we today would call empathy, but I think this agent-focused account of approval and disapproval won't quite do, because of certain possibilities of moral supererogation. After all, I might view someone else as, say, more forgiving than I would be about some matter, yet this need not prevent me from approving of the person whom I view as different from myself (and perhaps as more admirable than myself).

What I want to propose, then, is that we retain Smith's (un-Humean) idea that approval or disapproval most basically involves a feeling of (something like) empathy vis-à-vis agents, but that we make the adjustments necessary to avoid the just-mentioned implausible consequences (and others) of Smith's specific theory. Approval and disapproval of actions and their agents, I want to say, involve (the sentiment and mechanism of) empathy, but, to put the matter somewhat too baldly, the empathy involved here is empathy *with the agent's empathy or lack of it*. Ever since Shaftesbury, sentimentalists have noted the warm and tender quality of felt (empathic) concern for others – and the absence of that quality in those who exhibit a lack of concern for or hostility toward the welfare of others. But this is warmth/tenderness or its opposite in *agents*, and the view I want to suggest argues that an empathic moral judge or observer will pick up on those agentive distinctions and register them in herself as, respectively, approval and disapproval. When I, as judge or non-agent observer, empathetically feel the warmth of an agent as displayed in a given action, then the derivative or reflecting warmth that I feel *is* a (morally non-judging) feeling of approval toward the action or its agent qua doer of that action; and, similarly, when the agent's actions display an absence of warmth/tenderness, my observer empathy will register or reflect the contrast with agentive warmth as a cold feeling or (as we say) "chill" of disapproval.

This theory has its own distinctive way of accounting for the corrections of bias and perspective that Hume thought essential to true moral approval and judgement – it can say, for one thing, that the warmth a mother feels towards her son on death row is *not* approval of his murdering ways, because it is not (causally speaking) an empathic reflection in the mother of any warmth the son displays as an agent. Rather, it involves the mother's (agentive) concern for the son as a non-agent, as someone potentially affected for better or worse by the actions of other agents. If we make such causal distinctions as to source of empathic feeling(s of warmth), I believe we can accomplish what Hume sought to achieve via the idea of correction (among other things, we can explain why people might confuse

© Metaphilosophy LLC and Blackwell Publishing Ltd. 2003

approval or disapproval with other feelings); but this must for the present remain a promissory note. For the moment, our most pressing question is how to incorporate such a sentimentalist theory of approval and disapproval into an account of the meaning of explicit moral utterances or claims.

There are a variety of possible sentimentalist views about how (morally non-judging) feelings play a role in moral utterances or claims, and most of them can be found in Hume. Hume's ideas about the nature of moral utterances are difficult to interpret, and that is at least in part because he at various points suggests different theories, all of which are mutually inconsistent. For example, Hume at one point in the *Treatise* says that morality is more properly felt than judged of, and this certainly suggests and anticipates the emotivist idea that moral utterances or sentences express (positive or negative) feelings (of approval or disapproval) rather than making claims or judgements or expressing beliefs about the world.

In other famous passages, however, Hume seems to espouse the kind of projectivism that Simon Blackburn (1984) has in recent years defended (in neo-Humean terms). For Hume speaks of the mind's propensity to "spread itself" on external objects and of our tendency to "gild" or "stain" all material objects with "colours borrowed from internal sentiment," and this suggests (in contrast with emotivism) that moral claims really are claims, but that they involve systematically mistaking our internal sentimental states of approval or disapproval for something outside or independent of those states. (Perhaps – though I have not seen this mentioned before – the mistake involved in making moral judgements is the mistake of thinking that the *universe* disapproves or approves of some act or agent.) But this sort of "error theory" will leave many moral philosophers unsatisfied and sceptical because it is so uncharitable to our human tendency to think we are saying something that can be true (though it may be false) when we make moral claims. A sentimentalist view that is more in line with what we ordinarily, pre-philosophically, or intuitively, think about the nature of the moral judgements we make will to that extent (at least) be preferable to both projectivism and emotivism. Interestingly enough, Hume himself expresses and discusses such a view in various places.

What has come to be known as the "ideal-observer theory" (in more recent contexts, and with somewhat altered emphasis, the "response-dependent view") of moral judgements treats moral claims concerning any given entity as claims about how calm, disinterested, and relevantly informed "judicious spectators" or "ideal observers" would tend to react to the entity. On such a view, the moral claim that, for example, a given trait is morally bad asserts that human beings have the disposition or tendency to react with (a sentiment of) disapproval to that trait under certain ideal or idealised conditions, and, as I indicated, Hume in a number of places seems to favour (something approaching) such a view of moral utterances. Certainly, given the methodology briefly introduced above, this approach has at least something in its favour: it makes moral judgements susceptible to both truth and falsity and to both (epistemic) reasonableness and unreasonableness – as most of us, independently of philosophy, tend to think they are. But, independently of philosophy, most of us also think that moral judgements are true about something other than and independent of *our own moral reactions*. Surely claims about the wrongness of some act or trait seem to be primarily about the act or trait rather than primarily about our reactions or tendencies to react to them, and the ideal-observer theory does not do justice to this aspect of our "manifest image" of moral judgements.

What would be more in line with common opinion would be some form of (what is known as) *moral realism*, a view that would treat the goodness or wrongness of acts, traits, and motives as properties at least somewhat independent of our dispositions to react to such things. But this might seem a tall order for a sentimentalist theory of morality – with its emphasis, precisely, on internal states of feeling – to accomplish, and I believe Hume himself nowhere suggests such a view. The possibility, however, of what might be called "sentimentalist realism" has been suggested or at least hinted at by a number of philosophers, including David Wiggins, Nicholas Sturgeon, and Stephen Darwall (with the last two arguing that Hutcheson, though not Hume, may be interpretable as such a realist).

A fully developed sentimentalist realism would make use of an analogy between the sensory (for example, colours) and the moral that projectivism and the ideal-observer and response-dependent theories also rely on. But it would understand that analogy by reference to Saul Kripke's (1980) ideas about "reference fixing." According to Kripke, a phrase like "what explains (or underlies) the sensation of red I am having" fixes the reference, though it does not give the meaning, of our term *red*, and the latter picks out a property in objects that is possibly identical with some surface feature of those objects (in relation to surrounding objects) and that is "rigidly" the same in all possible worlds (even those where different external properties normally cause us to have sensations of red).

Applying such a theory to moral properties, we can say that (statements about) moral approval and disapproval fix the reference of moral properties or claims, but that, like colour properties, moral properties are external to or independent of these moral reactions. Moral claims would not, then, be *about* our reactive sentimental dispositions, but their (objective) reference would be fixed by facts about those dispositions, and such a view clearly deserves to be called a form of (sentimentalist) moral realism. Since (so far as I can tell) this approach sits better with our antecedent opinions about what moral utterances or claims *are* than any other known form of sentimentalist metaethics, I think there is reason for the modern-day sentimentalist to examine and develop it further. But, by way of bringing this essay to a close, I would like to say something about how such an approach stands in relation to issues of relativism or relativity.

An ideal-observer approach treats moral judgements as about human dispositions to respond to things, and one of its implications is that if human beings had different dispositions, things would have moral properties different from those they have in the actual world. But if that means that under different conditions cruelty and aggression would be morally good, we may have reason to worry that the ideal-observer theory treats moral judgements as unsatisfyingly relative or relativistic, something that moral rationalism deliberately seeks to avoid. The Kripkean approach avoids this conclusion by holding that, although our actual reactions serve to fix the reference of moral terms or concepts, the (basic) truths that can be stated using such concepts (for example, that red is a such-and-such physical reflectance property or that moral goodness consists in empathic concern for others) are *necessary truths*. This allow sentimentalism to be less relative and is more in line with what the rationalist aspires to, but the issue of precisely *how much* relativity it is realistic to ascribe to moral judgements is a very delicate issue that we do not have space to discuss here. (For example, sentimentalism and rationalism might both want to consider the extent of our obligations to, and the obligations of, beings incapable of empathy.)

A more pressing issue for sentimentalism arises from the way it makes moral distinctions follow distinctions in human empathy. As we saw above, this allows us to draw and justify certain important and intuitive moral distinctions. But may it not also lead us to draw certain invidious and unintuitive moral distinctions? If, for example, white people tend to empathise more easily with other whites than they do with blacks, will this not permit and recommend morally repugnant forms of *discrimination*? Interestingly, however, empirical studies of such cross-racial differences in empathy seem not to indicate any very marked or *basic* human tendency towards preference on the basis of (similar) skin colour (though it would be important to consider whether the fact that sentimentalism leaves certain moral issues in this way open to empirical investigation favours sentimentalism or whether it threatens it – as some, but not all, rationalists will hold). Also, Jorge Gracia and others have argued that a slight preference for those similar to one (physically or in terms of shared history or roots) may be morally acceptable and even desirable, if it does not go as far as callous indifference or hatred or (what we would call) prejudice.

Finally, I should mention a potentially more worrisome objection of relativism, based on differences of empathy between men and women. Following psychoanalyst Nancy Chodorow, Carol Gilligan (1982) has argued that men have to learn to separate themselves from their mothers in a way that women do not and that this makes men stress and embody autonomy more than women do, which leaves women with a greater over-all tendency towards empathic connection with and concern about others (whether they be men or women). But if, as I have suggested here, moral-ity is to be measured in terms of empathy and women tend to develop greater empathy than men, does this not treat men, invidiously and unfairly, as second-class moral citizens?

But it isn't just sentimentalism that faces this problem. If (as Kant held) morality requires us to emphasise our own autonomy and separateness from others, then women will be at a moral disadvantage vis-à-vis men if their tendency to stay (more) tied to their mothers leaves them less able to treat people as fully separate and autonomous. Given factual differences of this kind (though some consider this a questionable assumption), both rationalism and sentimentalism may be in difficulty.

Recent discussions of this issue, however, have noted that in certain ways, and given their strong tendency towards connection with the mother, women may have a more difficult time empathising with others than men do. Empathy does not involve obliterating the distinction between self and other, and if men may end up having some problems connecting with others, women may, if they do not sufficiently separate from their mothers, have the opposite problem of losing a sense of the boundaries between themselves and others. This too interferes with empa-thy, and the point is well illustrated in what is known as "substitute success syndrome," a problem that seems to beset women more than men and that involves living through one's spouse or children and being unwilling to see the latter as having their own independently valid sources of aspiration and interest.

In that case a sentimentalism focused on empathic caring may not so much see women as morally better than men as see men and women as subject to equally real but different vices that interfere with ideal empathic caring from opposite directions. Moreover, if the vice of too much connec-tion threatens women much more than men and the vice of too little threat-ens men more than women, then we can invoke Aristotle (towards a rather un-Aristotelian end) and say that morally good empathy lies in a mean between a vice typical of men and one typical of women. This means that a moral sentimentalism that regards men and women as morally *different* need not, in the end, have the invidious implication that one sex is morally superior to the other.

This is all I have space for here, but I hope that I have said enough to show where the present project is heading. I have not said or even hinted at much here about moral education of the sentiments or about how empa-thy might serve to undergird and support the use of moral rules and prin-ciples – though both topics are discussed in interesting detail in Hoffman's *Empathy and Moral Development*. But even the issues I *have* discussed I have had to deal with cursorily, and I hope the book that I am now in the process of writing will be able to do much greater justice to the topic – and aims – of moral sentimentalism.

Department of Philosophy
University of Miami
P.O. Box 248054
Coral Gables, FL 33124
USA
mslote@mail.as.miami.edu

References

Batson, C. D. 1991. *The Altruism Question: Toward a Social-Psychological Answer.* Hillandale, N.J.: Lawrence Erlbaum.
Blackburn, Simon. 1984. *Spreading the Word.* Oxford: Oxford University Press.
Fried, Charles. 1970. *An Anatomy of Values.* Cambridge, Mass.: Harvard University Press.
Gilligan, Carol. 1982. *In a Different Voice: Psychological Theory and Women's Development.* Cambridge, Mass.: Harvard University Press.
Hoffman, Martin. 2000. *Empathy and Moral Development: Implications for Caring and Justice.* New York: Cambridge University Press.
Kripke, Saul. 1980. *Naming and Necessity.* Oxford: Basil Blackwell.
Noonan, John T. Jr. 1973. "Responding to Persons: Methods of Moral Argument in Debate over Abortion." *Theology Digest*: 91–107.
Singer, Peter. 1972. "Famine, Affluence, and Morality." *Philosophy and Public Affairs* 1: 229–43.
Slote, Michael A. 2001. *Morals from Motives.* New York: Oxford University Press.

© Metaphilosophy LLC and Blackwell Publishing Ltd. 2003.
Published by Blackwell Publishing, 9600 Garsington Road, Oxford OX4 2DQ, UK and
350 Main Street, Malden, MA 02148, USA
METAPHILOSOPHY
Vol. 34, Nos. 1/2, January 2003
0026–1068

SOME WORRIES ABOUT NORMATIVE AND METAETHICAL SENTIMENTALISM

MICHAEL S. BRADY

ABSTRACT: In this response I raise a number of problems for Michael Slote's normative and metaethical sentimentalism. The first is that his agent-based account of rightness needs be qualified in order to be plausible; any such qualification, however, leaves Slote's normative ethics in tension with his metaethical views. The second is that an agent-based ethics of empathic caring will indeed struggle to capture our common-sense understanding of deontological constraints, and that appeal to the notion of causal immediacy will be of little help here. Finally, it seems to me that Slote's metaethical account will turn out to be much less externalist (and hence, by his own lights, much less plausible) than he suspects.

Keywords: agent-based virtue ethics, deontology, externalism, internalism, metaethics, sentimentalism.

For the past few years Michael Slote has been engaged in an ambitious and ground-breaking project aimed at explaining and defending an agent-based approach to normative ethics.[1] This approach maintains that all the important moral concepts and distinctions can be derived from or based upon the responses of virtuous agents. In his latest project, an outline of which appears in the preceding essay, Slote has an even broader remit: he proposes an agent-based or sentimentalist account of *metaethics* to accompany his normative theory, and he attempts to construct each around an ideal of empathic caring.

In what follows I shall raise some (necessarily provisional) doubts about the normative and metaethical theories Slote favours. In the first section I focus on Slote's agent-based account of rightness and wrongness, and I indicate how it needs to be modified in order to avoid a couple of criticisms; in section 2 I question whether an ethics based on the ideal of empathic caring can really accommodate deontological constraints; and in the final section I point out a tension between Slote's sentimentalist metaethics and its normative companion, which raises a suspicion about the possibility of a fully integrated sentimentalist theory.

[1] See Slote 1995; 1997; 2001.

I

In *Morals from Motives*, Slote writes that virtue ethics can be characterised by its focus on "the virtuous individual and on those inner traits, dispositions, and motives that qualify her as being virtuous" (Slote 2001, 4), rather than on acts themselves or consequences. *Agent-based* virtue ethics can be regarded as a unitary moral theory that regards the virtues as fundamental, and as such represents an approach that seems both more radical and more pure than traditional virtue theories. Slote defines the view as follows: "An agent-based approach to virtue ethics treats the moral or ethical status of acts as entirely derivative from independent and fundamental aretaic (as opposed to deontic) ethical characterisations of motives, character traits, or individuals" (Slote 2001, 5). On this view, rightness depends upon goodness, but contra utilitarianism it is the goodness of motives, rather than of outcomes, that matters. In this previous work, the emergent views of rightness appeal to the motives of partial and universal benevolence or caring. Slote now thinks that ideas of empathy and empathic caring "can enrich our (virtue-ethical) picture of what is virtuous and obligatory beyond anything the notion of caring by itself can accomplish" (132), and so seeks to ground his ethical theory in such notions. But how, exactly, does rightness depend upon empathic caring? To answer this question, let us turn to Slote's examples.

In Slote's discussion of the trapped miners, he claims that the right thing to do would be to help the trapped miners rather than let them die and install the safety devices; and in his discussion of Singer's article he holds that it would be morally worse not to save the drowning child than not to save some child by donating to Oxfam. In each case, Slote thinks that there are differences in the "natural flow or evocation of human empathy" (133): the clear and present danger to the miners "engages or arouses our empathy more readily or thoroughly than a danger or disaster that lies in the future" (133), and "we have stronger empathy for those whose plight is perceptually immediate for us than for those we only know about" (134). Since Slote's account is agent-based, he will deny that such differences merely *reflect* differences in moral status; for on his view the former *ground* the latter, and so he claims that "the distinction between right and wrong . . . can (to a first approximation) be understood . . . as the distinction between what reflects fully developed human empathic concern for others and what reflects less than fully developed empathic concern for other people" (133).

To a first approximation, then, Slote's view seems to be this:

1. An act *A* is right if and only if it expresses or reflects fully developed empathic concern on the part of an agent *S*.

This account of rightness might appear problematic, however, and for a couple of reasons. The first is that common sense tells us that sometimes an act is right even if it does not express *fully* developed empathic concern. An obvious example is when an agent strives to develop her empathic responses, because she realises that she is at present too cold-hearted and wants to be better able to respond to the plight of others: here the agent's motive is still empathy, but by definition not fully developed empathy. If we think that actions which express this goal are, given her circumstances, the right thing for the agent to do, we can doubt that rightness is as (1) claims (and can doubt that wrongness is as [1] implies).

A second reason is this: common sense also tells us that sometimes an act is right even if it does not *express* fully developed empathic concern. I can, for instance, perform actions that a person with fully developed empathic concern *would* perform in these circumstances – saving the miners, rather than letting them die and installing safety devices – and yet do so from morally questionable motives. (I'm a politician, it's election year, I have only one more term to serve and can confidently predict that my chances of re-election would be damaged were I not to save the miners, and so on.) Here I might be described as doing the right thing but for the wrong reason. This distinction is not something that Slote's theory is well placed to capture, however, since it makes the rightness or wrongness of an act depend upon the goodness or badness of the motives expressed or reflected *by that act*: if, then, the motive is good, the action is right, and if the motive is bad, the action is wrong. If we think that the distinction is indeed plausible, we can again doubt that (1) is correct.[2]

Now an agent-based approach might address the second worry by claiming that rightness depends not upon the actual motives for which an action was performed but upon the fact that the act *would* be performed by someone with fully developed empathy. Since I can do what the fully empathic person would do, but from any number of motives, this allows an ethic of empathic caring to capture the distinction between doing the right thing and doing the right thing for the right (or wrong) reason. Furthermore, the approach might respond to the first worry by claiming that rightness depends not upon the fact that someone with fully developed empathy would perform a certain act but that he or she would *approve* of the performance of such an act. As a result, the objections raised above do not necessarily tell against an agent-based approach to rightness that is centred on an ideal of empathic caring, and they suggest that any such approach ought to be reformulated along the following lines:

[2] Perhaps in this instance we are tempted to deny that saving the miners for political gain *is* the right thing to do. (See Antony Duff's contribution to this collection for arguments against an obvious distinction between doing the right thing and doing the right thing for the right or wrong reason.) Nevertheless, it is possible to make the same point by substituting a less morally questionable motive: suppose I feel no empathy for the plight of those down the mine, and my saving them does not express my empathic caring, but as a good Kantian I realise it is my duty to save those in need and as a result am motivated to do so. Here it is much less plausible to deny that I do the right thing.

2. An agent S's performing act A in circumstances C is right if and only if an observer with fully developed empathic concern would approve of S's performing act A in these circumstances.[3]

Whether Slote would be willing to accept this qualified standard of rightness remains to be seen. If I am right, then despite what he says in his outline and elsewhere,[4] Slote needs to accept something like (2) if his agent-based normative standard is to be plausible. There is, however, a downside to accepting (2): as I argue in section 3, this normative standard is in tension with Slote's sentimentalist metaethical views, in which case we might doubt whether Slote can maintain a plausible sentimentalist normative theory *and* a sentimentalist metaethics.

II

My second main worry concerns whether Slote's agent-based account can really capture or explain deontological constraints. The problem, as we recall, is that deontology is typically viewed as a limit or condition on feelings and concern, rather than as stemming from or based in sentiments. As such, a normative theory that appeals to an ideal of empathic caring appears to be badly placed when it comes to explaining such restrictions.

Slote's solution, as we have seen, is to vindicate the central deontological distinction between killing and letting die in light of our (fully developed) empathic response to a further kind of immediacy, namely, *causal* immediacy. He thinks that killing involves a closer causal connection to death than letting die, and that this difference is something that we are empathetically sensitive to. Given his previous arguments that such differences in empathic response have moral relevance, Slote thinks that this gives the sentimentalist "some reason to conclude that it is worse to kill or harm than (other things being equal) to allow these actions to happen" (136). As a result, we can see how deontological constraints might be grounded in certain empathic sentiments.

Is this plausible? One reason for doubt stems from the fact that our empathic responses to certain kinds of immediacy can be *outweighed*: thus, if the number of miners to be saved in the future by installing safety

---

[3] So fully empathic observers can approve of my doing things so as to develop my empathic responses, even though they would have no need to perform these actions themselves. For a view that makes rightness depend upon what the fully virtuous person would choose to do, see for instance Zagzebski (1996, 235) and Hursthouse (1999, 28). For an account of normative reasons that acknowledges and rests upon the distinction between the acts that a fully rational agent would perform and those that he would advise that one perform (or, in my terms, ones that he would approve of one's performing), see Smith (1994, 151–52).

[4] Slote has explicitly addressed the second problem in a number of places (see references in footnote 1), although I do not find what he says in defence of his position on this point entirely convincing.

devices now is in the (tens of) thousands, we might very well discover that our empathy for the plight of the small number who are currently trapped is overcome by our concern for those who face danger in the future. Similarly, if we are faced with a choice of saving the life of someone we can see or the lives of thousands of strangers, we might find that our empathic reaction to perceptual immediacy is swamped. By the same token, we might assume that our empathic aversion to causing death (or to causing harm in general) can be outweighed by our empathy for the plight of a great number of people whose lives we could thereby save.

Now this fact by itself does nothing to cast doubt upon the plausibility of Slote's view, since deontological restrictions on killing are (plausibly) not absolutist but rather have limited or conditional force, and given the previous comments we can see that Slote's empathy-based model can accommodate this. It seems, however, that Slote's account might allow our empathic aversion to causing death to be *too easily* outweighed and thus can come into conflict with our intuitions about the strength or stringency of deontological restrictions. This is most likely to happen when those who stand to be saved are people we love, and when the person whose death is necessary if they are to be saved is a stranger to us. For we are naturally (much) more empathically sensitive to the plight of those near and dear to us than we are to the plight of strangers, and once we factor in this additional kind of immediacy, the worry is that the natural flow of empathic feeling and concern will outweigh our empathic aversion to killing, thereby justifying (on Slote's account) the killing of a stranger in order to save a number of loved ones. If so, a sentimentalist account will have difficulty in capturing what I assume is a *non-absolutist* deontological prohibition on killing strangers to save loved ones.[5]

Is this just intuition mongering? Is my argument simply that I think that the strength of empathic caring for loved ones might outweigh the strength of empathic aversion to the causal immediacy involved in killing, and outweigh it more easily than Slote would allow? Can Slote insist that fully developed empathic observers would be more sensitive or averse to causing harm even when the lives of family members are at stake? Given that Slote has only given us a sketch of how sentimentalism can capture deontological restrictions, I am not sure what he would say here, but in any case I think that we have an additional (and possibly more principled) reason to

[5] It might be argued that I have ignored the *ceteris paribus* condition in Slote's formulation of the distinction between killing and letting die; as a result, this example does not tell against his sentimentalist treatment of that distinction. However, whilst it is true that other things are certainly not equal in my example – the person to be killed is a stranger, the person or people to be saved are, say, family members – this is compatible with the *common-sense* understanding of the principle, which is that killing is *much worse* than letting die, such that one cannot kill even if killing is necessary to save a number (although in non-absolutist versions, not *any* number) of loved ones. As a result, my example does not violate the 'spirit' of the distinction.

be suspicious of Slote's attempt to derive deontological restrictions from the idea of causal immediacy.

Suppose we grant the plausible claim that when we kill someone, "we are in causal terms more strongly connected to a death than if we merely allow someone to die" (136), and that empathy is sensitive to this difference in the way in which we affect the well-being of others. Causing *harm*, however, is not the only instance of the kind of causal immediacy to which we are empathically sensitive. For we are in a stronger or closer causal relation with an increase in someone's well-being when we *benefit* them than when we allow them to be benefited by others. Thus we prefer, especially when those involved are near and dear, that we benefit people rather than that they are benefited by someone else, and we prefer this (at least with regard to those we love) even when someone else can benefit them to a greater extent. We *welcome* the former in a way or to an extent that we don't welcome the latter, and thus the benefit that we cause has a greater causal immediacy for us than benefit that we do nothing to bring about.

A second reason to doubt Slote's proposal is, then, as follows: Why doesn't *this* kind of causal immediacy cancel out, or indeed outweigh, the kind of causal immediacy involved in killing, when there are greater numbers to be benefited than harmed? Why, in other words, doesn't the greater causal immediacy of benefiting a number of other people – especially, to reintroduce another form of immediacy and thus another level of empathic caring, if they are near and dear – justify killing an innocent person? The introduction of a factor of causal immediacy would thus seem to cut both ways: it does indeed seem worse to cause harm than to allow it to happen; but that fact by itself seems insufficient to ground deontological constraints, since by the same token it seems better to cause someone to be benefited than allow him or her to be benefited. What Slote needs to show, in order to secure a deontological constraint against killing one for the sake of a greater number, is that some factor *other than* causal immediacy is relevant, and moreover that this is a factor to which we are empathically sensitive. It will be interesting to see whether Slote's final treatment of sentimentalist deontology will contain such a demonstration.

III

Let us now turn to Slote's sentimentalist metaethics. Slote intends his account of moral judgements to be *cognitivist* (moral judgements are capable of truth or falsity), *realist* (some of them *are* true), and, at least to an extent, *externalist* (the truth makers are "properties at least somewhat independent of our dispositions to react to such things" [140]).[6] Moral properties

---

[6] Realists need not be externalists, so here I part company with Slote's use of "moral realism" (140).

are not, however, wholly independent of such dispositions, and so Slote's metaethics is also, at least to an extent, sentimentalist. For judgements about the responses of agents serve, on Slote's view, to "fix the reference" (140) of our moral terms, and so play a part in determining which external features our moral terms pick out.

In order to see how this is supposed to work, consider (as Slote briefly does) an analogy with colour judgements. One plausible story as to how we discover the nature of colour properties maintains that we first rely on so-called platitudes about colours to fix the reference of our colour terms.[7] For instance, if we are seeking a naturalistic account of the property of redness, we might appeal to the reference-fixing description that "redness is that property which causes objects to look red to normal perceivers under standard conditions" and then proceed to investigate the natural world so as to see which (surface reflectance) property actually does cause things to look red to such perceivers under said conditions. It is this latter property – which is a genuine property possessed by objects – that we thereby identify with the property of redness.

By the same token, Slote's approach seems to appeal to the following kind of reference-fixing claim: "Rightness is that property of actions, whatever it turns out to be, that elicits the approval of fully empathic observers," and it suggests that we then attempt to discover *what it is* about actions that is so approved of. It is this latter property – which will be a genuine property possessed by actions – that can be identified with the property of rightness. On this view, then, moral claims are not *about* the fully empathic responses of observers but ultimately refer to those properties that are picked out by our reference-fixing description.

Proponents of this type of moral realism (in Slote's terms, *sentimentalist*, in Michael Smith's, *internalist*) aim to take feelings, emotions and responses seriously, whilst at the same time trying to capture cognitivist and externalist platitudes about the nature and meaning of moral judgements. They aim, therefore, to capture the core metaethical ideas that moral judgements are practical *and* objective, and as such it would be a remarkable, and welcome, achievement if their theories were successful. I have my doubts, however, and my particular worry about Slote's endorsement of his metaethical position is that it sits uneasily with his normative ethics of empathic caring.

To see this, note that what is missing from the previous story is any account of *how* we go about discovering what it is about actions that elicits the approval of empathically sensitive observers. The obvious answer here is that we must engage in the kind of a priori theorising that is appropriate to normative ethics, in an attempt to discover the correct

---

[7] The following account is due to Smith (2000), and I trust that Slote wishes to employ something like this methodology.

normative theory (Smith 1994, 202).[8] For we can view the aim of normative moral theorising as that of seeing whether *one particular feature* of intentional behaviour can be regarded as fundamental: whether, for instance, we are justified in regarding the outcomes of actions as of primary moral importance, and the acts themselves or the agent's character traits as of secondary or derivative worth. This, in turn, requires consideration of whether the relevant feature is capable of unifying and systematising the set of intuitions, beliefs and principles that constitute our common-sense moral understanding: it requires, in other words, a view of the relevant feature as providing the fundamental justification for all of our more particular moral judgements and opinions.[9] As a result, the question of whether there is any property or feature we can identify with rightness would seem to come down to the question of whether, after reflection, one particular normative moral theory wins out.

Now Slote thinks that one normative theory does indeed win out, namely, an ethics of empathic caring, according to which what makes an action right is the fact that a fully empathic observer would approve of that action. But if so, then (given the story above) it will turn out that the feature of acts which elicits the approval of fully empathic observers, and which Slote will thereby identify with rightness, is the feature of *being approved of by fully empathic observers*. On this view, what fully empathic observers approve of is the approval of fully empathic observers. This is problematic (to put it mildly), for a number of reasons:

1. If the above is correct, Slote's claim that moral judgements are not about "our reactive sentimental dispositions" turns out to be false, since the approval of fully empathic observers figures both in the reference-fixing description *and* as the property picked out by such a description. Slote's account will, therefore, struggle to capture common-sense externalist intuitions about moral properties.
2. It is not obvious that the emerging view makes sense, since it is difficult to understand what it is for someone to have empathy with *his or her own* feelings of approval, and thus what it is for fully empathic observers to approve of *their own* fully empathic approval.
3. It is not obvious that the emerging view make sense for another reason, which is that a feeling of approval must be *elicited* (rather than sustained) by something other than itself, in which case it is this other

---

[8] The answer is obvious because we want the property thus picked out to accord with our considered moral intuitions: it would be a serious strike against any metaethical reference-fixing description if the property picked out as identical with rightness was the property of, say, causing pain.
[9] This represents what has been called the 'dominant conception' of moral theorising. See, for details, Jamieson 1991.

thing that will be the subject of approval. So the feature or property of actions that *elicits* the approval of fully empathic observers cannot be the approval of fully empathic observers.

4. If the feature of actions that elicits the approval of fully empathic observers is something other than the approval of fully empathic observers, where this other thing is the subject of approval, then it is this other thing that can be *identified* with the property of rightness – at least if metaethical sentimentalism is correct. For that view maintains, to repeat, that we can identify rightness with the property that elicits the approval of fully empathic agents. But then Slote's normative ethics of empathic caring turns out to be mistaken, since this theory regards the approval of fully empathic agents as *making* something right, and thus (given the story about how we identify moral properties) as being that which elicits the approval of fully empathic agents. The truth of metaethical sentimentalism, therefore, seems to be inconsistent with the truth of a normative ethics of empathic caring.

I suspect, in light of the above, that any marriage between normative and metaethical sentimentalism will be short lived. This does not, in itself, cast doubt upon either (although I hope to have done enough to raise doubts about the former in sections 1 and 2), but it does give us reason to be rather more pessimistic than Slote seems to be about the prospects for an integrated account.

IV

In the previous sections I have raised a number of doubts as to the plausibility of normative and metaethical accounts grounded in an ideal of empathic caring. It should, however, hardly be surprising that doubts can be raised against Slote's outline of his project, given that it is no more than a sketch of the form the final theories will take, and given that it is an extremely ambitious project. The question of whether the worries expressed above are ultimately warranted will have to wait, then, until we see the finished product, and this is reason enough to look forward to the completion of Slote's project. Given the richness and originality of Slote's work both here and elsewhere, however, this is not the only reason for anticipation.

Department of Philosophy
University of Stirling
Stirling FK9 4LA
United Kingdom
m.s.brady@stir.ac.uk

References

Hursthouse, R. 1999. *On Virtue Ethics*. Oxford: Oxford University Press.

Jamieson, D. 1991. "Method and Moral Theory." In *A Companion to Ethics*, edited by P. Singer, 476–87. Oxford: Basil Blackwell.

Slote, M. 1995. "Agent-Based Virtue Ethics." *Midwest Studies in Philosophy* 20: 83–101.

———. 1997. "Virtue Ethics." In *Three Methods of Ethics*, edited by M. Baron, P. Pettit, and M. Slote, 175–238. Oxford: Basil Blackwell.

———. 2001. *Morals from Motives*. Oxford: Oxford University Press.

Smith, M. 1994. *The Moral Problem*. Oxford: Basil Blackwell.

———. 2000. "Moral Realism." In *The Blackwell Guide to Ethical Theory*, edited by H. LaFollette, 15–37. Oxford: Basil Blackwell.

Zagzebski, L. 1996. *Virtues of the Mind: An Inquiry into the Nature of Virtue and the Ethical Foundations of Knowledge*. Cambridge: Cambridge University Press.

© Metaphilosophy LLC and Blackwell Publishing Ltd. 2003.
Published by Blackwell Publishing, 9600 Garsington Road, Oxford OX4 2DQ, UK and
350 Main Street, Malden, MA 02148, USA
METAPHILOSOPHY
Vol. 34, Nos. 1/2, January 2003
0026–1068

EPISTEMIC INJUSTICE AND A ROLE FOR VIRTUE IN THE POLITICS OF KNOWING

MIRANDA FRICKER

ABSTRACT: The dual aim of this article is to reveal and explain a certain phenomenon of epistemic injustice as manifested in testimonial practice, and to arrive at a characterisation of the anti-prejudicial intellectual virtue that is such as to counteract it. This sort of injustice occurs when prejudice on the part of the hearer leads to the speaker receiving less credibility than he or she deserves. It is suggested that where this phenomenon is systematic it constitutes an important form of oppression.

Keywords: credibility, epistemic injustice, ethical sensibility, historicism, internal reasons, oppression, prejudice, social identity, testimonial sensibility, virtue.

There is a growing sympathy with the idea that epistemology should look to ethics for conceptual tools to use in solving traditional epistemological problems. My aim here is to identify a role for virtue in accounting for both the rationality and the ethics of what must surely be our most basic and ubiquitous epistemic practice – the practice of gaining knowledge by being told.

I shall try to argue that a central difficulty in the epistemology of testimony is best handled by reference to a notion that belongs in the first instance to ethics, the notion of a *sensibility*. To this end I shall advance the idea of a *testimonial sensibility*: something that governs our responsiveness to the word of others so that, given the sensibility is properly educated, we may gain knowledge that *p* simply by being told that *p*. Next, on the assumption that such a sensibility incorporates a variety of intellectual skills and virtues that govern how much credibility the responsible hearer will attribute to different sorts of speakers in different sorts of circumstances, I shall identify a phenomenon of epistemic injustice with a view to homing in on the particular virtue whose role it is, or should be, to pre-empt such injustice. The form of epistemic injustice in question happens when a speaker receives the wrong degree of credibility from his hearer owing to a certain sort of unintended prejudice on the hearer's part. The virtue I shall try to home in on, whose role it is to safeguard against such operations of prejudice, embodies a special sort of *reflexive critical openness* to the word of others. The possession of this virtue is presented as an important regulator in the politics of testimonial practice, though I shall suggest ultimately that its powers are limited.

1. Avoiding Intellectualism: The Word of Others

There is a certain impasse to be detected in a traditional approach to the epistemology of testimony.[1] When we try to account for what goes on in an informal discursive context when someone comes to know that p by an interlocutor's telling him that p, it can seem as if we must plump for one of two epistemological stories. It can seem as if we must either endorse the idea that the hearer gains knowledge just by being uncritically receptive to the speaker's word, so long as there are no explicit signals that scepticism is in order, or else endorse the idea that the hearer gains knowledge only in virtue of rehearsing an appropriate inference – an argument whose conclusion licenses believing what he has been told. Thus the choice of philosophical pictures can seem to be between sheer uncritical receptiveness on the one hand and intellectualist argumentation on the other.

The shortcoming of each is the allure of the other. The uncritical-receptivity model surely leaves us too open to believing anything people tell us, so that, in the absence of signals of untrustworthiness, we are licensed to be entirely uncritical.[2] Philosophical accounts of testimonial knowledge will require the speaker to be both competent and honest with respect to her assertion that p. But the experience of everyday life leaves us only too aware that human beings cannot systematically be relied on in respect of either. Crudely, people often get things wrong, out of innocent error, or perhaps because they fancy they know when really they don't. And of course people can also succumb to the temptation to mislead deliberately – for instance, because it is in their interests to do so. When these two types of unreliability are compounded with the obvious fact that such mundane things as haste, or misunderstanding the inquirer's purposes, or simple carelessness can lead a speaker to mispronounce even on something he is perfectly competent and ready to be honest about, it becomes clear that a blanket policy of accepting the word of others unmediated by any critical filtering would be justificationally lax. The mere absence of explicit signals for doubt is not enough to justify a general habit of uncritically accepting what other people tell one.

This shortcoming in the uncritical-receptivity model might draw one's sympathies towards the inferential model. As C. A. J. Coady (1992, 122–23) describes it, this common picture of testimony has it "that all knowledge by testimony is indirect or inferential. We know that p when

---

[1] For an account of how the impasse is merely an artefact of a certain misguided conception of the philosophical options, see McDowell 1998.

[2] See Elizabeth Fricker 1994, and also 1987, in which she presents a powerful case against the idea that we have a "presumptive right" to believe what we are told in the absence of countervailing evidence.

© Metaphilosophy LLC and Blackwell Publishing Ltd. 2003

reliably told that *p* because we make some inference about the reliability and sincerity of the witness." In an alternative formulation, John McDowell presents the inferentialist model as resting on the following assumption:

> If an epistemically satisfactory standing in the space of reasons, with respect to a proposition, is mediated rather than immediate, that means the standing is constituted by the cogency of an *argument* that is at its occupant's disposal, with the proposition in question as conclusion. (McDowell 1998, 415)

On either formulation the inferential model is clearly invulnerable to accusations of justificational laxity, since it precisely requires that the hearer go in for a piece of reasoning that provides a justification for believing what she has been told. Inevitably this will usually be some sort of inductive argument – for instance, an argument about the individual speaker's past reliability on these matters, or about the general reliability of people like that about things like this. But the trouble now is that this requirement that the hearer avail herself of such an argument seems too strong, because too laborious intellectually. It simply does not match our everyday phenomenology of informal testimonial exchange, which presents learning something by being told as distinctly *un*-laborious and spontaneous. Surely an epistemic practice as basic to human life as being-told-things-by-someone-who-knows cannot possibly require all that *activity* at the level of propositional attitudes. If the hearer were genuinely supposed to consider (in however rule-of-thumb-ish a way) the likelihood that she has been told a truth, that would take at least a moment's hard-nosed assessment of a sort that simply does not tally with the effortless spontaneity characteristic of so much of our everyday testimonial exchange.

The advocate of the inferential model will naturally respond by empha-sising that the mature hearer will normally rehearse her argument very readily and easily. But the more he is at pains to emphasise that such justi-ficatory argumentation can be so swift as barely to be noticed, and might even be altogether unconscious, the more the model strikes one as a piece of intellectualism in a tight corner.

This problem with the inferential model now leads one back again to the picture on which the hearer is entitled, other things being equal, to be uncritically receptive to what she is told, for this picture of things can now be seen to retain something rather strongly in its favour: it more faithfully represents the phenomenology of our everyday exchanges. In the absence of explicit cues for doubt we do seem simply to accept most of what we are told without going in for any active critical assessment. An ordinary case might be that, as I make my way hurriedly to the train station, I ask a stranger what the time is, he tells me it is 4:30, and I simply, unreflectively, accept what he says. This unreflectiveness is underlined by the fact that if

I do pick up on some cue for doubt – such as his saying it is 4:30 when I already know it cannot be later than four o'clock – then I experience a sort of intellectual shift of gear, out of that unreflective mode and into some more active one of critical assessment. It is only with this shift of gear that I might start to bring some argumentation to bear on the matter of my interlocutor's trustworthiness.

But now we may feel that the intuitive relevance of the evidence of past experience in how we are conditioned to receive the word of others has gone missing from the ordinary unreflective case. Surely one's knowledge of a particular speaker's track record, or one's general background assumptions about how likely it is that someone like this will speak the truth about something like that, must be somewhere in the offing? If such inductive considerations are wholly absent from our unreflective exchanges, imposing no constraint whatsoever upon what the hearer is entitled to accept, then this does seem to leave our ordinary unreflective exchanges in an unacceptable rational vacuum. This thought, then, casts the inferentialist model once again in a more favourable light. And so, perhaps, the oscillation continues.

The conclusion I suggest we should draw from these brief considerations is that what is needed to provide a suitable exit from the impasse is a picture of informal testimonial exchange that honours the everyday phenomenology of unreflective transparency between speaker and hearer, while none the less avoiding justificational laxity. We need a positive account of how the responsible hearer may spontaneously and non-inferentially give an appropriately critical reception to the speaker's word. This critical reception must be such that, reliably, when the hearer simply accepts what he is told by someone who knows, he is justified in simply accepting it. The reception will be one of openness to his interlocutor's assertions, yet critical too – the hearer's normal stance needs to find a philosophical characterisation such that it constitutes a *critical openness* to the word of others. Such a characterisation will be able to explain how, when we are told things, we are indeed able to acquire knowledge, and as effortlessly as the phenomenology suggests.

2. The Responsible Hearer

McDowell argues for the view that a hearer gains knowledge by testimony in virtue of exercising "doxastic responsibility"; and what it is to exercise doxastic responsibility is explained in characteristic Sellarsian terms of a "sensitivity" to one's place in the "space of reasons." As I understand this way of putting things, the idea of a "mediated standing in the space of reasons" is the idea of a state – a state of knowledge, for example – that has been arrived at by way of an appropriate sensitivity to the reasons for and against the proposition. This sensitivity need not manifest itself in the making of inferences or arguments – precisely not. As McDowell says:

What I am proposing is a different conception of what it is for a standing in the space of reasons to be mediated. A standing in the space of reasons can be mediated by the rational force of surrounding considerations, in that the concept of that standing cannot be applied to a subject who is not responsive to that rational force. (McDowell 1998, 430)

So, if the standing in the space of reasons is "knowing that p," then McDowell's proposal is that this knowing that p has as a background precondition that the knower has somehow exercised a sensitivity to surrounding reasons for and against taking it that p.

If one accepts this eminently acceptable proposal, then it is natural to move to the next question and ask, If not by our usual faculties of argumentation and inference, then by what rational capacity *is* the hearer able to be responsive to the rational force of surrounding reasons? The idea that the fulfilment of doxastic responsibility need not require argumentation is surely crucial to explaining how testimonial knowledge can be mediated yet direct (or, as I am putting it, critical yet non-inferential), but something further needs to be said to explain how the hearer does it. If she is not exercising her capacity for inference and argumentation, what rational capacity is she exercising?

McDowell is minded to say there is nothing to be explained here:

If we are not to explain the fact that having heard from someone that things are thus and so is an epistemic standing by appealing to the strength of an argument that things are that way . . . do we need some other account of it? I would be tempted to maintain that we do not. The idea of knowledge by testimony is that if a knower gives intelligible expression to his knowledge, he puts it into the public domain, where it can be picked up by those who can understand the expression, as long as the opportunity is not closed to them because it would be doxastically irresponsible to believe the speaker. That idea seems obvious enough to stand on its own epistemological feet; the formulation makes as much sense of the idea that knowledge can be transmitted from one subject to another as any purported explanation could hope to confer on it. (McDowell 1998, 437–38).

But I am not sure that nothing more is needed here. One does not have to be an advocate of inferentialism to think that something more is called for in order to explain how a hearer can count as exercising doxastic responsibility if her acceptance of what she has been told is not based on any sort of inference or argumentation.

Let me be clear that the non-satisfaction I am registering is not about what doxastically responsible behaviour *consists in*, as if I were demanding that some rule-like norms or principles be explicated. No doubt there are a number of norms general enough to be expressed as guiding principles of a hearer's doxastic responsibility, but we don't need them in order to have a reasonably firm idea of what that responsibility requires. Indeed, those of us sympathetic to virtue-theoretical accounts of responsibility might be quite happy with the possibility that there were no such principles available at all. The question of what constitutes doxastic responsibility for a hearer, then, is not my worry. The worry is rather that the claim that a hearer exercises such responsibility without making any inferences leaves one wondering *how* – by what capacity of reason – she is supposed to do it.

If we look to Coady, we find tacit support for the view that something is needed on this score, since he does make a brief suggestion, albeit rather too brief to provide more than a pointer. He asserts we have a "learning mechanism" that operates critically though non-inferentially in the hearer to determine the balance of trust. He says:

> What happens characteristically in the reception of testimony is that the audience operates a sort of learning mechanism which has certain critical capacities built into it. The mechanism may be thought of as partly innate, though modified by experience, especially in the matter of critical capacities. It is useful to invoke the model of a mechanism here since the reception of testimony is normally unreflective but is not thereby uncritical. (Coady 1992, 47)

This seems exactly right, but as it stands the metaphor of a learning mechanism remains philosophically and psychologically mysterious. So much so that we are not much better off with this idea of a mechanism than we were with the non-metaphorical but equally elusive idea of a hearer's doxastic responsibility exercised non-inferentially.

It is time to take stock. What we are looking for is some mode of rational sensitivity that yields spontaneous, non-inferential judgements. And we are also looking for a mode of rational sensitivity that is learned, and learned in an ongoing way so that it is constantly developing and adjusting itself in the light of experience and critical reflection. I propose that at this point epistemology should turn to ethics for sustenance. For in ethics we find a notion that seems to me to fit the bill: the notion of a *sensibility*. An ethical sensibility yields genuine *judgements* – interpretative judgements, such as "That was cowardly," or immediately practical judgements, such as "I ought to confess" – yet these judgements are not conclusions to arguments. (They may permit of reconstruction as conclusions to arguments, but that is quite another thing. A rational reconstruction of a human practice does not automatically constitute a proper characterisation of it.) A well-trained ethical sensibility will presumably incorporate a range of relevant conceptual and social-perceptual skills, but most importantly it will comprise ethical virtues. The central place of virtue explains how a sensibility issues in non-inferential judgements. The virtuous person does not have to *work out* that an act was cowardly, or that the culprit should own up; he just sees that this is the case; he just knows. Continuing in this broadly Aristotelian vein, we might add that the virtuous person is able to

© Metaphilosophy LLC and Blackwell Publishing Ltd. 2003

perceive the moral colourations of things spontaneously in this way in virtue of his sensibility being formed by a proper ethical training or upbringing.

This idea of ethical training will be important for present purposes, but we shall need a more historicist or socially situated conception than we find in Aristotle. Let me suggest, then, that we think of the training of a sensibility as involving at least two distinct streams of input: social and individual – in that order. One develops an ethical sensibility by becoming inculcated with a historically and culturally specific way of life – or as Alasdair MacIntyre puts it, an ethical "tradition"[3] – where this is to be construed as a matter of ongoing ethical socialisation. There again, it is from an irreducibly individual life experience that one gains a particular sentimental education, and in that respect the ongoing formation of one's sensibility is something distinctly individual. Together these two streams of input – collective and individual – continually generate a person's sensibility.

The deliverances of an individual's sensibility, then, are shaped by a set of background interpretative and motivational attitudes, which are in the first instance passively inherited from the ethical community but thereafter actively reflected upon and lived out in one way or another by the reflective individual. Ethical responsibility demands that there be an appropriate critical link between the traditional moment in which the individual gains her ethical socialisation and the experiences life offers her – experiences that may sometimes be in tension with her ethical socialisation so as to prompt critical reflection on the sensibility which she has otherwise simply inherited.[4]

This idea of a sensibility gives us a picture of how judgements can be rational yet unreflective, critical yet non-inferential. It presents us with a rational capacity that is comprised of virtues, that is inculcated in the subject through a process of socialisation, and that permits of ongoing correction and adjustment in the light of experience and critical reflection. Thus we are confronted with a rational capacity unlike anything commonly entertained in epistemology, and a version of it seems to me to fit the bill as the explanation of how a hearer might be able to give an unreflective yet critical reception to the word of another. With this in mind, we must now ask what the epistemic analogue of an ethical sensibility would be like for testimony. I would like to think that this is not only a worthwhile philosophical question in its own right but also an important question at the level of epistemic practice. For if one wants to know how to improve one's performance as a receiver of the word of others – if one wants to become more responsible and successful as a hearer – then one had better know what, if not one's skills of inference and argument, one should be trying better to develop.

---

[3] See MacIntyre 1981, especially chapter 15.
[4] I have tried to develop this theme in my 2000.

3. Testimonial Sensibility: Critical Openness to the Word of Others

We are setting our sights on the possibility that responsible hearers in unreflective testimonial exchanges exercise a *testimonial sensibility*. This possibility introduces the idea that our responses to the testimony of others are learned and internalised through a process of *epistemic* socialisation – a social training of the interpretative and affective attitudes in play when we are told things by other people. We might think of it as part of our epistemic "second nature."[5] Here, again, I suggest there is in the first instance a passive social inheritance and then a sometimes-passive-sometimes-active individual input from the hearer's own experience. Together these two streams of input mean that our normal unreflective reception of what people tell us is conditioned by a great range of collateral experience. Just as the experiences pertinent to the training of ethical virtues are internalised in the sensibility of the virtuous person, so the body of collective and individual testimonial experience is internalised by the responsible or virtuous hearer, rendering it immanent in her testimonial sensibility.

It is through the inductive influence of this body of experience that we may learn, reliably enough, to assume trust when and only when it is in order. Our perception of speakers and their assertions comes to be informed by an inductive conditioning relating to what sorts of people are likely to convey the truth about which sorts of subject matters, just as in the ethical case our perception of agents and their actions comes to be informed by a motivational conditioning relating to what sorts of actions are ethically called for in which sorts of situations.

There is more to be said, however, about what sorts of experiences properly feed into a testimonial sensibility. They will chiefly be experiences of testimonial exchanges had by the individual and the wider community. But it must be acknowledged that these experiences can only have a rational impact on sensibility under a socially rich description. This is because the only way they can have inductive significance is by being such as to support or undermine existing habits of response concerning what sorts of people are trustworthy in what sorts of situations; which sorts of incentives to deceive are likely to be acted upon by which sorts of people; and so on. A testimonial sensibility, then, needs to be shaped by collective and individual experiences of testimonial encounters described in rich, socially specific terms relating to the trustworthiness of speakers of different social types in different sorts of contexts. These descriptions cannot but involve common cultural stereotypes of intellectual authority or its lack, perhaps by way of related characteristics, such as openness or inscrutability, steadiness or flakiness, rationality or emotionality, dependability or deviousness, logicality

[5] I echo John McDowell's use of this term, which he finds "all but explicit in Aristotle's account of how ethical character is formed," and which he extends to apply not simply to our ethical upbringing (Aristotle's "practical wisdom") but also, more generally, to our epistemic upbringing (McDowell 1994, 84).

or intuitiveness. . . . I use *stereotype* neutrally, but of course stereotypes are fertile ground for prejudice, so it is easy to see how a testimonial sensibility may come to embody the prejudices of the day. Where a testimonial sensibility is informed by stereotypes that are unfair – that is, where they are empirically unfounded – the sensibility will be both epistemically and ethically defective.

We shall return to this theme, but for the moment the point is rather that such elements of the social imagination as stereotypes of authority can be a perfectly proper part of a testimonial sensibility, for the necessary social richness of the body of testimonial experience which informs sensibility means that stereotypes are positively needed to oil the mechanism of our day-to-day exchanges. Hearers need spontaneously to perceive their interlocutors in a socially fine-grained way so that they can be appropriately responsive to all the subtleties of the interaction. Without this richness of social perception, many epistemically relevant cues will be missed. Consider, for instance, what complexity there can be in cues indicating how far one should interpret an interlocutor as *taking seriously* what he is asserting. Perhaps the hearer sees the speaker as entirely competent in all relevant matters, yet still her perception of him has to be responsive to all sorts of features of social location and discursive style that would not figure in any but the richest of social-psychological descriptions of the encounter.

If these remarks provide a reasonable working idea of *which* experiences feed into sensibility, is there something further we can say about *how* an individual takes them on in sensibility? Here again the task is to develop a parallel with the ethical case. An individual's testimonial sensibility will in the first instance be passively inherited. This passivity is justified, firstly, for the a priori reason that the body of judgements and attitudes which comprise a sensibility constitute the basis *from which* a hearer's doxastic responsibility emerges. And, secondly, for the empirical reason that even a minimally successful epistemic community must be operating with a broadly functional testimonial sensibility. But once light has dawned for a hearer, she will come to find that sometimes her experiences of testimonial exchange will be in tension with the deliverances of the sensibility she has passively taken on, in which case responsibility requires that her sensibility adjust itself to accommodate the new experience.

This might happen spontaneously, without active critical reflection on the part of the hearer, but it is more likely that she will need actively to bring critical thought to bear on her internalised habits of hearer response in order to shake them up sufficiently to effect the adjustment. If, for instance, a hearer is a teenager whose testimonial sensibility has contracted the defect of not taking seriously what old people say, and if this teenager finds himself one day struck by the veracity of his grandfather's stories of the war, he may experience a small epistemic revolution that requires some significant deliberative follow-through in terms of how he receives the word of the elderly quite generally. In so far as this teenager is doxastically responsible, he will effect an adjustment to his testimonial sensibility either directly, by way of a shift of social perception, or indirectly, by way of critical reflection. If the adjustment is direct, then he will undergo a Gestalt switch in how he perceives elderly speakers so that the adjustment to his testimonial sensibility is more or less instantaneous. If it is indirect, then active critical reflection on his habits of hearer response will first produce some sort of corrective policy external to the hearer's sensibility. (Perhaps this teenager disciplines himself when in conversation with the elderly, "Don't be dismissive. . . .") Given time, and all being well, such a corrective policy will become internalised as an integral part of his sensibility, so that it comes to be implicit in his newly conditioned perception of elderly speakers.

Whether direct or indirect, then, we can see how the responsible hearer's sensibility matures and adapts in the light of ongoing testimonial experience. Its claim to be a capacity of reason crucially depends on this adaptiveness, for otherwise it would be little more than a dead-weight social conditioning that looked more like a threat to the justification of a hearer's responses than a source of that justification.

This model for how inductive rationality can be embodied in sensibility shows that the making of an explicit inferential step is not the only way that the justificatory force of induction can enter into the hearer's reception of a speaker's word: an appropriately trained testimonial sensibility enables the hearer to respond to the word of another with the sort of critical openness that is required for a thoroughly effortless sharing of knowledge.

To sum up this section, then, the idea of a testimonial sensibility has in its favour not only that it represents a way out of the impasse with which we began (where we were stuck oscillating between the uncritical-reception model and the inferentialist model of testimonial knowledge) but also that it retains those features of each model that explained its attractiveness. Testimonial sensibility, as I have characterised it, pictures inductive rationality as the basic source of justification for hearer response, and this was the main thing we found attractive in the inferentialist model. Yet it also pictures hearer response in such a way that where knowledge is gained it is usually non-inferential. This means that the idea of a testimonial sensibility honours our everyday phenomenology of spontaneity and unreflectiveness, thus incorporating the non-intellectualism we found attractive in the uncritical-reception model.

Perhaps enough has now been said to show that the idea of a testimonial sensibility is able to explain how everyday testimonial knowledge can be non-inferential. But more needs to be said about what constitutes such a sensibility. I would like to think that introducing the notion opens up some new terrain for work of a virtue-ethical kind in exploring which virtues are properly incorporated into such a sensibility – work that could

be regarded as either replacing or complementing more technical, proba-
bilistic approaches to these matters. My next task here, then, will be to
home in on one virtue in particular, which – although it is in a certain way
thoroughly familiar – does not have a name. The role that this virtue has to
play in testimonial practice comes into view only if we follow through the
implications of our historicist, socially situated conception of the epistemic
socialisation that forms testimonial sensibility. More particularly, it comes
into view if we return to the role of social stereotypes in how a sensibility
determines habits of hearer response. I have said that such stereotypes,
where empirically founded, are a perfectly legitimate heuristic and a
necessary determining factor in how a hearer perceives a speaker. But we
must also confront the fact that in any actual human society, human societies being what they are, it is inevitable that such speaker stereotypes are
susceptible to distortion by the prejudices of the day. Stereotypes inform-
ing testimonial exchange will tend to imitate relations of social power at
large in the society. Our everyday, face-to-face testimonial encounters
bring to bear a whole social consciousness in an instant, and this creates a
deep structural liability to prejudicial dysfunction in our testimonial practices.

4. Epistemic Injustice: The Word of *Others*

Broadly speaking, prejudicial dysfunction in testimonial practice can be of
two kinds. Either the prejudice results in the speaker's receiving more credibility than she rationally deserves – *credibility excess* – or it results in her
receiving less credibility than she rationally deserves – *credibility deficit*.[6]
Consider the immediate discursive impact of accent, for instance. Not only
does a speaker's accent carry a great deal of baggage in terms of how a
hearer perceives the speaker socially; I would suggest that part and parcel
of this social perception are implications for how the hearer perceives the
speaker epistemically. Accent can have a significant impact on how much
credibility the hearer affords the speaker, especially in a one-off exchange.

---

[6] Someone might ask how far the idea of a credibility excess or deficit depends on there
being some exact degree of credibility which the speaker is due. I share Coady's scepticism
about there being any precise science here, any precise credibility ratio to determine what
degree of belief the hearer is entitled to. As Coady says, people are not like coins, exhibiting quite general tendencies to be right and honest about things (see Coady 1992, 210). And
I see no reason to think this difficulty can be made good by building a sensitivity to subject
matter into one's calculations, for the likelihood of speaker veracity is always dependent on
which of an indeterminate number of discursive contexts the interlocutors happen to be in
(including maximally contingent shifts of context that depend, for instance, on whether the
speaker is in the mood for being undetectably sarcastic, and so on). This dependence on such
finely differentiated contexts seems not merely to indicate that if there is a precise probability available then it can hardly be available to the hearer. Rather, it would seem to indicate that there is no such precise probability available at all, and that the matter is in some
significant degree indeterminate.

I do not mean that someone's accent is especially likely to lead a hearer, even an intensely prejudiced one, simply to *disbelieve* some perfectly believable assertion, or simply to *believe* some otherwise incredible assertion. Given that it is overwhelmingly in the interests of hearers in general to believe what is true and not believe what is false, it would have to be an unusual prejudice to be strong enough to have that sort of effect. (We should note, however, that social contexts structured by relations of systematically unequal social power do have a habit of generating situations in which a hearer with the greater social power is in a position such that it costs him nothing to disbelieve a manifestly believable speaker, as one of my examples will demonstrate.)

More usually, however, power will influence hearer-response in a less obvious way. Rather than turning belief into non-belief or vice versa, it will surreptitiously raise or lower the hearer's *degree* of belief, by inflating or deflating the credibility he affords the speaker. Epistemic trust, like other kinds of trust, has an affective[7] aspect that is influenced – sometimes rightly, sometimes wrongly – by how the hearer perceives the interlocutor. Its key affective aspect is a kind of minimal interpretative sympathy with the speaker that allows signs of her trustworthiness to be picked up on in the hearer's perception of her. Even such a minimal sympathy will be signally uneven across differences of social identity and especially where those differences of identity are characterised by dramatically unequal relations of power. Both of the examples I shall present illustrate how the social "otherness" of the speaker is fundamental to the prejudiced reception their word is given – the hearers re-enact their general social advantage in the reception they give the speaker's word.

To the examples, then. Both present cases of credibility deficit (rather than credibility excess), since that is the phenomenon that most urgently calls for the specific anti-prejudicial virtue I aim to identify. My first example is drawn from a novel, *To Kill a Mockingbird*, by Harper Lee (1974); the second is drawn from a screenplay, *The Talented Mr Ripley*, by Anthony Minghella (2000).[8] I offer the first as an example in which the epistemic failings on the part of the hearer (or rather hearers) is clearly culpable, the second as an example in which it is plausible to suggest that the hearer inflicts the injustice non-culpably. Each presents an instance of epistemic injustice in testimony – an instance, then, of *testimonial injustice*.

First example: The year is 1935, and the scene a courtroom in Maycomb County, Alabama. The defendant is a young black man named Tom Robinson. He is charged with raping a white girl, Mayella Ewell, whose family's run-down house he passes every day on his way to and

---

[7] See Jones 1996.

[8] Minghella's screenplay is closely based on Patricia Highsmith's novel, though, crucially for present purposes, the character of Marge Sherwood and her relationship with Dickie Greenleaf is developed differently.

from work. It is obvious to the reader, and would be obvious to any relatively unprejudiced person in the courtroom, that Tom Robinson is entirely
innocent. For Addicus Finch, our politely spoken counsel for the defence,
has proved beyond doubt that Robinson could not have beaten the Ewell
girl so as to cause the sort of cuts and bruises she sustained that day,
because whoever gave her this beating led with his left fist, whereas Tom
Robinson's left arm is disabled, injured in an accident when he was a boy.
The trial proceedings present a fairly clear-cut struggle between the power
of evidence and the power of racial prejudice, with the all-white jury's
sympathies ultimately succumbing to the latter. But there is a great
complexity of social meanings at work in determining the jury's perception of Tom Robinson as a speaker. In a showdown between the word of a
black man and a white girl, the courtroom air is thick with the do's and
don'ts of racial politics. Telling the truth here is a minefield for Tom
Robinson, since if he casts aspersions on the white girl he will be
perceived as a presumptuous, lying Negro, yet if he does not publicise
Mayella Ewell's attempt to kiss him (which is what really happened), then
a guilty verdict is even more nearly assured. (This discursive predicament
mirrors his practical predicament at the Ewell's house when Mayella
grabbed him. If he pushes her away, he will be found to have assaulted her;
yet if he is passive he will equally be found to have assaulted her. So he
does the most neutral thing he can, which is to run away, though knowing
all the while that this action too will be taken as a sure sign of guilt.)

At a pivotal moment during the prosecution's interrogation, Tom
Robinson makes the mistake of being honest about his motivations for
stopping off at Mayella Ewell's house as regularly as he did to help her out
with odd jobs. The scene, like the whole story, is reported from the point
of view of Scout, Addicus Finch's little daughter, who is secretly survey-
ing the proceedings with her brother Jem from the "Negro gallery." Mr
Gilmer, the prosecutor, sets him up:

> "Why were you so anxious to do that woman's chores?"
> Tom Robinson hesitated, searching for an answer. "Looked like she didn't have
> nobody to help her, like I says –" . . .
> Mr Gilmer smiled grimly at the jury. "You're a mighty good fellow, it seems –
> did all this for not one penny?"
> "Yes suh. I felt right sorry for her, she seemed to try more'n the rest of 'em –"
> "*You* felt sorry for *her*, you felt *sorry* for her?" Mr Gilmer seemed ready to rise
> to the ceiling.
> The witness realised his mistake and shifted uncomfortably in the chair. But the
> damage was done. Below us, nobody liked Tom Robinson's answer. Mr Gilmer
> paused a long time to let it sink in. (Lee 1974, 201)

Here the "damage" in question is done to any interpretative sympathy the
white jury has so far been human enough to feel towards the black defendant. For *feeling sorry for* someone is a taboo sentiment if you are black

and the object of your sympathy is a white person. And the fact that Tom Robinson has made the sentiment public raises the stakes in a way that is disastrous for justice, disastrous for him. The trial is a contest between the word of a black man against that of a white girl, and there are those in the jury whose testimonial sensibility is such that the idea that the black man is to be trusted and the white girl distrusted is virtually a psychological impossibility – Robinson's expressed sympathy for a white girl only reinforces that impossibility.

As it turns out, the members of the jury stick with their prejudiced perception of the defendant, formed principally by the racial stereotypes of the day. Addicus Finch challenges them to dispense with these stereotypes, to dispense with the "assumption – the evil assumption – that *all* Negroes lie, that *all* Negroes are basically immoral beings, that *all* Negro men are not to be trusted around our women" (Lee 1974, 208). But when it comes to the verdict, the jurors go along with the automatic distrust delivered by their corrupted testimonial sensibility. They find him guilty. And it is important that we are to interpret the novel so that the jurors really do find him guilty. That is to say, they do not privately find him innocent but cynically convict him anyway. They really do fail to do what Finch in his summing-up describes as their duty: they fail to *believe Tom Robinson*. Given the evidence put before them, their immovably prejudiced social perception of Robinson as a speaker leads at once to a gross epistemic failure and an appalling ethical failure.

Second example: It is the 1950s, and we are in Venice. Herbert Greenleaf, a rich American industrialist, is visiting, accompanied by a private detective he has hired to help solve the mystery of the whereabouts of his renegade son, Dickie. Dickie Greenleaf recently got engaged to his girlfriend, Marge Sherwood, but subsequently spent a great deal of time travelling with their "friend" Tom Ripley – until Dickie mysteriously disappeared. Marge is increasingly distrustful of Ripley because he seems to be obsessed with Dickie and suspiciously bound up with his strange disappearance. She also knows very well that it is unlike Dickie – unreliable philanderer though he undoubtedly was – simply to do a bunk, let alone to commit suicide, which is the hypothesis Ripley is at pains to encourage. Ripley, however, has all along done a successful job of sucking up to Greenleaf senior, so Marge is entirely alone in her suspicion – her correct suspicion – that Tom has in fact killed Dickie.

Herbert Greenleaf has just asked Ripley to be as helpful as he can in "filling in the blanks" of Dickie's life to Macarron, the private detective, and Ripley responds:

Ripley: I'll try my best, sir. Obviously I'll do anything to help Dickie.
Marge looks at him in contempt.
Herbert Greenleaf: This theory, the letter he left for you, the police think that's a clear indication he was planning on doing something . . . to himself.

Marge: I just don't believe that!
Herbert Greenleaf: You don't want to, dear. I'd like to talk to Tom alone –
perhaps this afternoon? Would you mind? Marge, what a man may say to his
sweetheart and what he'll admit to another fellow –
Marge: Such as? (Minghella 2000, 120–21)

Here Marge is being gently, kindly, sidelined by Greenleaf senior, who
pathologizes her disbelief that Dickie would kill himself as a sweetheart's
wishful thinking. He also seems to assume that Marge is generally innocent of the more tawdry facts of Dickie's life, so that his primary attitude
towards her on the one hand and the-truth-about-Dickie on the other is that
she needs protection from *it*. Greenleaf's everyday theory about what a
man may say to his sweetheart, et cetera – though in itself quite possibly
true enough – has the effect of undermining Marge as a possessor of
knowledge about the lover she had been living with for some time.
Greenleaf is only too aware how little he knows of his son – pathetically
enthusiastic as he is at the prospect that the private detective might help
make good this ignorance – and yet he fails to see Marge as the source of
knowledge about Dickie that she manifestly is.

This attitude has the knock-on effect that Greenleaf fails to trust one of
Marge's key reasons for her correct hypothesis that Dickie has died at the
hands of Ripley. Even when Marge finds hard evidence back at Ripley's
place, coming across a ring which she had given Dickie and which he had
sworn never to remove, still she receives no credibility. Ripley's deliberate
tactic is to dismiss her as "hysterical" – a line he continues to peddle in
front of Greenleaf in order to get him to share this interpretation. The tactic
works, not only on Greenleaf but also on her friend Peter Smith-Kingsley,
so that the result is a collusion of men against Marge's word being taken
seriously. The theme of knowledge ever to the fore in the dialogue, we at
one point hear her off-screen, soon after she finds the ring, saying emphat-
ically to the incredulous Greenleaf, "I don't know, I don't know, I just
know it," and Greenleaf replies with a familiar put-down: "Marge, there's
female intuition, and then there are facts – ."

A number of these sorts of exchanges build up to the scene in which
Marge, being taken back to America, is ushered on to a boat but breaks
away to lunge at Ripley, saying, "I know it was you – I know it was you,
Tom. I know it was you. I know you killed Dickie. I know it was you."
Macarron, the private detective, comes out of the waiting boat to restrain
her, and the stage direction reads: "Ripley looks at him as if to say: What
can you do, she's hysterical. Macarron nods, pulls her onto the boat." As
the viewer is aware, however, Marge was right: she did know; she knew
Dickie well; and she knew Ripley had killed him. Her suspicions should
have been listened to; *she* of all people should have been given some credibility. But Ripley cynically exploits the gender attitudes of the day so that
the kindly and well-meaning men around her effectively collude with him
to make her seem epistemically untrustworthy.

What both these examples present us with, in their different ways, is a case of a hearer failing to correct for one or another sort of prejudice in his testimonial sensibility. Both Greenleaf and the members of Maycomb County's jury fail to distrust their own distrust[9] of the speaker. They fail to adjust for the way in which their testimonial sensibility is badly trained. In the formal courtroom context of Tom Robinson's trial, they have ample opportunity to sense the dissonance between the distrust that their defective sensibility spontaneously delivers and the trust that attention to the evidence ought to inspire. Even if members of the jury were to be forgiven for the way their sensibility is saturated with the prejudices of the day, they remain starkly culpable in failing to respond appropriately to the new testimonial experience afforded by the trial. In the case of Herbert Greenleaf, he fails to correct for the way in which his habits of hearer response are saturated with the sexist constructions of gender – notably, ideas of women's innocence concerning the truths of men, and their need to be protected from such truths; ideas of feminine intuitiveness being an obstacle to rational judgement; and even ideas of a female susceptibility to hysterics.

But it is not simply a matter of failure properly to accommodate the speaker's social identity. In both examples, the hearers fail to adjust for the way in which their *own* social identity affects the testimonial exchange. The jury fails to account for the difference it makes to Tom Robinson's "performance" as a speaker (in the wide sense of performance, to include both what he does and how the audience responds) not only that he is black but equally *that they are white*. What Greenleaf fails to account for in his sceptical responses to Marge is the difference it makes to her performance not only that she is a woman but also that *he is a man*. The relation – a relation of power – between the social identities of hearer and speaker influence both how the speaker expresses herself and how the hearer responds.

Our two examples, then, demonstrate that testimonial responsibility requires a distinctly reflexive critical awareness. Had Marge shouted her accusations in the presence of Mrs Herbert Greenleaf, one speculates that she might have received from her some greater degree of credibility. That things would have gone differently at Tom Robinson's trial if the members of the jury had been black goes without saying.

Thus we have arrived at the final feature of the anti-prejudicial testimonial virtue we have been looking for: it is essentially reflexive. Its possession means that the hearer reliably succeeds in correcting for the way testimonial performance can be prejudiced by the inter-relation of the hearer's social identity and the speaker's social identity. In testimonial exchanges, for hearers and speakers alike, no party is neutral – everybody has a race, everybody has a gender. What is needed on the part of the

---

[9] I borrow this formulation from Jones 2002, in which she explores the themes of power and credibility specifically concerning astonishing reports.

hearer, then, in order to avert an epistemic injustice (and in order to serve his own epistemic interest in the truth) is a virtue of *Reflexive Critical Openness*. This is the virtue we have been aiming to identify by attending to the phenomenon of testimonial injustice.

5. The Virtue of Reflexive Critical Openness – Historicism

The virtue of Reflexive Critical Openness is an especially hard virtue to achieve at the best of times, inasmuch as prejudice is a powerful visceral force, functioning less at the level of propositional attitudes and more at the level of the social-imaginative and emotional commitments that colour one's perceptions of speakers. (Even if one were only faced with correcting for prejudice at the level of belief, this can still be very hard while those beliefs are propped up by motivational attitudes in this way. As Christopher Hookway [2001, e.g., 182] has argued, there is the usual room for *akrasia* in the practical business of managing one's epistemic habits.)

Clearly, however, it is in principle achievable, and the virtue will be an integral part of any well-trained testimonial sensibility in so far as the risk of prejudice-induced credibility deficit is an inevitable feature of epistemic life. The human condition is a social condition, and social relations inevitably create space for prejudice.

Yet, there are circumstances under which the virtue cannot be achieved, for it is a notable and ethically significant feature of this virtue that it displays a special sort of cultural-historical contingency. In order to explain this, let me follow Linda Zagzebski's (1996) definition of virtue such that virtues have both a motivational component and a component of reliable success in bringing about the end of that motivation. In the case of intellectual virtues there will always be a motivation to achieve truth, but usually there will also be a more proximal aim to achieve something that is conducive to truth – notably here the aim of ensuring that one's levels of trust are untainted by prejudice. As a matter of definition, then, the intellectually virtuous subject will be reliably successful in fulfilling that proximal aim of ensuring against prejudice, and she will succeed in this by achieving reflexive critical awareness of the prejudicial distortions in her existing testimonial sensibility and by correcting for those distortions.

It must now be acknowledged, however, that the ability to do that is dependent upon the cultural-historical setting. A setting in which there is little critical awareness of gender is a setting in which no-one is in a position to possess the virtue of Reflexive Critical Openness *vis-à-vis* gender prejudice of any subtle kind. While the Herbert Greenleafs of this world were always at fault in failing to exhibit the virtue, I would suggest they were not *culpably* at fault until the requisite critical consciousness of gender became available to them. They were not culpably at fault until they were in a position to know better. Now there will of course be no precise answer to the question of at what point a Herbert Greenleaf comes to be in a position where he should know better than to overlook the possibility that Marge was right. But no doubt someone like him will be in that position long before he actually lives up to it by taking on board the gender-critical insights newly available to him. Thus there will tend to be some period of historical transition in which a Herbert Greenleaf, well-intentioned and paternal as he may remain, moves from innocent fault to culpable fault. He lacked the virtue of Reflexive Critical Openness with regard to women speakers all along, but the relevant advance in collective consciousness will mean that this shortcoming in his epistemic conduct, and in the testimonial sensibility behind it, will have become blameworthy.

This shows that the power to possess the virtue of Reflexive Critical Openness depends upon the social-historical context. The case of Herbert Greenleaf, as I have characterised it, exemplifies the idea that one cannot be blamed for failing to do something one wasn't in a position to have reason to do. Essentially this is an instance of the maxim that "ought" implies "can," since in our example the "can" part is a matter of whether Greenleaf could reasonably be expected to *achieve* the critical perspective on gender that would have given *him* a reason to cast doubt on his lack of trust in Marge's word. More specifically, and more controversially, we might think of ourselves as having arrived at an insight into the structure of responsibility that is advanced by Bernard Williams (1995, 35) in terms of the internality of practical reasons. It would not be right to blame someone for an action or omission unless there existed a "sound deliberative route" from that person's actual motivational set ("the set of his desires, evaluations, attitudes, projects, and so on"). Whatever one thinks about the disagreements between so-called internal and external reasons theorists, it is worth noting that our intellectual case could not be controversial in anything like the way the ethical case is. This is because it could not be controversial to presume that all epistemic subjects possess in their motivational set a general motivation to aim at truth, and *a fortiori* to aim at more proximal ends which are in the service of that general motivation (such as correcting for prejudice in one's habits of trust, for instance).

Given this, it is clear that not just Herbert Greenleaf but even the most virulent, dyed-in-the-wool sexist version of Herbert Greenleaf possesses a motivation (the motivation to truth) from which there might be a sound deliberative route to distrusting his lack of trust in Marge. It is not the lack of a motivation, then, that explains why Greenleaf "cannot" do what he ought – cannot exhibit the appropriate virtue. It is rather the unavailability to him of a sound deliberative route from that veridical motivation to the conclusion that he should doubt his lack of trust in Marge. There is no such sound deliberative route available to him, in as much as the critical concepts in which that deliberation would have to be couched are genuinely not yet available. On this (perhaps rather charitable) interpretation, then, Greenleaf is unlucky, epistemically and morally. His non-culpable inability to exhibit the virtue of Reflexive Critical Openness not only means that he misses out on a truth that he is especially interested in acquiring (Marge is right; Ripley is Dickie's murderer) but also means he inflicts a significant injustice on Marge. She is treated as a hysterical female who cannot handle the truth, someone who deserves protection and sympathy but not epistemic trust. If one's rationality is an essential part of one's humanity, then Marge is gently undermined in her very humanity.

Evidently testimonial injustice will tend to imitate the broader structures of power in society, and where it is systematic we should recognise it as a face of oppression. In an essay on the nature of oppression Sandra Lee Bartky (1990, 30) quotes Frantz Fanon's notion of "psychic alienation," where the alienation in question consists in "the estrangement of separating off a person from some of the essential attributes of personhood." I take it that basic forms of epistemic agency, such as functioning as an informant on everyday matters, is indeed one of the essential attributes of personhood – it is part and parcel of being accepted as a compatriot in the community of the rational. If this is so, then an epistemic climate in which some people suffer systematic testimonial injustice must be regarded as seriously defective both epistemically and ethically. It is the site not simply of error and frustration, advantage and disadvantage, but of a distinctively epistemic kind of oppression. We have seen that the virtue of Reflexive Critical Openness (and doubtless many other virtues besides) has an important role in combating this sort of oppression. But as something possessed of mere individuals whose social-historical situation can deprive them of the very resources they need in order to attain the virtue, its anti-oppressive power remains hostage to the broader social structures in which our testimonial practices must take place.

School of Philosophy
Birkbeck College
University of London
Malet Street
London WC1E 7HX
United Kingdom
m.fricker@philosophy.bbk.ac.uk

References

Bartky, Sandra Lee. 1990. "On Psychological Oppression." In *Femininity and Domination: Studies in the Phenomenology of Oppression*, 22–32. London: Routledge.
Coady, C. A. J. 1992. *Testimony: A Philosophical Study*. Oxford: Clarendon Press.
Fricker, Elizabeth. 1987. "The Epistemology of Testimony." *Proceedings of the Aristotelian Society* (supplementary volume) 61: 57–83.

———. 1994. "Against Gullibility." In *Knowing from Words*, edited by B. K. Matilal and A. Chakrabarti. Dordrecht, The Netherlands: Kluwer.

Fricker, Miranda. 2000. "Confidence and Irony." In *Morality, Reflection, and Ideology*, edited by E. Harcourt, 87–112. Oxford: Oxford University Press.

Jones, Karen. 1996. "Trust as an Affective Attitude." *Ethics* 107: 4–25.

———. 2002. "The Politics of Credibility." In *A Mind of One's Own: Feminist Essays on Reason and Objectivity*, edited by L. Antony and C. Witt, 154–76. Boulder, Col.: Westview Press.

Lee, Harper. 1974. *To Kill A Mockingbird*. London: Pan Books.

Hookway, Christopher. 2001. "Epistemic *Akrasia* and Epistemic Virtue." In *Virtue Epistemology: Essays on Epistemic Virtue and Responsibility*, edited by A. Fairweather and L. Zagzebski, 178–99. Oxford: Oxford University Press.

MacIntyre, Alasdair. 1981. *After Virtue: A Study in Moral Theory*. London: Duckworth.

McDowell, John. 1994. *Mind and World*. Cambridge, Mass.: Harvard University Press.

———. 1998. "Knowledge by Hearsay." In *Meaning, Knowledge, and Reality*, essay 19. Cambridge, Mass.: Harvard University Press.

Minghella, Anthony. 2000. *The Talented Mr Ripley*. London: Methuen.

Williams, Bernard. 1995. "Internal Reasons and the Obscurity of Blame." In *Making Sense of Humanity and Other Philosophical Papers*, chapter 3. Cambridge: Cambridge University Press.

Zagzebski, Linda. 1996. *Virtues of the Mind: An Inquiry into the Nature of Virtue and the Ethical Foundations of Knowledge*. Cambridge: Cambridge University Press.

© Metaphilosophy LLC and Blackwell Publishing Ltd. 2003

© Metaphilosophy LLC and Blackwell Publishing Ltd. 2003.
Published by Blackwell Publishing, 9600 Garsington Road, Oxford OX4 2DQ, UK and
350 Main Street, Malden, MA 02148, USA
METAPHILOSOPHY
Vol. 34, Nos. 1/2, January 2003
0026–1068

EPISTEMIC INJUSTICE
THE THIRD WAY?

S. E. MARSHALL

ABSTRACT: In response to Miranda Fricker's advocacy of a virtue of 'reflexive critical openness', I emphasise the importance of other virtues, such as loyalty, in evaluating an agent's response to testimony, and I query Fricker's claim that in certain circumstances agents can lack a means to correct their faulty evaluations of another's testimony.

Keywords: epistemic injustice, loyalty, testimonial sensibility, virtue.

"And if anyone knows anything about anything," said Bear to himself, "it's Owl who knows something about something" he said, "or my name's not Winnie-the-Pooh," he said. "Which it is," he added. "So there you are." (Milne 1975, 42)

In her essay Miranda Fricker advances a view that might seem to forge a 'third way' – or, given the Aristotelian drift of the argument, a 'mean' – between the two traditional approaches to the epistemology of testimony. At the one extreme, there is the model of 'uncritical receptivity', which seems to leave us vulnerable to the vice of gullibility. At the other, there is the inferential model, which, in requiring us to engage in a process of reasoning about the reliability of the speaker, leaves us vulnerable to the vice of suspiciousness. Neither of these characterisations adequately captures our ordinary dealings with one another, as Fricker rightly argues, for we are not inclined simply to trust *whatever* anyone tells us, irrespective of circumstances, nor do we consciously rehearse the arguments for the speaker's reliability before accepting what he or she says.

It is important to notice, furthermore, the extent to which this practice of accepting what we are told, the gaining of knowledge by testimony, is utterly fundamental to the possibility of social life. It would be hard to imagine a society that was totally lacking in what Fricker calls "the effortless spontaneity characteristic of so much of our everyday testimonial exchange" (156), or in which we never relied upon what we were told by others *at all*. I might go so far as to say that it would not be just *hard* to imagine such a society but impossible, that whatever it was we were imagining, it would not be a society and the beings would not be people. To a considerable extent, then, I am sympathetic to the arguments that Fricker presents in her essay. What follows will, for that reason, be more by way of further observations on the theme that she develops than a critical argument with what she says.

Before moving to some of the detail of Fricker's own view, it is worth pointing out that neither of the two rejected positions should be completely written off as irrelevant. It may be right to reject them as accounts of what the epistemology of testimony fundamentally *is*, but this is not to say that they do not speak at all to our practice. The point must be that the whole practice of coming to know something by being told is not a single activity with a uniform structure. For example, there are circumstances in which we may well react in just the way characterised by the model of uncritical receptivity. Fricker's example of asking a stranger the time illustrates this point. Similarly, were I to be discussing the finer points of domestic plumbing with a stranger on a train, I might well engage in the kind of inferential process at issue in the inferential model, especially considering what I know about, as Fricker puts it, the "general reliability of people like that about things like this" (156). (More so, if it turned out not to be the case that the stranger was a plumber.) Of course, it must also be borne in mind that not every occasion upon which someone *tells* us something is one that is epistemologically relevant – my train conversation with the would-be plumber no doubt has a function quite different from that of acquiring knowledge, even if the form of the conversation is that of my asking questions and the plumber's giving me long and detailed answers. There are different social practices that constitute 'telling someone something', informed by different social virtues.

The account offered by Fricker, then, is one which draws precisely on that rich and ineradicable social context to steer the path between the two extremes, although at first sight her view may seem closer to the 'uncritically receptive' model. This is not necessarily a problem, for we should remember that the Aristotelian mean is not simply that which is *exactly* in the middle of two extremes. The trained 'testimonial sensibility' that constitutes the everyday hearer response is, nonetheless, on Fricker's account grounded in inductive rationality as the basic source of justification for hearer response. Whether this means that, in any event, a hearer must at least be able, if asked, to give the kind of justification for her acceptance of what she is told by a speaker that has the inferential *form* is not entirely clear. It is not obvious either that in fact the kind of training which is involved in acquiring testimonial sensibility starts with anything like a process of inductive inferential reasoning, for that training is essentially social and perhaps rather more active than Fricker suggests. The hearer has to learn to be both a speaker and a hearer; to learn, that is, by participation in a range of social practices that require her to develop habits of thought and action. She learns to *be* trustworthy at the same time as learning to judge when she is to trust the word of others, and in becoming so habituated we come to exercise a *range* of virtues, as Fricker points out, although her main concern is largely with the one she calls "Reflexive Critical Openness." This virtue is necessary if we are to avoid 'epistemic injustice' – that is, failing to believe people when they ought to be believed, but also believing someone who ought not to be believed.

Here, however, one can see the possibility of conflict between the different virtues that structure the social relations in which testimonial sensibility is embedded, for sometimes it may be that loyalty might demand that one have faith in a speaker even when there might be reason not to, and this may mean that someone else is not believed when he or she ought to be. There is a range of cases here that might conflict with the demands of testimonial sensibility in different ways. One might, for instance, consciously disregard the epistemic deliverances of a reflexively critical perception and at least act as if one believed what another says. So, the parent of a convicted murderer might say that they simply 'have to believe' their child's claims of innocence, for their child's sake. What such 'believing' comes to is another matter. The demands of loyalty, however, can go deeper (or become more extreme, some might say), so that the stance of reflexive critical openness itself can have no role to play. The point about such loyalty is not simply that contrary evidence is disregarded but that a certain line of thought or range of considerations does not enter into the relationship at all. Loyalty can, of course, be misguided, but more argument would be needed to show that it is necessarily misguided, just in case it conflicts with the demands of testimonial sensibility.

Are we here to speak of a case of a 'prejudicial dysfunction in testimonial practice'? The examples of such dysfunction that Fricker considers are based upon unequal relationships of power, so perhaps it is rather that the lesson of Fricker's essay is that in such a case of trust born of loyalty we do not have a case of testimonial practice at all, even though one person relies upon what the other says to her and even where what she accepts is, as a matter of fact, the truth. Alternatively, it might seem that there are differences in what we have a right to expect depending on the closeness of the relationship we have to others, and it may be that some relationships cannot easily accommodate the degree of distance that the virtue of reflexive critical openness demands.

This raises a more general question about the degree, and kind, of detachment required by the virtue of reflexive critical openness. The examples of epistemic injustice discussed by Fricker suggest that it will vary according to the case, and in their own way they reflect the two extremes Fricker wishes to avoid. The jury, indeed, is in the position closest to that demanded by the inferential model, since what it is quite explicitly required to do is weigh what the witness says – to test it for plausibility, to make conscious assessments of its veracity. It will not do for the jury to adopt the stance of simply believing what the witness says, in the way in which I might just believe what the stranger tells me when I ask him the time. The members of the jury in *To Kill a Mocking Bird* are wrong not because they do not believe Tom Robinson but because they do not *weigh* his testimony in the right way – they are not properly impartial. Is such impartiality, or detachment, what is required of Herbert Greenleaf? Is it that he fails to make the correct judgement about Marge's testimony because, prejudiced as he is, he fails to *weigh* what she says correctly? Or is it rather that he fails to take what she says seriously without needing to make any kind of judgement at all? One might say that he *ought* to have trusted someone who was so close to his son, and not simply that he was wrong in letting prejudice get in the way of an inferential judgement.

In any case, it does not seem to me that the agents involved in either the *To Kill a Mocking Bird* example or *The Talented Mr Ripley* example lack the 'sound deliberative route' that would have enabled them to correct their perceptions. Clearly this is not the case for the members of the jury, since the arguments put forward by Addicus Finch precisely point them to that route, and if it is open to him then it is open to them (these arguments are thus a part of their 'social-historical situation'). Similarly, the ideas of womanhood that informed Herbert Greenleaf's thinking were not unchallengeable – that is, they would not have been unintelligible. None of this is to say that either the members of the jury or Herbert Greenleaf would have found it very easy to change their views and attitudes, but rather that the failing they exhibit is a failing of moral character. To that extent testimonial virtue is indeed dependent upon moral virtue.

Department of Philosophy
University of Stirling
Stirling FK9 4LA
United Kingdom
s.e.marshall@stir.ac.uk

Reference

Milne, A. A. 1975. *Winnie the Pooh*. London: Methuen.

Published by Blackwell Publishing, 9600 Garsington Road, Oxford OX4 2DQ, UK and
350 Main Street, Malden, MA 02148, USA
METAPHILOSOPHY
Vol. 34, Nos. 1/2, January 2003
0026–1068

VIRTUE JURISPRUDENCE
A VIRTUE-CENTRED THEORY OF JUDGING

LAWRENCE B. SOLUM

ABSTRACT: "Virtue jurisprudence" is a normative and explanatory theory of
law that utilises the resources of virtue ethics to answer the central questions of
legal theory. The main focus of this essay is the development of a virtue-centred
theory of judging. The exposition of the theory begins with exploration of defects
in judicial character, such as corruption and incompetence. Next, an account of
judicial virtue is introduced. This includes judicial wisdom, a form of *phronesis*,
or sound practical judgement. A virtue-centred account of justice is defended
against the argument that theories of fairness are prior to theories of justice. The
centrality of virtue as a character trait can be drawn out by analysing the virtue of
justice into constituent elements. These include judicial impartiality (even-handed
sympathy for those affected by adjudication) and judicial integrity (respect for the
law and concern for its coherence). The essay argues that a virtue-centred theory
accounts for the role that virtuous practical judgement plays in the application of
rules to particular fact situations. Moreover, it contends that a virtue-centred
theory of judging can best account for the phenomenon of lawful judicial disagreement. Finally, a virtue-centred approach best accounts for the practice of equity,
departure from the rules based on the judge's appreciation of the particular characteristics of individual fact situations.

Keywords: ethics, justice, jurisprudence, law, virtue.

1. Introduction

"Virtue jurisprudence" is a normative and explanatory theory of law that
utilises the resources of virtue epistemology,[1] virtue ethics,[2] and virtue
politics[3] to answer the central questions of legal theory.[4] In a sense, virtue

---

[1] See Zagzebski 1996. See also Fairweather and Zagzebski 2001.
[2] The literature on virtue ethics is now vast. My own work has been especially influenced by the following contemporary works: Foot 1978; 2001; Hursthouse 1999; MacIntyre
1984; and Sherman 1989. See also Crisp and Slote 1997; Statman 1997; and Crisp 1996.
[3] See Crisp and Slote 1997, "Introduction."
[4] The phrase *virtue jurisprudence* is coined on the model of "virtue ethics" and "virtue
epistemology." Virtue jurisprudence today is in much the same early stage as "virtue politics." See Crisp and Slote 1997, "Introduction."

jurisprudence is a new theory, drawing on the resources provided by recent developments in moral philosophy, but virtue jurisprudence is also a very old theory, rooted in Aristotle's conception of ethics, politics, and the nature of law.[5] A central thesis of virtue jurisprudence is that rival accounts of the nature of law are seriously deficient, because they do not and cannot provide an adequate account of the relationship between law and character. This essay explores one aspect of that thesis in the context of theories of judging.

I shall begin my exposition of virtue jurisprudence by comparing the situation of legal theory today to the condition of ethics a few decades ago when Elizabeth Anscombe (1997) wrote her essay "Modern Moral Philosophy." Then I shall proceed to a very broad-brush sketch of the issues that might be encompassed by virtue jurisprudence. After these introductory topics have been explored, I shall turn to the central part of the essay, an outline of a virtue-centred theory of judging. Finally, I contend that a virtue-centred theory of judging offers an adequate account of the practice of equity, but competing theories of judging run into trouble on this score.

A. Law and Modern Moral Philosophy

In "Modern Moral Philosophy" Elizabeth Anscombe famously noted persistent problems with the deontological and utilitarian approaches that dominated normative ethics when she wrote in 1958. Modern legal theory has strong connections with modern moral philosophy. Historically, the connection is evident in the work of Jeremy Bentham,[6] which combined a conceptual separation of law and morality with a utilitarian program of legal reform.[7] Contemporary legal scholarship frequently invokes general

---

[5] My understanding of Aristotle's theory of the virtues reflects a variety of sources. See, e.g., Broadie 1991; Hardie 1980; Kraut 1989; 2002. See also Rorty 1980. I am also indebted to Gavin Lawrence for his course on Aristotle's ethics at the University of California at Los Angeles and to Christine Korsgaard for her seminar on Aristotle's ethics at Harvard University.

[6] See generally Bentham 1988; 1996.

[7] The relationship between legal positivism and normative criticism of the law is controversial. Frederick Schauer (1996) has articulated the idea that legal positivism enables moral criticism of the law by making the separation between legality and morality clear. Julie Dickson (2001) criticises this line of argument on the grounds that it involves "wishful thinking." Dickson believes that legal positivism is a theory of what law is, i.e., a theory that specifies the necessary and sufficient conditions for a social practice to count as a law. Therefore, she argues, the beneficial consequences of legal positivism cannot count as an argument for the acceptance of legal positivism as a theory of the nature of law. The acceptance of legal positivism must depend on whether it does, in fact, capture the necessary and sufficient conditions for law; any beneficial consequences would be mere epiphenomena. Discussion of this issue is beyond the scope of this essay, except for one brief observation. Dickson's argument assumes that the concept of "law" designates a social practice, the nature of which is fixed by the necessary and sufficient conditions that constitute its conceptual structure. If, however, law is a social practice, the nature of which is contestable and subject to revision, then it would follow that legal positivism is indeed a normative position and that Schauer is not guilty of wishful thinking.

moral theories, including preference-satisfaction utilitarianism[8] and deontological theories like Kant's,[9] to make arguments about what the law
should be. Such normative legal theories are addressed to lawmakers (in
the broad sense), including legislators and adjudicators. Developments in
political philosophy, sparked by John Rawls's *Theory of Justice*[10] and its
libertarian[11] and communitarian[12] critics, have met with avid attention from
the legal academy.

There is, however, an exception to general reflection of developments
in moral philosophy in legal theory. Legal philosophy (as practised by
philosophers or academic lawyers) has only recently paid attention to one
of the most significant developments in moral theory in the second half of
the twentieth century, the emergence of virtue ethics.

An outpouring of articles and monographs attests to the interest of
philosophers in virtue ethics.[13] In the law, the situation has been different.
The hegemony of deontological and utilitarian theories prevails, at least
among legal theorists working in the common-law tradition.[14] There are,
however, a growing number of exceptions to this hegemony,[15] including
work on antitrust law,[16] civil-rights law,[17] corporate law,[18] criminal law,[19]

[8] Preference-satisfaction utilitarianism provides the moral foundation for most of normative law and economics. For a general statement, see Kaplow and Shavell 2002.

[9] See, e.g., Bricker 1999; Haemmerli 1999; Housman 1992; Lillich 1997; Wright 2002.
See also Symposium on Kantian Legal Theory 1987.

[10] Use of Rawls's theory in general and the original position in various forms has become
commonplace in legal scholarship. See, e.g., Jackson 1986 (bankruptcy law); Gordon 1989
(intellectual property law); Schroeder 1986 (tort law). See also Solum 1994b (discussing use
of Rawls in legal scholarship and judicial opinions).

[11] The contemporary classic is Nozick 1977. For applications in legal scholarship, see,
e.g., Byrne 1995; Carens 1987; Garcia 2000. An influential libertarian theory of law is
offered in Barnett 1998; see also Fleming 2000 (discussing Barnett) and Solum 1999
(discussing Barnett).

[12] One prominent communitarian critique is found in Sandel 1988. For discussions by
legal academics, see, e.g., Baker 1985; Forbath 2001; Quinn 2000.

[13] See the sources cited *supra* note 2.

[14] For a particularly self-conscious choice to discuss deontology and utilitarianism at the
expense of virtue ethics, see Strudler and Orts (1999, 381–82 n. 20): "For the purposes of
this Article, we identify utilitarianism as the main normative alternative to deontological
theory. We do so for two reasons. First, proponents of economic analysis, the dominant
approach to insider trading, often regard utilitarianism as the moral foundation of economic
analysis. . . . Second, utilitarianism has historically been perceived as the strongest
competitor to deontology. . . . Because of considerations of space, we have had to make
some editorial choices about moral theories we discuss and to omit discussions of theories
other than deontology and utilitarianism. We intend no slight to virtue ethics, moral development theory, social contract theory, or any of the other moral theories we do not
discuss."

[15] See, e.g., Araujo 1994; Brosnan 1989; Galston 1994; Garcia 2001; Heyman 1992;
Hirschman 1990; 1992.

[16] Robertson 2000.

[17] Araujo 2002, 433–34.

[18] Aaronson 1995; Bainbridge 1997; Beck-Dudley 1996; Nesteruk 1996a; 1996b.

[19] See Huigens 1995; 1998; 2000a; 2000b; 2002 and Muller 1993.

employment law,[20] environmental law,[21] torts,[22] legal ethics,[23] military justice,[24] pedagogy,[25] and public-interest law.[26]

"Virtue ethics" and "virtue epistemology" are not, of course, monolithic theories, and I cannot attempt to present a fully developed version of either approach on this occasion. I shall assume (but not argue for) the proposition that Aristotle's ethics counts as an example of virtue ethics.[27] In so far as it is possible, I shall attempt to avoid the various controversies surrounding the different varieties of virtue ethics and virtue epistemology. I shall certainly not be able to offer a defence of either theory against its critics.

B. Virtue Jurisprudence

A full account of the implications of virtue ethics and epistemology for legal theory is a very large topic. Among the issues raised by virtue jurisprudence are the following:

- Virtue ethics has implications for an account of the proper ends of legislation. If the aim of law is to make citizens virtuous (as opposed to maximizing utility or realising a set of moral rights), what are the implications for the content of the laws?[28]
- Virtue ethics has implications for legal ethics. Current approaches to ethical lawyering emphasise deontological moral theory, that is, duties to clients and respect for client autonomy, and these deontological approaches are reflected in the various codes of professional conduct that have been devised for lawyers, judges, and legislators. How can we reconceive legal ethics from a virtue-centred perspective?[29]
- Accounts of the virtue of justice (in particular, Aristotle's and Aquinas's theories of natural justice) have implications for debates between natural lawyers and legal positivists over the nature of law.[30]

[20] Sulentic 2001.

[21] Gaba 1999a; 1999b and Harsch 1999.

[22] Feldman 2000; see Simons 2001.

[23] Araujo 1997; Cochran 1996; 1998; 2000; Feldman 1996; 1999; Perkins 1998; Shaffer 1993; Smith and Montross 1999; Tremblay 1999b.

[24] Hudson 1999; Osiel 1998.

[25] Aaronson 1998; Hirschman 1993.

[26] Tremblay 1999a.

[27] Whether Aristotle had a virtue ethics in the contemporary sense is controversial; I shall not enter into that debate. The position that I attribute to Aristotle serves my purpose even if it turns out to be a neo-Aristotelian variation that is in some way inconsistent with Aristotle's own theory.

[28] For discussion of the relationship between lawfulness and virtue in Aristotle, see Kraut 2002. For a contemporary approach that emphasises the cultivation of virtue as the end of law, see George 1995.

[29] For an account that emphasises virtue and especially phronesis but is not rooted in contemporary virtue ethics, see Kronman 1993. For accounts that more directly connect legal ethics and virtue ethics, see sources cited *supra* note 23.

[30] The relationship between Aristotle's account of justice and debates over the nature of law is notoriously obscure. For a reading of Aristotle that is highly suggestive, see the

On this occasion, however, I shall limit my attention to the implications of a virtue-centred approach for a normative theory of judging. Such theories answer the question: How should judges decide the controversies that are presented to them? A virtue-centred theory of judging provides an answer along the following lines: Judges should decide cases in accord with the virtues, or judges should render the decisions that would be made by a virtuous judge.

By way of clarification, I am not making any claim that theories of law should be judge centred.[31] Nor am I making any claim about the relative merits of judicial lawmaking and legislation.[32] Those are important topics, ones with which a virtue jurisprudence must grapple. A virtue-centred theory of judging is simply a place to start.[33]

C. What Is a Virtue-Centred Theory of Judging?

Beyond a Thin Theory of Judicial Virtue

There is a sense in which the notion of judicial virtue is likely to prove uncontroversial. For any given normative theory of judging, there is a corresponding account of the qualities that make for a good judge. If we are not too picky about the sort of qualities that we are willing to call "virtues" or "excellences," then we can offer accounts of judicial virtues that correspond to various theories of judging.

Ronald Dworkin's theory of law as integrity provides an example of a theory of judging.[34] Roughly, we might say that Dworkin believes that judges should decide cases in accord with the normative theory of law that best fits and justifies the law as a whole. For judges to be able to do this reliably, they will need to possess certain characteristics that we might call judicial virtues – the excellences appropriate to the role of judge. On Dworkin's theory, for example, the intellectual virtue of theoretical wisdom is clearly a prerequisite for excellence in judging. Dworkin's imaginary judge, Hercules, decides cases by constructing the theory that fits and justifies the law as a whole; this task can only be accomplished by someone who is able to appreciate legal complexity and to see the subtle

---

illuminating and important discussion of book 5 of the *Nicomachean Ethics* in Kraut 2002, 98–177.

[31] Although my discussion is of theories of judging, I do not mean to imply that virtue jurisprudence should focus only on the virtues of judges. A complete virtue jurisprudence would offer accounts of the virtues of legislators, executives, citizens, and other legal actors in addition to a theory of judging. Judging, however, is an important case, at least in part because theories of judging are prominent in contemporary jurisprudence.

[32] See generally Waldron 1999.

[33] Other recent uses of Aristotelian resources in the development of a theory of judging can be found in Modak-Truran 2000 and Henry 1999. My own prior work on a virtue-centred theory of judging includes Solum 1988; 1990; 1994a.

[34] See Dworkin 1978; see also Dworkin 1986.

interconnections between various legal doctrines summarised in the slogan "the law is a seamless web."[35]

Different normative theories of law may result in different lists of the excellences that are appropriate to judging. If it were the case that some qualities of judicial character are necessary for reliably good judging given any plausible normative theory of judicial decision, then an account of these qualities would be what I shall call a "thin" theory of judicial virtue. We might analogise such a thin theory to Rawls's notion of primary goods,[36] which are sometimes (albeit erroneously) understood as all-purpose means for the realisation of one's conception of the good life. In this picture, the judicial virtues are simply those qualities of character that are required to realise one's conception of good judging. Thus, a thin theory of judicial virtues might include the intellectual virtue of theoretical wisdom, which plausibly is necessary for judges to understand complex legal material. Likewise, irrespective of one's particular theory of good judging, it might turn out that certain vices are inconsistent with reliably good judging. Judges who are civic cowards, slavishly seeking approval from others, may be incapable of reliably adhering to any coherent and plausible theory of good judicial decision making. A similar claim might be made about judges who are intemperate or avaricious and thus prone to sharp dealing or susceptible to bribery. Hence, civic courage and temperance might be considered thin judicial virtues.

How a Virtue-Centred Theory Is Distinctive
This essay focuses on a virtue-centred theory of judging as a component of virtue jurisprudence. The aim is to provide arguments that make a virtue-centred theory plausible, but in order to accomplish this task, we need criteria that distinguish a virtue-centred theory of judging from a theory of judicial character that could be incorporated as a module within rival theories of judging. What makes a virtue-centred theory distinctive?

I shall approach this question by explicating the differences between a virtue-centred theory of judging and a thin theory of judicial virtue. A virtue-centred theory of judging differs from a thin theory of judicial virtue in two respects. First, a virtue-centred theory is not limited to those qualities of judicial character that would count as means to good decisions for any plausible theory of what counts as a good decision. Thus, the account that I offer might be characterised as a "thick" rather than a "thin" theory of judicial virtue. But thickness is not sufficient to make a theory virtue centred. For example, it might be that law as integrity can incorporate a

---

[35] Maitland (1898, 13): "Such is the unity of all history that any one who endeavours to tell a piece of it must feel that his first sentence tears a seamless web"; see also *Transworld Airlines v. American Coupon Exchange* (1990, 685) (discussing "law's oft-proclaimed seamless web"); *Kleinwort Benson Ltd. Appellant v. Lincoln City Council Same Respondent* 1999 (opinion of Lord Goff of Chieveley).
[36] See Rawls 1999, §60, 347–50.

thick theory of judicial virtues. Hercules may need the virtue of judicial integrity, that is, a special concern for the coherence of the law. This virtue might not be important to an act-utilitarian theory of judging.[37]

Second, a thin theory of judicial virtue cannot be focused on judicial character as opposed to judicial decision. Many normative theories of judging are decision (or outcome) centred. A decision-centred theory offers criteria for what should count as a good, right, just, or legally valid decision. For a decision-centred theory of virtue, the notion of a correct decision is primary, and the judicial virtues are derived from it. Thus, Dworkin's description of Hercules begins with the criteria for good decisions and then constructs the ideal judge who is able to render such decisions. A virtue-centred theory does not proceed in this way. I shall begin with an account of a virtuous judge as primary and then proceed to derive the notion of a virtuous decision.

By way of clarification, consider some of the claims that a virtue-centred theory of judging does *not* need to make. For a theory to be virtue centred, it need not make the claim that judging can be explained solely and exclusively by reference to the virtues. Thus, the full story about correct or just or virtuous decision making will necessarily make reference to facts about the world (including the facts of the disputes that judges decide) and legal facts (including facts about what statutes have been validly enacted, what prior decisions are binding precedent, and so forth). A virtue-centred theory must claim that judicial virtues are a necessary part of the best theory of judging and that judicial virtue plays a central explanatory and normative role. A theory does not lose its status as virtue centred simply because it does not limit its explanatory resources to the virtues alone.[38]

The Aims of the Project

I shall conclude these introductory remarks with a comment about the aims of my project in this essay. The development of a virtue-centred theory of judging may allow us to make progress on two fronts. First, it may contribute to our understanding of normative and explanatory jurisprudence; in particular, a virtue-centred theory of judging organises our views about how judges do and should go about their business. This is my primary aim, and it is the explicit focus of this essay.

---

[37] I do not mean to claim that an act utilitarian could not make a case for judicial integrity. My claim is simply that one could plausibly argue that concern for coherence need not be a virtue for a theory that makes the consequences of judicial decisions the measure of their correctness. A rule-utilitarian theory of judging, on the other hand, might need the virtue of judicial integrity.

[38] Indeed, it is difficult to imagine how a theory could explain judging without reference to concepts other than virtues. Facts about the world and the law are obviously necessary to describe the cases that judges decide. The question is not whether we admit such facts into our virtue-centred theory. Rather, the question is how such facts relate to the judicial virtues.

There is a second aim, however. The development of virtue jurisprudence may provide a perspicuous context for testing theories of virtue
ethics or virtue epistemology. For example, if virtue ethics offers a genuine
alternative to rival moral theories (deontology and consequentialism), then
it ought to be able to handle the special case of judging adequately. If
virtue ethics can provide an account of judging that does a better job of
fitting our considered judgements than do the theories of judging offered
by deontological or consequentialist moral theories, then we have a reason
that counts in favour of virtue ethics and against these rivals.

With respect to this second aim, there is a sense in which virtue
jurisprudence addresses a challenge that it is especially important for
virtue ethics to answer adequately. Crudely, we might say that virtue ethics
is especially well suited to handling those features of ethical life that are
not well served by moral rules. Virtue ethics thrives on the observation that
there is no master decision procedure for ethics.[39] Where virtue ethics
seems more awkward is in the cases where adherence to rules and decision
procedures has great intuitive plausibility. Judging seems to be the paradigm case in which we want adherence to constraining rules and transparent decision procedures. If virtue ethics can be extended to handle the case
of judging, it will have succeeded where many would expect it to fail.

2. A Sketch of a Virtue-Centred Theory of Judging

At this point, I shall sketch a virtue-centred theory of judging. The enterprise in this section is to develop an account of good judicial character.
This task will be accomplished in four steps. The first step is a brief survey
of the ways in which judges can be systematically defective: What are the
characteristic defects of judicial character? The second step is an account
of the kind of judicial character that will avoid these defects: What makes
for a reliably excellent judge? The third step is an exploration of the virtue
of justice: What qualities of mind and character make a judge just? The
fourth and final step is to state a theory of good judging as a function of
good judicial character: What is the relationship between correct judicial
decision and good judicial character? We can restate the four questions in
the language of the virtues:

* What are the judicial vices?
* What are the judicial virtues?
* What is the virtue of justice?
* What is the structure of a virtue-centred theory of judging?

Each topic will be considered in order.

---

[39] Cf. Rawls 1951.

A. What Are the Judicial Vices?

I turn initially to the judicial vices. Although there is considerable controversy about what constitutes a good judicial decision, there is considerable agreement about some of the characteristics that mark truly bad judges. Let us begin with these easy cases and work from them to an account of the judicial virtues.

Corruption

The first (perhaps the worst) judicial vice is avarice or corruption. We know from experience that corruption is a real danger for judges. Judicial avarice expresses itself in the blatant and obvious form of soliciting or accepting bribes, and in more subtle financial conflicts of interest, such trading on advance knowledge of the outcome of judicial proceedings or setting a precedent that will benefit a company in which one owns stock.[40] Corruption is not, of course, a uniquely judicial vice, but judicial corruption is particularly bad, because judges occupy a position of trust and because judicial corruption will often lead to grave injustice to innocent third parties unable to protect themselves. That is, an avaricious decision may lead to a defendant or litigant being denied that to which she is due under the law. Corruption is an especially heinous fault in judicial character, because we expect judges to display exemplary respect for the law. A corrupt or avaricious judge cares too much for material rewards or the pleasures they afford and accepts the wrong rewards from the wrong people for the wrong reasons.

Notice, however, that our objection to judicial avarice is not reducible to our concern that litigants get their due. Many judicial decisions are discretionary. Putting aside the controversial question whether "hard cases" in Dworkin's sense involve discretion, there are many issues (for example, the number of witnesses that are permitted to testify on a particular issue) where the decision of a trial-court judge is not significantly constrained by any rule. A corrupt decision on such an issue is evil, even if it does not deny any party something to which she is entitled. Indeed, a corrupt decision is wrong, even if it does, in fact, give the parties that to which they are entitled as a matter of law. A judge is not better for accepting bribes to render the correct decision.

Civic Cowardice

A second vice is judicial cowardice. I do not mean a disposition to excessive fear of solely or primarily *physical* danger. Judges in the United States and the United Kingdom rarely make official decisions that expose them to significant risk of harm. Such risk may be more common in other legal cultures; for example, narco-terrorist retaliation against judges in

---

[40] For general background on judicial corruption and efforts to control it, see National Commission on Judicial Discipline and Removal 1993; Simon 1994.

Colombia is common. Even in relatively stable societies it is not unusual to learn of a death threat against a judge. More frequently, however, judges may fear the loss of office or the loss of the opportunity to gain promotions. The election of judges is common in state judicial systems in the United States, for example. In some legal systems, judges earn promotions from lower courts to higher courts through a civil-service system. Even in a system with life tenure (such as the federal system in the United States) opportunities for promotion to a higher court or other position of prestige may depend on avoiding unpopular decisions on matters of public interest. More simply, judges may fear the opinions of the public and the powerful as well as the consequences of such opinions for their social positions. Judges with the vice of civic cowardice fear too much for their careers and social prestige, and hence are swayed by concern for their reputation on the wrong occasions and for the wrong reasons.

Cowardly decisions are bad ones for reasons that are much the same as those advanced for the conclusion that corrupt decisions are evil. Judges who rule against unpopular criminal defendants because they fear they will not be re-elected are likely to render decisions that are unjust because they deny to defendants that to which they are due. Moreover, a cowardly decision is properly criticised even if the outcome of the decision is within a judge's range of discretion or is, in fact, legally correct. Good judging requires that the right decision be reached for the right reason.

Bad Temper

A third judicial vice is bad temper. Trials in particular and the processes of civil and criminal justice in general are emotionally charged. Criminal defendants, litigants, and lawyers are all likely to disagree with, criticise, and even disrespect judicial officers. Judges who are quick to anger or who harbour resentments that occasionally burst into inappropriate explosions are likely to damage the judicial process. Their anger may cloud their judgement, leading them to render decisions that are wrong or to exercise their discretion in a biased manner. Even when inappropriate anger does not directly affect the outcome of judicial proceedings, it may undermine the confidence of the participants and public in the judge's fairness, and hence impair the effectiveness of the judicial process as a mechanism for resolving conflicts in a manner that gains acceptance and support from those affected.

Incompetence

The three judicial vices that I have considered so far (avarice, cowardice, and bad temper) involve defects in judges' affective states, their emotions or desires. What of defects in their intellectual equipment? Sometimes the law is subtle or complex, and a judge may go wrong by failing to grasp the law. When judges fail to understand the law, their decisions are likely to be unjust. The judge who fails to comprehend a complex rule or subtle distinction lacks the equipment to reliably hit the target, a legally correct result. Of course, even a blindfolded archer may hit the target, and even an incompetent judge may stumble on a legally correct result. If the decision is the kind that requires justification in the form of a written opinion, however, even a lucky guess about the outcome will not save a judge who lacks the ability to grasp the law intellectually. A well-reasoned opinion on a complex issue of law cannot be the product of good luck. In a system that incorporates the rule of *stare decisis*, a badly written opinion can result in injustice in the decision of many other cases, even if the outcome in the case in which the opinion was rendered was correct.

Although lawyers are well familiar with the problem of intellectually deficient judges, our public vocabulary is not rich with respect to this vice. We might say that the intellectually deficient judge suffers from judicial incompetence, or we might employ a less direct locution, saying such judges are "less than brilliant," "somewhat dense," or, more pejoratively, "stupid."

Foolishness

If one intellectual failure is related to legal complexity or subtlety, there is another sort of intellectual failure, associated with a lack of sound judgement. A judge can be foolish because the judge lacks the ability to distinguish between what is workable and what is impracticable. A related failure is the inability to distinguish between the aspects of a dispute that are important and those that are trivial. A judge who is a poor judge of character will be unable to tell honest witnesses from liars or to discern the difference between zealous advocacy and sharp dealing. Even judges who have a strong theoretical grasp of the law may go badly wrong if they lack common sense and sound practical judgement.

Failures in practical judgement by judges can have serious consequences. Judicial responsibility extends beyond the task of simply getting the law right and then applying it to the undisputed facts. Perhaps the clearest example of the dangers of bad judgement is the complex injunction. When a judge is required to supervise a complex institution, such as a penal system or a school district, the consequences of bad judgement can be serious indeed. Getting the law right may help the judge to see the legal goal that ongoing supervision of a complex injunction requires, but this is not sufficient. An impractical mandate or a poor allocation of resources can have devastating consequences, even without a mistake of law.

Let us pause and examine our brief and incomplete list of judicial vices. Judges who are avaricious, cowardly, bad tempered, stupid, or impractical are likely to go systematically wrong in their decisions. What are the qualities of character that avoid these defects? What qualities of character dispose a judge to make excellent decisions? In other words, what are the judicial virtues?

B. What Are the Judicial Virtues?

Our investigation of the judicial vices suggests that judicial virtue has much in common with human excellence in general. The intellectual virtues of theoretical and practical wisdom and the moral virtues of courage, temperance, and good temper are required for excellence in judging, just as they are required for any flourishing human life. To put the same point negatively, a vicious person – someone who is foolish, lacks common sense, is avaricious, cowardly, and prone to disproportionate anger – lacks the equipment for excellence in any social endeavour,[41] including a career as a judge.

Assuming that judicial excellence requires the possession of the virtues to at least some degree, the next step is to give an account of the virtues as they operate in the context of judging. I shall briefly describe five aspects of judicial virtue: (1) judicial temperance, (2) judicial courage, (3) judicial temperament, (4) judicial intelligence, and (5) judicial wisdom. I shall also discuss the virtue of justice, but that discussion will be postponed because of the special problems posed by justice.[42]

Before we proceed, two qualifications are in order. First, by calling these qualities "judicial virtues" I do not mean to imply any strong claim about their underlying nature. The psychology of the judicial virtues may well be the same as the virtues in general. The distinctive features of the judicial virtues may be attributable to the contexts in which they are exercised.[43] Because judges assume a special role and face situations that are distinct from the circumstances faced by the rest of us, the virtues they exercise can be described in a distinctive way. Second, the list of judicial virtues offered here is intended to be illustrative, not exhaustive.[44] Good judging requires more than just these five qualities of character.

Judicial Temperance

Consider first the virtue of temperance. Good judging requires that one's desires be in order. This is clear when the temperate judge is contrasted to the judge who lacks the ability to control her appetites. Judges who care too much for their own pleasures are prone to temptation; they are likely

[41] It is not clear to me that virtue is required for excellence in all human endeavours. It may, for example, be possible to be a great painter or singer, despite a vicious character. The claim that I make in the text is that virtue is required for human endeavours that are social and practical in nature, although I offer no defence for that claim on this occasion.

[42] For other discussions of judicial virtues, see Araujo 1994; see also Glendon 1994; Luban 1992, 242–56; Pinkard 1992, 281–82.

[43] The use of "may" indicates that I do not take a stand here. I am not ruling out the possibility that good judges develop emotional responses that are psychologically different from those who do not occupy this (or a relevantly similar) social role.

[44] A number of readers have suggested judicial virtues that might be added to my list. For example, judges in common-law systems are sometimes required to write opinions that justify their decisions. In order to do this well, judges need certain skills and capacities that might be called virtues – eloquence and wit come to mind.

to be swayed from the course of reason and justice by the temptations of pleasure. A libertine judge may indulge in pleasures that interfere with the heavy deliberative demands of the office. Hence, the saying "sober as a judge" reflects the popular understanding that excessive indulgence in hedonist pleasures would interfere with excellence in the judicial role.

As in the case of temperance generally, it is a bit difficult to see the virtue of judicial temperance as a mean between two opposing vices. Asceticism may interfere with a flourishing human life, but it is not so clear that it interferes in any distinctive way with the demands that we place on judges. Perhaps extreme judicial asceticism would interfere with the judge's ability to sympathise with and understand motivations and desires of lawyers, parties, and witnesses. If asceticism were a judicial vice, the explanation would lie in the connection of this quality to a lack of sound practical judgement.

Judicial Courage
A second virtue, judicial courage, corresponds to the vice of civic cowardice. The ordinary moral virtue of courage is sometimes thought to serve as a relatively clear example of Aristotle's doctrine of the mean.[45] Courage is a mean with respect to the morally neutral emotion of fear. The disposition to inordinate fear is cowardice. The opposing vice, rashness, is the disposition to insufficient fear. The coward is easily intimidated and does not take worthwhile risks. The rash person fails to perceive genuine danger and so is prone to injury from foolhardy risk taking.

Judicial courage is a form of "civic courage," distinguishing this quality of character from courage with respect to physical danger. The courageous judge is willing to risk career and reputation for the ends of justice. In the case of judging, it is a bit difficult to see the virtue as a mean between two opposing vices. If civic cowardice, too much fear of risk, is a familiar judicial vice, it is a bit difficult to imagine the judge who cares too little for his career and reputation. In special circumstances, we can imagine a judge who is too willing to throw away reputation and influence on a case that is not worthy of the sacrifice. But this case will need to be a special one, because in ordinary circumstances we believe that judges should do as the law and justice require in every case, not just important cases. Even the small injuries of little people should be important to judges.[46] Perhaps in a defective society, where one's ability to prevent grave injustice depends on one's willingness to inflict minor injustice, we might say that judges should be neither too fearful nor too careless of the risks of unpopular decisions. Such a society is defective, however, simply because it puts judges in just such a position.

[45] For doubts about this, see Pears 1980.

[46] As Learned Hand put it, "It is the daily; it is the small; it is the cumulative injuries of little people that we are here to protect . . . if we are to keep our democracy, there must be one commandment: thou shalt not ration justice." See Baldwin 1997, 58.

This is not to say that a judge should not care about her reputation or public opinion. A judge whose public reputation is good may be enabled to do good judicial work. Civic rashness is indeed a vice. It is a mistake for judges to sacrifice their reputations on the wrong occasions, for the wrong reasons, or by doing the wrong things. A judge may engage in extrajudicial behaviour that brings shame or ridicule. But the defect here is not likely to be too little fear of civic disrepute for unpopular decisions. Rather, some other defect is likely to be involved. Bad temper, immoderation, and poor judgement may all result in a poor reputation or damage one's opportunities for civic rewards, but all these vices should also be avoided in themselves and not simply because they reflect a lack of civic courage.

Judicial Temperament
A third virtue, judicial temperament, corresponds to the vice of bad temper. The traditional concern in judicial selection with judicial temperament is illuminated by Aristotle's account of the virtue of good temper, or *proates*: the disposition to anger that is proportionate to the provocation and the situation.[47] Good temper is a mean between excessive and deficient dispositions to anger. The vice of excess was illustrated circa 1968 and 1969 in the United States by Judge Hoffman's disproportionate rage in the Chicago Seven trial: his extreme anger produced a spectacle that undermined public confidence in the orderly administration of justice. But being too slow to anger is also a judicial vice. A judge who fails to respond with appropriate outrage in the face of misconduct can have a similar, if less dramatic, effect: a courtroom that is out of control is almost as bad as one in which defendants are bound and gagged. The virtue of good temper requires that judges feel outrage on the right occasions for the right reasons and that they demonstrate their anger in an appropriate manner.

Judicial Intelligence
The corrective for the vices of judicial stupidity and ignorance is a form of *sophia*, or theoretical wisdom. I shall use the phrase *judicial intelligence* to refer to excellence in understanding and theorising about the law. A good judge must be learned in the law; she must have the ability to engage in sophisticated legal reasoning.[48] Moreover, judges need the ability to grasp the facts of disputes that may involve particular disciplines such as accounting, finance, engineering, or chemistry. Of course, judicial intelligence is

---

[47] Aristotle 1976, 1125b27–31.
[48] Judges must be learned in the law in two senses. First, they must be learned in the sense that they actually know a great deal about the law that is relevant to their jurisdiction. Second, they must be learned in the sense that they have the cognitive capacities, experience, and skills that enable the acquisition of legal knowledge. Being learned in the first sense is not an intellectual virtue, but being learned in the second sense is. Being learned in the first sense is, however, likely to be a precondition for the development of being learned in the second sense.

related to theoretical wisdom in general, but the two are not necessarily identical. The talents that produce theoretical wisdom in the law may be different from those that produce the analogous intellectual virtue in physics, philosophy, or microbiology. Or it may be that theoretical wisdom is the same for all these disciplines. If this is the case, then judicial intelligence may simply be general theoretical wisdom supplemented by the skills or knacks that produce fine legal thought combined with deep knowledge of the law.

Judicial Wisdom
The final virtue on my short list is the corrective for bad judgement or foolishness. I shall use the phrase *judicial wisdom* to refer to a judge's possession of the virtue of *phronesis*, or practical wisdom: the good judge must possess practical wisdom in her selection of the proper legal ends and means.[49] Practical wisdom is the virtue that enables one to make good choices in particular circumstances. The person of practical wisdom knows which particular ends are worth pursuing and which means are best suited to achieve those ends. Judicial wisdom is simply the virtue of practical wisdom as applied to the choices that must be made by judges. The practically wise judge has developed excellence in knowing what goals to pursue in the particular case and excellence in choosing the means to accomplish those goals. In the literature of legal theory, Karl Llewellyn's notion of "situation sense" captures much of the content of the notion that judicial wisdom corresponds to the intellectual virtue of phronesis.[50]

This abstract account of judicial wisdom can be made more concrete by considering the contrast between practical wisdom and theoretical wisdom in the judicial context. The judge who possesses theoretical wisdom is the master of legal theory, with the ability to engage in sophisticated legal reasoning and insight into subtle connections in legal doctrine. But even a judge who possesses judicial intelligence is not necessarily a reliably good judge, even if she employs the correct decision procedure in her judicial decision making. Why not? An answer to this question begins by clarifying the distinction between judicial intelligence and judicial wisdom.

As an illustration of the distinction between theoretical and practical wisdom, consider the United States Supreme Court's articulation of a constitutional rule governing the free speech of lawyers in *Gentile v. State Bar of Nevada* (1991).[51] Gentile was disciplined by the Nevada Bar for holding a press conference in which he charged that a witness against his client had really committed the offence. Although the Court reversed the

---

[49] My account of phronesis has been influenced by many sources. See, e.g., MacIntyre 1984; Hardie 1980, 212–39; Engberg-Pedersen 1983. For a discussion of phronesis and the legal craft, see Scharffs 2001.
[50] Llewellyn 1960, 59–61, 121–57, 206–08; Twining 1973, 216–27; see also Farber 1991 (contemporary application of Llewellyn's idea).
[51] See Solum 1991, 16.

conviction on other grounds, Chief Justice Rehnquist's opinion for a majority of the Court held that the "substantial likelihood of material prejudice" standard used in the Model Rules of Professional Conduct does not violate a lawyer's right to freedom of speech; Rehnquist rejected the argument that some version of the "clear and present danger" standard was constitutionally required.

Whatever the merits of the theoretical debate in *Gentile* over the proper first-amendment standard, it misses an essential practical point expressed by former California Supreme Court Justice Otto Kaus in *Younger v. Smith* (1973), a case involving an issue very similar to the one raised in *Gentile*.[52] As Justice Kaus wryly put it,

> [P]endantic appellate debates over the correct criterion are good clean fun for those who enjoy that sort of thing, but of precious little help to a trial judge who must silence the sources of prejudicial pre-trial publicity as soon as possible, or risk spending weeks or months trying a case which is doomed to be reversed, should it result in a conviction. (*Younger v. Smith* 1973, 160)

Requiring a trial judge to find that a lawyer's conduct creates some quantum of risk "is simply to require him to palm off guesswork as finding" (1973, 164), said Justice Kaus. For our purposes, the point of Kaus's opinion was this: theoretical sophistication is no substitute for practical judgement. The abstract standard that best fits the contours of the freedom of speech doctrine can be a practical disaster if it is based on false assumptions about what trial judges can do.

Otto Kaus was one of many common-law judges whose careers exemplify the virtue of practical wisdom or, as I call it, judicial wisdom. As the eminent appellate lawyer Ellis Horvitz said of Kaus, "To an extraordinary degree, he possessed all of the important judicial virtues."[53] Kaus's opinion in *Younger* illustrates the relevance of the virtue of judicial wisdom at the appellate level. The need for common sense at the trial level is relatively obvious: trial judges need managerial skills that are not supplied by legal theory.[54] But the virtue of practical wisdom is a prerequisite for excellence in appellate judging as well.[55] The practically wise judge has an intuitive

---

[52] *Younger* was decided while Justice Kaus was on the bench of the California Court of Appeal.

[53] See Horvitz 1997.

[54] See Resnick 1982.

[55] In oral comments on prior work, Kent Greenawalt and Barbara Herman have suggested that the virtues of trial and appellate judges may be importantly different from the virtues of trial-court judges. See also Herman 1988, 1663–64: "If social role defines judicial virtue, one might well ask whether there is enough unity in the role across courts to provide useful content to the term 'good judge.' If there are radical differences, then there is room to question the transitivity of virtue from lower to higher courts. An exhaustive list of virtues obscures rather than answers the question." As the text suggests, I do not believe that the differences are fundamental, but a full discussion of that question is beyond my task in this essay.

sense as to how real-life lawyers and parties will react to judicial decisions. Judicial wisdom is required in order to know whether a particular doctrinal formulation will work in practice.[56]

C. What Is the Virtue of Justice?

I have left one virtue off the list, and it is the virtue that seems crucial in the case of judges. This is the virtue of justice. We are not tempted to name the distinctively judicial form of this virtue "judicial justice," as we could so name judicial courage, judicial wisdom, or judicial temperament. This is not because there is no association but rather because the association is too close. We call high judges "justices," we call the buildings they occupy the "halls of justice," and we call what they do "the administration of justice." If we know anything about judges, it is that they ought to be just. If judges should possess any virtue, then surely they should possess the virtue of justice.

The Centrality of Justice

If justice is a judicial virtue, how does it relate to the others? It seems clear that the virtue of justice is central. We can imagine a judge who has the natural virtues of temperance, courage, and good temper. Suppose this judge has the right intellectual equipment as well, a strong intellect, a good sense of practicality, and situation sense in matters legal. But if such a judge lacked the virtue of justice, then all the rest would be for naught. Put aside the question of whether one could lack justice but possess all the other judicial virtues (as natural virtues).[57] If, for the sake of argument, we can imagine the unjust man who is fully endowed with intellect and the natural virtues but lacking in justice, it is clear that such an adjudicator would be an especially bad judge.[58] Taking the problem from the other end, if there could be a judge who lacked the natural virtues but possessed a strongly developed virtue of justice, we might have a good judge who was not a very good human. Off the bench, the life of the just (but otherwise vicious) judge might be a disaster, but we would seem to lack grounds for criticism if all of the judge's decisions were just.

Laying this thought experiment aside, our working hypothesis is that justice is an essential virtue for excellence in judging. Without justice, judging cannot be good. With justice, judging must be good. Justice, we might say, is the cardinal virtue of judging.

[56] There is a great deal more to say about the need for practical wisdom at the appellate level. On this occasion, I can only offer a promissory note.

[57] It may well turn out that a judge cannot have the virtue of "judicial wisdom," or phronesis, and lack a sense of justice. Questions about the unity of the judicial virtues will be touched on below.

[58] This judge has no disposition to act justly. Although she may follow the law, she will only do so for reasons other than justice. For example, she might be motivated by considerations of honour and prestige to make decisions that will be seen as legally correct. But as soon as justice and honour part company, she will go for the latter at the expense of the former.

Is Justice a Virtue?

There are, however, a number of difficulties with incorporating the virtue of justice into a virtue-centred theory of judging. One such difficulty is that it is not easy to pin down the sense in which "justice" is a virtue at all. Aristotle classified justice as a moral virtue but (famously) found it difficult to fit justice into the schema of virtue as a mean between two opposing vices with respect to a morally neutral affective state, such as an emotion or desire.[59] If justice is giving persons their due, or doing what is fair, then what are the opposing vices? In the case of an individual, we might be tempted to postulate justice as a mean between the disposition to take more than one's share and the disposition to take less, but this solution has many well-known difficulties, including the problem that taking too little for one's self is not usually characterised as an instance of injustice. In the case of judges, this solution is unavailable in any event. In the usual case, judges do not take for themselves when they do injustice.[60]

If justice does not fit the pattern of temperance, courage, and good temper, then what kind of disposition could justice be? Is justice a disposition or character trait of any kind? Bernard Williams suggests that the notion of a just outcome "is prior to that of a fair or just person. Such a person is one who is disposed to promote just distributions, look for them, stand by them, and so on" (1980, 196–97). "The disposition of justice," Williams continues, "will lead the just person to resist unjust distributions – and to resist them *however they are motivated*" (1980, 197, emphasis in original). On Williams's account, then, justice is a virtue, but it does not fit the pattern of the other moral virtues. Justice is not a mean with respect to a morally neutral emotion or desire; rather, justice, the virtue, is the disposition to aim at fairness (for a judge, to give the parties that which is due to them). The concept of a fair judicial decision, Williams would argue, exists prior to the virtue of justice.

Williams's picture of the virtue of justice poses an important problem for a virtue-centred theory of judging. If the concept of justice were prior to the virtue of justice, then it would follow that a normative theory of judging cannot be virtue centred. When we ask how judges should decide cases, it would seem that we ought to begin with a theory of what will count as a just outcome. We might then proceed to consider what methods of judging are most likely to lead to such outcomes. The virtues come in as means, but not as ends. The relationship between good judging and the general moral and intellectual virtues would only be contingent, depending on the empirical question as to whether such qualities as courage and temperance are, in fact, conducive to decision in accord with justice. The

---

[59] See Williams 1980.

[60] There are, however, unusual cases. As the discussion of the vice of judicial avarice reminds us, judges sometimes do "take for themselves" when they decide cases. This occurs when a judge takes a bribe or fails to disqualify herself from a case in which she has a financial stake.

virtue of justice in judging would be derived from one's theory of fairness, and not the other way around.

Of course, it might turn out that just decisions are not wholly independent of the virtues, even if they are prior to them. Thus, it might turn out that only someone with the right character will be good at devising just solutions to difficult problems or discerning the just outcome in a hard case. "But even there," Williams points out, "it is important that, although it took [a virtuous judge], or someone like [a virtuous judge], to think of it, the [decision] can then be recognised as fair independently of that person's character" (1980, 197). Moreover, it may turn out that only someone with the virtues will be capable of the disposition to promote just outcomes. That is, nothing in Williams's account precludes the possibility that disposition to do justice is simply not, as a matter of fact, consistent with possession of the vices of avarice, civic cowardice, bad temper, stupidity, and foolishness.[61] Using the terminology I introduced earlier, Williams can accept a thin theory of judicial virtue and might also accept a thick theory that identified particular virtues as instrumental to just decision making.

Hence, if we accept the centrality of justice for judging and Williams's view that theories of justice are prior to the virtue of justice, it would seem that we could not have a virtue-centred theory of judging. How can virtue jurisprudence answer Williams's challenge? My answer to Williams begins with a second look at the virtue of justice and its structure.

The Structure of Justice

If justice is the disposition to fairness (to give each their due), can we say anything more about this disposition? That is, can we say anything more particular about the question as to what qualities of character make up the virtue of justice, as the disposition to fairness? What constitutes a sense of fairness? What emotional and intellectual equipment disposes and enables a judge to be fair? Is "fairness" really a synonym for "justice," or is the relationship between justice, law, and fairness more complex?

Consider the quality that we might call "judicial impartiality," the disposition to even-handed sympathy or empathy with the parties to a legal dispute. Judges should not identify more strongly with one side than with the other;[62] a good judge must be able to understand the interests and the passions of all who appear before her. The degree of "partiality" or identification with the viewpoints and interests of the litigants that is appropriate to the role of judge is different from that which is appropriate to other situations. Parents should be partial to their children, and friends partial to

[61] To avoid confusion, I should note that I do not believe that the paragraph in the text is an answer to the challenge that William's argument poses for a virtue-centred theory of judging.
[62] "The judicial virtues are those that allow people to stand back from their personal commitments and projects and judge them from an impersonal point of view." Macedo 1990, 275.

one another. Judges should be partial to none, but should possess an appropriate degree of sympathy and empathy with all who appear before them.[63] A disposition to fairness is constituted in part by having the right sort of emotional equipment for sympathy, an appropriate, even-handed concern for the interests of others.

There is another quality that is closely connected with the disposition to do what is just. The good judge must have a special concern for fidelity to law and for the coherence of law. Let us call this "judicial integrity."[64] Why is this quality a component of the virtue of justice? Part of the answer lies in a complicated story about the relationship between law and justice. In a common-sense way, we can appreciate that there is a relationship. Assuming we live in a reasonably just society with good laws, then what people are due as a matter of fairness will, in the usual case, correspond to what the law gives them. Characteristically, there are two reasons for this correspondence. On the one hand, good laws meet standards of moral and political fairness. Fidelity to law is clearly a component of a disposition to fairness in such cases. On the other hand, decision according to law is fair because of the values we associate with the ideal of the rule of law. These values, which include legal regularity, publicity, and generality, would be threatened by departure from decision according to law. Even when a judge believes that a particular legal rule might be improved, the just decision will, in the usual case, require fidelity to law; a judge who does otherwise will create uncertainty and inconsistency. Moreover, the absence of such fidelity creates room for other defects (partiality, for example) to have a distorting influence on one's decisions.

Finally, a sense of justice requires the ability to perceive the salient features of particular situations. In the context of judging, we can use Karl Llewellyn's phrase *situation sense* or, by way of analogy to the phrase *moral vision*, we can say that a sense of justice requires "legal vision," the ability to size up a case and discern which aspects are legally important. This requires an intellectual grasp of the content of the law, an understanding of the underlying purposes the law serves, and an ability to pick out the features of particular cases that are important for those rules and purposes.[65] Because the virtue of justice requires legal vision, it is closely tied to the virtue of judicial wisdom.

---

[63] I do not mean to imply that judges may never be partial or that persons who do not occupy the judicial role should never be impartial. All of us, judges and non-judges alike, should be partial on the right occasions, towards the right persons, for the right reasons. Similarly, we all need the capacity and propensity for impartiality when the situation demands it.

[64] The virtue of judicial integrity expresses in virtue-jurisprudential terms many of the same aims as Dworkin's (1986) theory, "law as integrity."

[65] See Sherman 1989.

Justice and the Unity of the Virtues
Thus, we can discern at least three ingredients in the virtue of justice as it applies to judges: judicial impartiality, judicial integrity, and legal vision. Notice, however, that these ingredients do not combine like the various nuts in a party mix. Rather, the ingredients of the virtue of justice combine as do the ingredients of a cake. The whole is not simply the sum of its parts. Hence, sympathetic identification with the interests of litigants makes vivid the rule-of-law values of predictability and certainty that motivate the aspect of judicial integrity I have called fidelity to law. And fidelity to law is not even possible without legal vision, the ability to discern the legally relevant aspects of a particular case in terms of the purposes and values that animate the rules of law.

Although the virtue of justice can be analysed into component parts, the value of these components is only fully realised if they all are present together. This point about the unity of justice can be extended to the judicial virtues as a whole. Each judicial virtue requires all of the others, and the virtue of judicial wisdom (phronesis) plays a special unifying role. This point is expressed by the familiar formula that one can go right in only one way, but one can go wrong in many ways. The judicial virtues are complete only when they are all present together.

With this point at hand, I can now turn to a preliminary statement of a virtue-centred theory of judging.

D. What Is the Structure of a Virtue-Centred Theory of Judging?
For the sake of simplicity and clarity, I shall formulate a virtue-centred theory of judging in the form of five definitions:

- A *judicial virtue* is a naturally possible disposition of mind or will that when present with the other judicial virtues reliably disposes its possessor to make just decisions. The judicial virtues include but are not limited to temperance, courage, good temper, intelligence, wisdom, and justice.
- A *virtuous judge* is a judge who possesses the judicial virtues.
- A *virtuous decision* is a decision made by a virtuous judge acting from the judicial virtues in the circumstances that are relevant to the decision.
- A *lawful decision* is a decision that would characteristically be made by a virtuous judge in the circumstances that are relevant to the decision.[66]

---

[66] The distinction between virtuous and correct decisions is introduced to distinguish between a fully virtuous decision (made by a virtuous judge acting from the virtues) from a merely correct decision (made for the wrong reasons). In order to be legally correct, a decision need only be the decision a virtuous judge would have made under the circumstances. Thus, a legally correct decision could be made for vicious reasons. For example, a corrupt judge could accept a bribe to render the same decision that a virtuous judge would have made.

The phrase *legally correct* is synonymous with the word *lawful* in this context.
- *A just decision* is identical to a *virtuous decision*.

The central normative thesis of a virtue-centred theory of judging is that judges ought to be virtuous and to make virtuous decisions. Judges who lack the virtues should aim to make lawful or legally correct decisions, although they may not be able to do this reliably, given that they lack the virtues. Judges who lack the judicial virtues ought to develop them. Judges ought to be selected on the basis of their possession of (or potential for the acquisition of) the judicial virtues.

We can now return to Williams's thesis: *the notion of a just outcome is prior to and independent of the notion of the virtue of justice*. There is a sense in which a just decision may, under certain conditions, be recognised as just without reference to the virtues of the judge. In order to clarify this point, we need to sort out a variety of situations in which Williams's thesis holds true. We shall then be able to consider the cases in which Williams's thesis does not ring true.

The first context to consider we might call *easy cases*. Some decisions will obviously be just. Even persons who have incomplete legal knowledge or who have obtained only an incomplete degree of virtue will be able to recognise the justice of the decision. Even in easy cases, however, someone who is thoroughly blinded by self-interest might not concur in a widely shared judgement about what outcome is just.

There are cases where the justice of a decision is not so obvious as in easy cases. The second context might be called *complex cases*. When the law is complex, a high degree of legal intelligence may be required to recognise the legally correct result. When the facts are complex, other intellectual skills – for example, a highly developed situation sense – may be required to see what even relatively simple legal rules require. Thus, in complex cases, it may be the case that only someone with sufficient legal knowledge and in possession of a high degree of judicial virtue will be able to grasp fully which outcome is just and why this is so.[67] Although we might say that a just decision is independent of the virtue of the particular judge who made the decision, it is not the case that the justice of the decision is independent of judicial virtue. There are cases in which the just outcome can only be recognised by a virtuous judge.

In both easy cases and complex cases Williams could argue that the criteria for a legally correct decision are antecedent to the virtuous judge. In complex cases, it may take virtue to recognise these criteria, Williams

---

[67] In such cases, I am inclined to say that any virtuous person could be brought to see which result is just and why this is so, but the process of bringing about such an understanding may involve quite a lot of explanation.

can concede, but it is the legal rules and the facts that determine the legal correctness of outcomes. In the section that follows, I shall argue that there are cases in which Williams's thesis does not hold.

3. The Adequacy of a Virtue-Centred Account

Does virtue jurisprudence offer an adequate theory of judging? I shall answer this question with respect to two kinds of cases, illustrating both the way in which a virtue-centred theory of judging can capture the insights of its rivals and the way in which it might differ from them. The first sort of cases I shall call cases of "justice as lawfulness." These are cases in which the outcome required by the legal rules is in full accord with our sense of fairness. The second sort of cases I shall call cases of "justice as fairness."[68] Cases of justice as fairness involve the situation in which the outcome dictated by the rules of law alone is not consistent with our understanding of what is fair in a wider sense.

A. Justice as Lawfulness

Can a virtue-centred theory of judging offer an adequate normative account of cases, either easy or complex, in which the legal rules determine the lawful outcome? The answer is surely yes. For the most part, a virtue-centred theory of judging will be in accord both with common sense and with other normative theories of judging with respect to the question as to what constitutes the just outcome in such cases. The virtue of justice ordinarily requires decision in accord with the letter of the law.[69] Of course, the reasons offered by various normative theories of judging are likely to differ even in easy cases. Utilitarians will emphasise the good consequences that justify the rules and the bad consequences that would result if judges undermined the predictability and certainty created by the laws by failing to adhere to them. Deontologists might emphasise the rights that legal rules protect and the unfairness of failing to follow legal rules once they become a source of legitimate expectations.

The rivals of a virtue-centred theory of judging can agree on the idea that judges ought to possess the judicial virtues in so far as these are required for judges to follow the law reliably. No plausible normative theory of judging is inconsistent with a thin theory of the judicial virtues. No sensible theory would be indifferent to judges who are avaricious, cowardly, bad tempered, stupid, or foolish, and no sensible theory would claim we should not prefer temperate, courageous, good-tempered, intelligent, and wise judges. How, then, does a virtue-centred account differ from accounts that do not focus on the virtues?

---

[68] This locution is only coincident with "justice as fairness" in Rawls's (2001) sense.
[69] See Kraut 2002, 105–08, 117.

Virtue Is Required to Explain Decisions According to Legal Rules
Unlike other theories of judging, a virtue-centred theory makes the claim
that virtue is an ineliminable part of the explanation for and justification of
the practice of judging. According to a virtue-centred theory, the whole
story about what the rules of law require in particular cases includes the
virtues. If they were to be left out, the story would be incomplete.
Moreover, a virtue-centred theory suggests that it may require judicial
virtue to recognise the legally correct result. The rules do not apply themselves; judgement is always required for a general rule to be applied to a
particular case. Practical wisdom or good judgement is required to ensure
that the rules are applied correctly.

The necessity for practical wisdom in rule application can be discerned
by imagining an appellate judge and her interlocutor discussing the appellate review of a trial judge's finding of fact. "Why was the trial judge's
finding of fact clearly erroneous?" the interlocutor asks. "Because it was
not sufficiently supported by evidence on the record," answers the judge.
"Why do you conclude that the support was insufficient?" asks the interlocutor. "Because a reasonable finder of fact could not move from that
evidence to the conclusions that judge drew," answers the judge. "But why
couldn't a reasonable finder of fact make the necessary inferences?" asks
the interlocutor. Imagine that the interlocutor responds to each explanation
with a demand for definite criteria for application of the clearly erroneous
standard. At some point the answers must stop. If the questioner were still
unsatisfied, the judge would be forced to explain her lack of further justifications by saying, "Because that's the way I see it, and I am a competent
judge. I cannot say any more than that." Explanations must come to an end
somewhere.[70] The clearly erroneous rule provides a particularly perspicuous example of the bottom-line role of practical judgement in rule application, because it is widely acknowledged that no criteria can be provided
for sorting errors that are clear from those that are not.[71]

In the end, agreement and disagreement about what rules mean and how
they are applied are rooted in practical judgements. Even with respect to
some easy cases, and more frequently with respect to complex cases, articulated reasons will not suffice to explain why, in cases of bottom-line
disagreement about the application of a rule to the facts, one judgement is
legally correct and competing judgements are not.

[70] See Wittgenstein 1968, §1.
[71] See *United States v. Aluminium Company of America* (1945, 433) (opinion by Learned
Hand, J., stating, "It is idle to try to define the meaning of the phrase 'clearly erroneous'; all
that can be profitably said is that an appellate court, though it will hesitate less to reverse the
finding of a judge than that of an administrative tribunal or of a jury, will nevertheless
reverse it most reluctantly and only when well persuaded"); see also Cooper 1988. A virtue-
centred theory also accounts for the observation that the clearly erroneous rule is applied
with an eye to the virtues of the trial-court judge. See James and Hazard (198), §12.8, 668):
"[A]n appellate court's inclination to accept a trial judge's findings depends . . . on the
court's unstated degree of confidence in the trial judge's fair-mindedness."

Indeed, a virtue-centred account allows us to appreciate the fact that explanations or justifications of legal decisions play more than one role. In some cases, when a judge explains a decision, the intention is to lay bare the premises and reasoning that moved the judge from accepted premises about the law and the facts to some conclusion about what result is legally correct. There are other cases, however, where explanations play a different role. When the decision of a case is based on legal vision or situation sense – that is, when the decision is based on the virtue of judicial wisdom, or phronesis – then the point of an explanation is to enable others to come to see the relevant features of the case. Such explanations do not recreate a decision procedure; rather, they are aimed at enabling others to acquire practical wisdom.

Thus, Bernard Williams's (1980) claim that the notion of a just decision "is prior to that of a fair or just person" is at best partially correct. Even when judges simply apply the rules to the facts, the notion of a just decision cannot be untangled from the notion of a virtuous judge grasping the salient features of the case. Virtue, in particular the virtue of phronesis, or judicial wisdom, is a central and ineliminable part of the story.

A Virtue-Centred Account of Lawful Judicial Disagreement
At this point one could object that a virtue-centred account fails for a different reason. It might be argued that a virtue-centred account requires that two inconsistent outcomes in the very same case could both be legally correct.[72] As we shall see, this apparent objection to a virtue-centred theory of judging actually illuminates one of its greatest strengths. A virtue-centred theory allows us to account for the fact that there are frequently cases in which more than one outcome would count as legally correct.

The objection begins with a premise that we shall call *the multiplicity of virtuous decisions*. The core idea of this premise is quite simple: there are cases in which different virtuous judges would make different decisions with respect to a given issue and a given set of facts. The second premise we shall call *the uniqueness of legally correct decisions*. The idea of this premise is that, given a particular issue and a given set of facts, only one decision of the issue can be legally correct. Call the claim that a decision is legally correct if and only if it is the decision that would be made by a virtuous judge under the relevant circumstances *the identity of virtue and legality*. The shape of the argument should now be clear. From the uniqueness of legally correct decisions and the multiplicity of virtuous decisions it would seem to follow that some virtuous decisions are incorrect. If these premises are true, it follows that the identity of virtue and legality is false.

The first premise, the multiplicity of virtuous decisions, asserts that two

---

[72] I am grateful to Phillip Pullman for his forceful presentation of this objection and to Linda Zagzebski for her assistance in working out the answer that is presented here.

different virtuous judges could reach different decisions in the same case. This claim seems plausible. Different virtuous judges are likely to differ in ways that might affect their decisions. They will have different experiences and beliefs, and those differences could easily affect the decision on a variety of legal issues. The multiplicity of virtuous decisions seems especially likely in so-called hard cases, in which there are good legal arguments on both sides of the issue.[73]

However, the second premise, the uniqueness of legally correct decisions, is false. There are a variety of situations in which more than one outcome is legally correct. This is true for a variety of reasons. First, it is sometimes the case that the pre-existing legal rules underdetermine the outcome of a particular case.[74] In the United States, a frequent pattern involves the situation where an issue of law has been resolved differently by different circuits of the United States Court of Appeal. This phenomenon is called a "circuit split." Unless the Supreme Court resolves the split, inconsistent results can be correct in different circuits. In a circuit that has not decided the issue, two different trial judges can reach different outcomes and neither judge has rendered a decision that is legally incorrect. In this first sort of case, however, one might argue that there is a sense in which the inconsistent decisions are only correct provisionally or temporarily. If the Supreme Court resolves the split, then one line of cases is approved and the inconsistent line becomes "bad law."

Of course, there are times when a circuit split is best explained as a competition between a correct line of authority and another position that is badly reasoned or that ignores relevant authority. But there are other times when both results are plausible. Because the Supreme Court leaves many circuit splits unresolved (for years, decades, or even permanently), the best description of the situation is that two inconsistent positions on the same issue of law are both correct; neither line of authority can be said to be bad law.

Second, it is sometimes the case that the law itself commits a decision to the discretion of the judge. A paradigm case of such discretion can be found in the power of trial judges to manage the mechanics of a trial. Trial-court judges have discretion to decide how long a trial will last, how many

---

[73] Although I concede the multiplicity of virtuous decisions, I should note that this premise might be attacked in a variety of ways. For example, we might argue that although different partially virtuous judges might decide the same issue in the same case differently, only one decision could and would be made by the fully virtuous judge. Put another way, we might say that the various decisions made by different judges who possess the virtues to different degrees converge on a single decision as the degree of virtue increases. This picture may fit some kinds of issues and cases, but I shall demonstrate that there are issues and cases that do not fit into the picture of increasing virtue converging on a unique outcome.

[74] See Solum 1987 (distinguishing indeterminate from underdeterminate). This assertion is, of course, controversial. I have not here addressed the important and persuasive arguments made by Ronald Dworkin (1985).

witnesses each side can present, and how long the examination of a witness will be permitted to take. If a virtuous judge makes such a decision, then it is legally correct, even though another virtuous judge would have made a different decision. If, however, the decision was the product of judicial vice – for example, it was a product of corruption – then the decision is in error – even though the very same decision would have been legally correct if it had been the product of virtue rather than vice. The law of procedure captures this phenomenon in the standard of appellate review for discretionary decisions. The relevant standard is called "abuse of discretion," and given an abuse-of-discretion standard it is settled law that inconsistent decisions of the same issue on identical legally relevant facts can both be legally correct.[75]

Moreover, some legal standards sanction more than one legally correct outcome on a particular set of facts. A clear example of this is the "best interests of the child" standard in child-custody disputes. Although formulated as a rule of law, this legal standard requires the application of practical judgement to a particular fact situation. As a consequence, an appellate court will affirm a trial court's decision to award custody, even when the appellate judges would have made a different decision.[76] In such a case, each of two inconsistent decisions (awarding primary custody to one parent versus the other) can be legally correct. Although "best" is superlative and therefore suggests a unique outcome, the best-interests-of-the-child standard is understood by courts to permit a multiplicity of outcomes in the large range of cases in which both parents have good claims that they would provide the best for the child.

A virtue-centred theory of judging explains and justifies this feature of our judicial practice. There are circumstances in which two or more different (and in one sense "inconsistent") outcomes are legally correct. A virtue-centred theory explains this on the grounds that two different virtuous judges could each make different decisions, even though each was acting from the virtues. In cases in which the judge was not acting from virtue but was acting from vicious motives, such as corruption, wilful disregard of the law, or bias, then a discretionary decision may be legally incorrect – even though the very same outcome would have been acceptable if the decision had been made by a virtuous judge.

B. The Virtue of Equity

The distinctive contribution of a virtue-centred theory is even clearer in the second category of cases, those in which the result required by the legal

---

[75] See, e.g., *Jones v. Strayhorn* 1959: "The mere fact or circumstance that a trial judge may decide a matter within his discretionary authority in a manner different from what an appellate judge would decide if placed in a similar circumstance does not demonstrate that an abuse of discretion has occurred."

[76] See *Ford v. Ford* 2002 (indicating that a difference of judgement does not justify reversal of a child-custody decision absent "abuse of discretion").

rule is inconsistent with our notion of what is fair. In these cases, a virtue-centred theory suggests that the virtuous decision is guided by the virtue of equity, or justice as fairness, distinguished from justice as lawfulness.[77]

The notion of equity as departure from the rules is rooted in Aristotle, and the best place to begin an exposition is with Aristotle's statement of the problem of equity and justice:

> What causes the difficulty is the fact that equity is just, but not what is legally just: it is a rectification of legal justice. The explanation of this is that all law is universal, and there are some things about which it is not possible to pronounce rightly in general terms; therefore in cases where it is necessary to make a general pronouncement, but impossible to do so rightly, the law takes account of the majority of cases, though not unaware that in this way errors are made. And the law is nonetheless right; because the error lies not in the law nor in the legislator but in the nature of the case; for the raw material of human behaviour is essentially of this kind. (Aristotle 1976, 1137b9–1137b24)

This is the core of Aristotle's view of *epieikeia*, usually translated as "equity" or "fair-mindedness." As is frequently the case with Aristotle, the text is ambiguous. Aristotle and his contemporary expositors[78] inform my account of equity, but I do not claim that my interpretation is Aristotle's own view.

One characteristic of equity is that it involves a departure from the rules. Any general rule may be overinclusive or underinclusive with respect to the goal the rule is meant to achieve.[79] Equity corrects the law's generality by making exceptions in cases in which the rule leads to unanticipated and unjust results. An equitable departure from the rules can relate to the intentions of legislators in two distinct ways. In some cases, doing equity requires the judge to realise the intention of the legislature. In other cases, it may require the judge to correct a defect in the law that the legislator did not or could not have anticipated – for example, in cases in which circumstances have changed or previously unknown facts have come to light.

A second characteristic of equity is its particularism. Equity tailors the . law to the requirements of the particular case. Understanding equity as a particularised practice allows us to distinguish it from other practices that involve a departure from legal rules. For example, equity is not identical to the resolution of conflicts between law and morality in favour of the latter. Judges might nullify a statute that legalised the practice of human slavery on the grounds that slavery is always morally wrong. This is not an example of the practice of equity, because such a decision would not involve a departure from the rule on the basis of the facts of the *particular*

---

[77] See Shiner 1994.
[78] See Shiner 1994; Kraut 2002, 108–11.
[79] See Schauer 1991.

case. Rather, the decision would be based on a general moral principle – for example, that wicked or immoral statutes should not be enforced.

Equity is the tailoring of the law to the demands of the particular situation. For this reason, equity can (or should) be done only by a *phronimos*, a judge with moral and legal vision. Only a virtuous judge can do equity. Putting the point a bit differently, we could say that "equity," the practice, should only be done by judges who possess "equity," the virtue. As Roger Shiner (1994, 1260–61) puts it: "Equity is the virtue shown by one particular kind of agent – a judge – when making practical judgements in the face of the limitations of one particular kind of practical rule – those hardened customs and written laws that constitute for some societies the institutionalised system of norms that is its legal system."

A virtue-centred theory of judging offers a distinctive approach to cases that involve considerations of equity. Here is one way to put it. Other normative theories of judging have difficulty explaining why there should be a distinctive practice of equity. If an exception ought to be made to a legal rule, then amend the rule. (This is the approach favoured by theories of statutory interpretation that require strict adherence to plain meaning.) Of course, sometimes rules should be amended, but a virtue-centred theory of judging stakes out the claim that there will always be cases in which the problem is not that the rule was not given its optimal formulation. Rather, the problem is that the infinite variety and complexity of particular fact situations outruns our capacity to formulate general rules. The solution is not to attempt to write the ultimate code, with particular provisions to handle every possible factual variation. No matter how long and detailed, no matter how many exceptions, and exceptions to exceptions, the code could not be long enough.[80] Rather, the solution is to entrust decision to virtuous judges who can craft a decision to fit the particular case.

No thin theory of judicial virtue can incorporate the virtue of equity. Indeed, I shall stake the claim that only a virtue-centred theory offers a fully adequate explanation of equity.[81] But Aristotle is right about rules; no set of rules can do justice in every case. Thus, I believe that the argument of this essay provides grounds for the following claim: Virtue jurisprudence offers a normative and explanatory theory of judging that explains and justifies the practice of equity, but many other theories of law stumble at precisely this point.

---

[80] Even if the code could be long enough, it would not be a good idea to make it "complete," when by "complete" we mean the code is sufficiently particularistic as to provide, in theory, a guide to decision making in every possible case. The complete code would be so long and so complex that it would be of no practical use as a guide to decision. Cf. Solum 1993, 324–27 (arguing for analogous thesis in context of notion of a complete contract).

[81] Of course, a defence of this claim requires an examination of all the alternative normative theories of judging. Because this task goes beyond the scope of this essay, I can only offer a promissory note on this occasion.

4. Conclusion

This essay has examined one component of virtue jurisprudence, a virtue-centred theory of judging. Its aim has been to clarify the sense in which a theory of judging may be said to be virtue centred and to argue that a virtue-centred theory is plausible. The advantages of a virtue-centred account have been illustrated in two contexts. Where justice requires a decision that accords with the legal rules, a virtue-centred theory accords with common sense but explains both the role of practical judgement in rule application and the phenomenon of legal disagreement. Where justice requires a departure from the rules, a virtue-centred theory explains and justifies the practice of equity. Virtue jurisprudence does the work we hope a theory of judging can do.

Loyola Law School
919 S. Albany St.
Los Angeles, CA 90015
USA
Lawrence.Solum@lls.edu

Acknowledgments

I am grateful to Sharon Lloyd and Roger Shiner for their comments on "Should Judges Be Virtuous?" an earlier and substantially different version of this essay, presented at the Pacific Division of the American Philosophical Association on 27 March 1998. I also owe thanks to the participants in the Southern California Law and Philosophy Discussion Group for comments on a draft presented on 13 February 2002. I am especially grateful to Antony Duff for the comments he presented at the Stirling Conference on 3 March 2002. On that occasion, I received valuable comments too from Linda Zagzebski and Phillip Pullman. I have also benefited from numerous comments on my previous work on virtue jurisprudence: in this regard, I owe special thanks to Steven Burton, Kent Greenawalt, Stephen Macedo, Richard Posner, Frederick Schauer, and Ian Shapiro.

References

Aaronson, Mark Neal. 1995. "Be Just to One Another: Preliminary Thoughts on Civility, Moral Character, and Professionalism." *St. Thomas Law Review* 8: 113ff.
———. 1998. "We Ask You To Consider: Learning About Practical Judgement In Lawyering." *Clinical Law Review* 4: 247ff.
Anscombe, Elizabeth. 1997. "Modern Moral Philosophy." In *Virtue Ethics: Oxford Readings in Philosophy*, edited by Roger Crisp and Michael Slote, 26–44. Oxford: Oxford University Press.

Araujo, Robert J. 1994. "Moral Issues and the Virtuous Judge: Reflections on the Nomination and Confirmation of Supreme Court Justices." *Catholic Lawyer* 35: 311ff.

————. 1997. "The Virtuous Lawyer: Paradigm and Possibility." *SMU Law Review* 50: 433ff.

————. 2002. "Justice as Right Relationship: A Philosophical and Theological Reflection on Affirmative Action." *Pepperdine Law Review* 27: 377ff.

Aristotle. 1976. *The Ethics of Aristotle: The Nicomachean Ethics*, translated by J. A. K. Thomson, revised by Hugh Tredennick. London: Penguin.

Bainbridge, Stephen M. 1997. "Community and Statism: A Conservative Contractarian Critique of Progressive Corporate Law Scholarship." *Cornell Law Review* 82: 856ff.

Baker, C. Edwin. 1985. "Sandel on Rawls." *U. Pa. Law Review* 133: 895ff.

Baldwin, Dick. 1997. "Lawyers, Justice & Money." *Oregon State Business Bulletin* (October): 58ff.

Barnett, Randy. 1998. *The Structure of Liberty*. Oxford: Oxford University Press.

Beck-Dudley, Caryn L. 1996. "No More Quandries: A Look at Virtue Through the Eyes of Robert Solomon." *American Business Law Journal* 34: 117ff.

Bentham, Jeremy. 1988. *A Fragment on Government*, edited by J. H. Burns, Ross Harrison, and Herbert L. Hart. Cambridge: Cambridge University Press.

————. 1996. *An Introduction to the Principles of Morals and Legislation*, edited by J. H. Burns, Herbert L. Hart, and J. Rosen, Cambridge: Cambridge University Press.

Bricker, David C. 1999. "A Kantian Argument for Native American Cultural Survival." *U. of Detroit Mercy Law Review* 76: 789ff.

Broadie, Sarah. 1991. *Ethics with Aristotle*. Oxford: Oxford University Press.

Brosnan, Donald F. 1989. "Virtue Ethics in a Perfectionist Theory of Law and Justice." *Cardozo Law Review* 11: 335ff.

Byrne, Donna M. 1995. "Progressive Taxation Revisited." *Arizona Law Review* 37: 739ff.

Carens, Joseph H. 1987. "Aliens and Citizens: The Case for Open Borders." *Review of Policy* 49: 251ff.

Cochran, Robert F. 1996. "Lawyers and Virtues." *Notre Dame Law Review* 71: 707ff.

————. 1998. "Crime, Confession, and the Counselor-At-Law: Lessons From Dostoyevsky." *Houston Law Review* 35: 327ff.

————. 2000. "Professionalism in the Postmodern Age: Its Death, Attempts at Resuscitation, and Alternate Sources of Virtue." *Notre Dame Journal of Law Ethics and Public Policy* 214: 305ff.

Cooper, Edward H. 1988. "Civil Rule 50(A): Rationing and Rationalizing the Resources of Appellate Review." *Notre Dame Law Review* 63: 645ff.

Crisp, Roger, editor. 1996. *How Should One Live?: Essays on the Virtues*. Oxford: Clarendon Press.

Crisp, Roger, and Michael Slote, editors. 1997. *Virtue Ethics: Oxford Readings in Philosophy*. Oxford: Oxford University Press.

Dickson, Julie. 2001. *Evaluation and Legal Theory*. Oxford: Hart Publishing.

Dworkin, Ronald. 1978. "Hard Cases." In *Taking Rights Seriously*, 81ff. London: Duckworth.

———. 1985. "Is There Really No Right Answer in Hard Cases?" In *A Matter of Principle*, 119–44. Cambridge, Mass.: Harvard University Press.

———. 1986. *Law's Empire*. Oxford: Hart Publishing.

Engberg-Pedersen, Troels. 1983. *Aristotle's Theory of Moral Insight*. Louisville, Ky.: Westminster/John Knox Press.

Fairweather, Abrol, and Linda Zagzebski, editors. 2001. *Virtue Epistemology: Essays on Epistemic Virtue and Responsibility*. Oxford: Oxford University Press.

Farber, Daniel A. 1991. "The Inevitability of Practical Reason: Statutes, Formalism, and the Rule of Law." *Vanderbilt Law Review* 45: 533ff.

Feldman, Heidi Li. 1996. "Codes and Virtues: Can Good Lawyers Be Good Ethical Deliberators?" *Southern California Law Review* 69: 885ff.

———. 1999. "Beyond the Model Rules: The Place of Examples in Legal Ethics." *Georgetown Journal of Legal Ethics* 12: 409ff.

———. 2000. "Prudence, Benevolence, and Negligence: Virtue Ethics and Tort Law." *Chicago-Kent Law Review* 74: 1431ff.

Fleming, James E. 2000. "The Parsimony of Libertarianism." *Constitutional Commentary* 17: 171ff.

Foot, Philippa. 1978. *Virtues and Vices*. Oxford: Clarendon Press.

———. *Natural Goodness*. Oxford: Clarendon Press.

Forbath, William E. 2001. "Constitutional Welfare Rights: A History, Critique, and Reconstruction." *Fordham Law Review* 69: 1821ff.

Ford v. Ford. 2002. 68 Conn. App. 173, 187, 789.

Gaba, Jeffrey. 1999a. "Environmental Ethics and Our Moral Relationship to Future Generations: Future Rights and Present Value." *Columbia Journal of Environmental Law* 24: 249ff.

———. 1999b. "Environmental Ethics and Our Moral Relationship to Future Generations: Future Rights and Present Virtue." *Columbia Journal of Environmental Law* 24: 249ff.

Galston, Miriam. 1994. "Taking Aristotle Seriously: Republican-Oriented Legal Theory and the Moral Foundation of Deliberative Democracy." *California Law Review* 82: 329ff.

Garcia, Frank J. 2000. "Trade and Inequality: Economic Justice and the Developing World." *Michigan Journal of International Law* 21: 975ff.

Garcia, J. L. A. 2001. "Topics in the New Natural Law Theory." *American Journal of Jurisprudence* 46: 51ff.

Gentile v. State Bar of Nevada. 1991. 111 S. Ct. 2720.

George, Robert P. 1995. *Making Men Moral: Civil Liberties and Public Morality.* Oxford: Clarendon Press.

Glendon, Mary Ann. 1994. *A Nation Under Lawyers: How the Crisis in the Legal Profession IS Transforming American Society.* Cambridge, Mass: Harvard University Press.

Gordon, Wendy J. 1989. "An Inquiry into the Merits of Copyright: The Challenges of Consistency, Consent, and Encouragement Theory." *Stanford Law Review* 41: 1343ff.

Haemmerli, Alice, 1999. "Whose Who? The Case for a Kantian Right of Publicity." *Duke Law Journal* 49: 383ff.

Hardie, W. F. R. 1980. *Aristotle's Ethical Theory.* Oxford: Oxford University Press.

Harsch, Bradley A. 1999. "Consumerism and Environmental Policy: Moving Past Consumer Culture." *Ecology Law Quarterly* 26: 543ff.

Henry, Rebecca S. 1999. "The Virtue in Discretion: Ethics, Justice, and Why Judges Must Be 'Students of the Soul.'" *New York University Review of Law & Social Change* 25: 65ff.

Herman, Barbara. 1988. "Comment on Gavison." *Southern California Law Review* 61: 1663ff.

Heyman, Steven J. 1992. "Aristotle on Political Justice." *Iowa Law Review* 77: 851ff.

Hirschman, Linda R. 1990. "The Virtue of Liberality in American Communal Life." *Michigan Law Review* 88: 983ff.

———. 1992. "The Book of 'A.'" *Texas Law Review* 70: 971ff.

———. 1993. "Nobody in Here but Us Chickens: Legal Education and the Virtues of the Ruler." *Stanford Law Review* 45: 1905ff.

Horvitz, Ellis J. 1997. "Otto Kaus Remembered." *Loyola of Los Angeles Law Review* 30: 961ff.

Housman, Robert F. 1992. "Kantian Approach to Trade and the Environment." 49 *Washington and Lee Law Review* 49: 1373ff.

Hudson, Walter M. 1999. "Book Review, Obeying Orders: Atrocity, Military Discipline, and the Law of War." *Military Law Review* 161: 225ff.

Huigens, Kyron. 1995. "Virtue and Inculpation." *Harvard Law Review* 108: 1423ff.

———. 1998. "Virtue and Criminal Negligence." *Buffalo Criminal Law Review* 1: 431ff.

———. 2000a. "The Dead End of Deterrence, and Beyond." *William and Mary Law Review* 41: 943ff.

———. 2000b. "Rethinking the Penalty Phase." *Arizona State Law Journal* 32: 1195ff.

————. 2002. "Solving the Apprendi Puzzle." *Georgetown Law Journal* 90: 387ff.

Hursthouse, Rosalind. 1999. *On Virtue Ethics*. Oxford: Oxford University Press.

Jackson, Thomas H. 1986. *The Logic and Limits of Bankruptcy Law*. Cambridge, Mass.: Beard Books.

James, Fleming, and Geoffrey Hazard. 1985. *Civil Procedure*. Boston: Little, Brown.

Jones v. Strayhorn. 1959. 159 Tex. 421, 321 S.W. 290.

Kaplow, Louis, and Stephen Shavell. 2002. *Fairness Versus Welfare*. Cambridge, Mass.: Harvard University Press.

Kleinwort Benson Ltd. Appellant v. Lincoln City Council Same Respondent. 1999. 2 A.C. 349.

Kraut, Richard. 1989. *Aristotle on the Human Good*. Princeton: Princeton University Press.

————. 2002. *Aristotle: Political Philosophy*. Oxford: Clarendon Press.

Kronman, Anthony T. 1993. *The Lost Lawyer: Failing Ideals of the Legal Profession*. Cambridge, Mass.: Harvard University Press.

Lillich, Richard B. 1997. "Kant and the Current Debate Over Humanitarian Intervention." *Journal Transnational Law and Policy* 6: 397.

Llewellyn, Karl. 1960. *The Common-Law Tradition*. Boston: Little, Brown.

Luban, David. 1992. "Justice Holmes and Judicial Virtue." *Nomos* 34: 235ff.

Macedo, Stephen. 1990. *Liberal Virtues*. Oxford: Clarendon Press.

MacIntyre, Alasdair. 1984. *After Virtue: A Study in Moral Theory*. London: Duckworth.

Maitland, F. W. 1898. "A Prologue to a History of English Law." *Law Quarterly Review* 14: 13ff.

Modak-Truran, Mark C. 2000. "Corrective Justice and the Revival of Judicial Virtue." *Yale Journal of Law and Humanities* 12: 249ff.

Muller, Eric L. 1993. "The Virtue of Mercy in Criminal Sentencing." *Seton Hall Law Review* 24: 288ff.

National Commission on Judicial Discipline and Removal. 1993. *Report*. Washington, D.C.: Government Printing Office.

Nesteruk, Jeffrey. 1996a. "Law, Virtue, and the Corporation." *American Business Law Journal* 33: 473ff.

————. 1996b. "The Moral Dynamics of Law in Business." *American Business Law Journal* 34: 133ff.

Nozick, Robert. 1977. *Anarchy, State, and Utopia*. Oxford: Basil Blackwell.

Osiel, Mark J. 1998. "Obeying Orders: Atrocity, Military Discipline, and the Law of War." *California Law Review* 86: 939ff.

Pears, David. 1980. "Courage as a Mean." In *Essays on Aristotle's Ethics*, edited by A. O. Rorty, 171ff. Berkeley: University of California Press.

Perkins, James W. 1998. "Virtues and the Lawyer." *Catholic Lawyer* 38: 185ff.

Pinkard, Terry. 1992. "Judicial Virtue and Democratic Politics." *Nomos* 34: 265ff.

Quinn, Kevin P. 2000. "Viewing Health Care as a Common Good: Looking Beyond Political Liberalism." *Southern California Law Review* 73: 277ff.

Rawls, John. 1951. "Outline of a Decision Procedure for Ethics." *Philosophical Review* 60: 177ff.

———. 1999. *A Theory of Justice*. Cambridge, Mass.: Harvard University Press.

———. 2001. *Justice as Fairness: A Restatement*. Cambridge, Mass.: Harvard University Press.

Resnick, Judith. 1982. "Managerial Judges." *Harvard Law Review* 96: 374ff.

Robertson, Elbert L. 2000. "A Corrective Justice Theory of Antitrust Regulation." *Catholic U. Law Review* 49: 741ff.

Rorty, A. O., editor. 1980. *Essays on Aristotle's Ethics*. Berkeley: University of California Press.

Sandel, Michael J. 1988. *Liberalism and the Limits of Justice*. Cambridge: Cambridge University Press.

Scharffs, Brett G. 2001. "Law as Craft." *Vanderbilt Law Review* 54: 2245ff.

Schauer, Frederick. 1991. *Playing by the Rules: A Philosophical Examination of Rule-Based Decision-Making in Law and Life*. Oxford: Clarendon Press.

———. 1996. "Positivism as Pariah." In *The Autonomy of Law: Essays on Legal Positivism*, edited by Robert P. George. Oxford: Clarendon Press.

Schroeder, Christopher H. 1986. "Rights Against Risks." *Columbia Law Review* 86: 495ff.

Shaffer, Thomas L. 1993. "The Legal Profession's Rule Against Vouching for Clients: Advocacy and 'The Manner That Is The Man Himself.'" *Notre Dame Journal of Law, Ethics and Public Policy* 7: 145ff.

Sherman, Nancy. 1989. *The Fabric of Character*. Oxford: Clarendon Press.

Shiner, Roger. 1994. "Aristotle's Theory of Equity." *Loyola of Los Angeles Law Review* 27: 1245ff.

Simon, Maria. 1994. "Bribery and Other Not So 'Good Behaviour': Criminal Prosecution as a Supplement to Impeachment of Federal Judges." *Columbia Law Review* 94: 1617ff.

Simons, Kenneth W. 2001. "The Hand Formula in the Draft Restatement (Third) of Torts: Encompassing Fairness as Well as Efficiency Values." *Vanderbilt Law Review* 54: 901ff.

Smith, Abbe, and William Montross. 1999. "The Calling of Criminal Defence." *Mercer Law Review* 50: 443ff., esp. 511–33.

Solum, Lawrence B. 1987. "On the Indeterminacy Crisis: Critiquing Critical Dogma." *U. of Chicago Law Review* 54: 462ff.

―――. 1988. "The Virtues and Vices of a Judge: An Aristotelian Guide to Judicial Selection." *Southern California Law Review* 1730.

―――. 1990. "Virtues and Voices." *Chicago-Kent Law Review* 66: 111ff.

―――. 1991. "What Remains of Freedom of Speech for Lawyers after Gentile?" *California Litigation* (November): 16ff.

―――. 1993. "The Boundaries of Legal Discourse and the Debate over Default Rules in Contract." *Southern California Multidisciplinary Law Review* 3: 311ff.

―――. 1994a. "Equity and the Rule of Law." *Nomos* 34: 120ff.

―――. 1994b. "Situating Political Liberalism." *Chicago-Kent Law Review* 69: 549ff.

―――. 1999. "The Foundations of Liberty." *Michigan Law Review* 97: 1781ff.

Statman, Daniel, editor. 1997. *Virtue Ethics: A Critical Reader*. Edinburgh: Edinburgh University Press.

Strudler, Alan, and Eric W. Orts. 1999. "Moral Principle in the Law of Insider Trading." *Texas Law Review* 78: 375ff.

Sulentic, Alison M. 2001. "Happiness and ERISA: Reflections on the Lessons of Aristotle's Nicomachean Ethics for Sponsors of Employee Benefit Plans." *Employee Rights and Employment Policy Journal* 5: 7ff.

Symposium on Kantian Legal Theory. 1987. *Columbia Law Review* 87: 421ff.

Transworld Airlines v. American Coupon Exchange. 1990. 913 F.2d 676.

Tremblay, Paul R. 1999a. "Acting 'A Very Moral Type of God': Triage Among Poor Clients." *Fordham Law Review* 67: 2475ff.

―――. 1999b. "The New Casuistry." *Georgetown Journal of Legal Ethics* 12: 489ff.

Twining, William. 1973. *Karl Llewellyn and the Realist Movement*. Norman: University of Oklahoma Press.

United States v. Aluminium Company of America. 1945. 148 F.2d 416.

Waldron, Jeremy. 1999. *The Dignity of Legislation*, 189ff. Cambridge: Cambridge University Press.

Williams, Bernard. 1980. "Justice as a Virtue." In *Essays on Aristotle's Ethics,* edited by A. O. Rorty. Berkeley: University of California Press.

Wittgenstein, Ludwig. 1968. *Philosophical Investigations*, translated by G. E. M. Anscombe. Oxford: Basil Blackwell.

Wright, R. George. 2002. "Treating Persons as Ends in Themselves: The Legal Implications of a Kantian Principle." *University of Richmond Law Review* 36: 271ff.

Younger v. Smith. 1973. 30 Cal. App. 3d 138, 106 Cal. Rptr. 225.

Zagzebski, Linda. 1996. *Virtues of the Mind: An Inquiry into the Nature of Virtue and the Ethical Foundations of Knowledge*. Cambridge: Cambridge University Press.

© Metaphilosophy LLC and Blackwell Publishing Ltd. 2003.
Published by Blackwell Publishing, 9600 Garsington Road, Oxford OX4 2DQ, UK and
350 Main Street, Malden, MA 02148, USA
METAPHILOSOPHY
Vol. 34, Nos. 1/2, January 2003
0026–1068

THE LIMITS OF VIRTUE JURISPRUDENCE

R. A. DUFF

ABSTRACT: In response to Lawrence Solum's advocacy of a 'virtue-centred theory of judging', I argue that there is indeed important work to be done in identifying and characterising those qualities of character that constitute judicial virtues – those qualities that a person needs if she is to judge well (though I criticise Solum's account of one of the five pairs of judicial vices and virtues that he identifies – avarice and temperance). However, Solum's more ambitious claims – that a judge's vice necessarily corrupts her decisions, and that in at least some contexts we must define a legally correct decision as one that would be reached by a virtuous judge – should be rejected: we can undermine the former by attending to the requirements of due process, and the latter by attending to the ways in which a judge would try to justify her decision.

1. 'Virtue Jurisprudence'

The rise of 'virtue jurisprudence' is one of the more striking features of legal philosophy during the past decade or so, since it seems so radically at odds with the kind of liberalism that became almost an orthodoxy in the 1960s. According to that orthodoxy, the law had no proper interest in virtue and vice, in particular in the virtue and vice of its citizens. It had a proper interest in their conduct, in so far as that affected the significant interests of others, and in their responsibility for such conduct – a responsibility that depended, on the prevalent and roughly Kantian view, on their capacity to control their conduct through their choices as rational beings: but the deeper character traits that lay behind such overt conduct, the moral condition of the citizens' souls, was not the law's business. This reflected the neutralism that characterised the then dominant strands of liberalism: the state and its laws should not favour or seek to impose any single conception of the good, but it had to leave citizens free to determine and pursue their own conceptions of the good, so long as they respected the rights of others. The orthodoxy also reflected a strong conception of the 'private': conduct that impinged on the world and on the interests of others was a 'public' matter that could properly concern the law; moral beliefs and moral character, by contrast, were 'private' matters that concerned only those others with whom the citizen chose to enter into relationships more intimate than that of citizenship. The task of the law was to keep the peace and preserve the social structures of expectation and conduct within which individuals could pursue their own conceptions of the good; its job was not to make us moral or to attend to the condition of our souls.

Against that background, some of the claims of virtue jurisprudence will seem both novel and disturbing, in particular the claim that "the aim of law is to make citizens virtuous," or "to promote the greater good of humanity . . . by promoting virtue."[1] The antennae of traditional liberals will quiver at the suggestion that this is any part of the law's proper aim: they might be uncomfortably reminded of Stephen's (in)famous dictum that "criminal law is in the nature of a persecution of the grosser forms of vice" (1967, 152) and see in the rise of such virtue jurisprudence a manifestation of the more illiberal and oppressive aspects of communitarianism. Even those who have more sympathy with some species of communitarianism, or 'perfectionist' liberals who deny that the law can or should be wholly neutral between competing conceptions of the good,[2] may be disturbed by the thought that the law might make the promotion of virtue, and in consequence the elimination of vice, part of its aim: we surely should not trust so crude and potentially oppressive a mechanism as the law to discharge so sensitive a task.

Such fears about virtue jurisprudence are, however, aroused by the suggestion that the law should take an interest in its *citizens'* virtues and vices; but that is not Solum's suggestion in his essay. His concern is rather with the virtues of *judges* and with the fruitfulness of "a virtue-centred theory of judging" (179), and it might seem that no-one, however traditionally liberal their outlook, could object to this aspect of virtue jurisprudence: we must, surely, want our judges to have the appropriate judicial virtues; a judge who exhibits judicial vices in her judicial activities is for that reason a bad judge who merits our censure and, if she cannot be reformed, dismissal from her post.

All of that is certainly true, but so far somewhat unilluminating. We have yet to see just what role the notions of virtue and vice should play in our understanding of judging, and how far that role is a substantial or indispensable one. To put the question simply, is talk of judicial virtue and vice simply a rhetorical flourish to an account of judging whose substantial content is set in quite other terms; or does it play an essential role in any adequate normative account or understanding of what it is to be a judge? I shall argue that there is some substantial work for the ideas of judicial virtue and vice to do in a theory of judging – but that their role is not and could not plausibly be as substantial as Solum thinks it is.

2. Thick and Thin Theories of Judicial Virtue

The 'thinnest' role for notions of virtue and vice in a normative account of judging would be one that made them wholly derivative from assessments

---

[1] The first claim is Solum's, p. 181 in this collection (in the rest of this comment, bare page references in the text are to Solum's essay); the second claim is Huigen's (1995, 1425). See also George 1993.
[2] See, e.g., Raz 1986.

© Metaphilosophy LLC and Blackwell Publishing Ltd. 2003

of judicial conduct. We could say, if we wished, that a judge who acts as a judge should act – a judge who reaches just decisions, by following appropriate judicial procedures – thereby exhibits judicial virtue; and that one who culpably fails to act as a judge should act – one who reaches unjust decisions or follows inappropriate procedures – thereby exhibits judicial vice. But this is to use 'virtue' and 'vice' as nothing more than rhetorical flourishes: all the substantial work is done by an account of how judges should act, and the notions of judicial virtue and vice are simply applied to those who regularly act well or badly; the criteria for ascribing virtue or vice are just derived from the criteria for appraising the judge's actions as judicially right.[3]

We arrive at a slightly 'thicker', more substantial, account of judicial virtue and vice when we turn to what Solum calls a "'thin' theory of judicial virtue" (183) – a theory that seeks to identify those "qualities of judicial character [that] are necessary for reliably good judging given any plausible normative theory of judicial decision" (183). Now Solum wants to offer a theory that goes beyond this in two ways: it will not be limited to those qualities of character that are necessary on *any* plausible account of judging, but could include qualities that are necessary only given some particular conception of judging; and it will make virtue a criterion of good decisions, rather than vice versa. I shall attend to the latter feature in the subsequent two sections; in this section I shall be concerned with the first.

There is certainly important and interesting work to be done in identifying and analysing the qualities of character that are needed for reliably good judging – work that will give ideas of virtue and vice a substantial role in a normative theory of judging. Although an account of proper judicial conduct is still logically prior to the account of judicial virtue and vice, that account now adds something – it tells us what qualities a person needs if she is to be reliably able to act appropriately. Solum's (admittedly provisional and incomplete) discussion of five judicial vices and their corresponding virtues makes a very useful start on this work; I have just two comments to make on it.

The first comment concerns the 'thickness' of his account. Although what he offers is a 'thick' account, in the sense that it identifies some substantial character traits that should count as virtues or vices, it seems to fit his description of a 'thin' theory rather well: for on any 'plausible normative theory of judicial decision' avarice, civic cowardice, bad temper, stupidity and poor judgement would surely count as defects that hinder or pervert judicial conduct – that is, as vices – whilst their correlates would count as judicial virtues. It is of course a difficult and probably in the end futile exercise to try to work out what belongs with the very concept of judging (that is, what would have to figure in anything that was to count as a theory of *judging*) and what belongs rather with particular

---

[3] The ascription of virtue or vice might add *something* to appraisals of a judge's particular actions, in so far as such an ascription implies a persisting pattern of conduct, but it still says nothing more than that the judge acts, or regularly acts, well or badly by whatever are the appropriate criteria of good or bad judicial action.

conceptions of judging. But Solum's account thus far is, in the non-pejorative sense that he is using, 'thinner' than he recognises.

My second comment concerns the content of Solum's account. One sign of the extent to which we are living 'after virtue', in a culture in whose moral understanding ('such as it is', as more pessimistic MacIntyreans would add) notions of virtue and vice no longer play a substantial role, is that we have lost whatever sure grip our predecessors might have had on the language and conceptual architecture of virtue and vice. Solum's grip is better than many people's, but he goes astray in his account of the judicial vice of avarice and the supposedly corresponding virtue of temperance. He takes avarice to be equivalent to corruption, but whilst avarice, or the aspect of avarice that involves an excessive greed for the acquisition of money or other goods, is often a motive for familiar kinds of corruption (the acceptance of bribes, for instance), corruption need not flow from avarice. A corrupt judge is a judge who is liable to accept improper inducements to allow his decisions to be guided by improper and irrelevant considerations. Whilst such inducements are often of a kind that appeals to avarice, they could instead consist in, for example, the defeat of a political enemy or the provision of sexual favours – neither of which is really an object of *avaricious* desire.

Nor is 'temperance' clearly the virtue that corresponds either to avarice or to corruption. Temperance involves having rightly ordered appetites. A temperate person does not deny the value of those appetites and their satisfaction (that would constitute the vice of asceticism), but her appetites are appropriately moderate; she is not overly concerned with such pleasures as those of food, drink and sex, and she would never over-indulge in them. Now an intemperate judge might be led into corruption if her appetites were too expensive for her salary, or if she exposed herself to blackmail through her over-indulgence. But this need not happen, since the intemperate person's appetites might be ones that could be indulged without any such risk of corruption. Intemperance would still, however, be a judicial vice, in so far as over-indulgence might impair judicial capacities – put simply, a judge suffering a hangover or indigestion will not judge well.

Finally, the vices of avarice and corruption need have nothing to do with intemperance: a miser is avaricious, but not intemperate; and a judge's corruption could flow from his miserly desire to accrue wealth, or from motives that have nothing to do with either intemperance or avarice (a desire to do down one's political opponents, for example). All of this suggests that, rather than identifying "avarice or corruption" (186) as a judicial vice to which temperance is the corresponding virtue, we should identify corruption as a distinctive judicial vice, to which integrity is the corresponding virtue, and recognise avarice and intemperance as distinct (and extrajudicial) vices that are also amongst the possible sources of corruption.

This discussion of judicial virtues and vices gives the idea of virtue a

© Metaphilosophy LLC and Blackwell Publishing Ltd. 2003

substantial, but still derivative, role in a normative theory of judging. That role is substantial, because virtue is not defined merely as a disposition or tendency to make right decisions – we identify substantive qualities of character that will equip or enable the person to make right decisions. But the role is still derivative, since it depends on a logically independent or prior account of what makes judicial decisions right or wrong, good or bad; only once we know what counts as a good or a bad judicial decision can we begin to work out which qualities of character will equip a judge to reach good decisions, and which are liable to hinder or pervert judicial decision making – which qualities, that is, should count as judicial virtues or as judicial vices.

Solum, however, is more ambitious than this: he argues that the quality of the decision is at least in part a function of the virtue or vice of the judge who makes it. It is to that argument we must now turn.

3. Right Decisions and Wrong Reasons

One merit of a virtue-oriented approach to ethics is that it provides a salutary corrective to an over-general application of the idea that one can do 'the right deed for the wrong reason', and to the sharp distinction between 'deeds' and 'reasons' on which that idea depends.

Such a corrective is especially needed in the context of personal (as distinct from official or institutional) actions, and especially when the action's expressive character is salient. Thus a visit to a sick relative takes its moral value, in essential part, from the loving concern that it expresses, or purports to express. If it is instead motivated solely by a desire to keep my place as a beneficiary in her will, its moral value is vitiated, if not destroyed altogether (even if she is in fact cheered up by my successful pretence at loving concern); we might think, as might she if she discovers the truth, that it would be better not to visit at all than to visit in that spirit and from that motive.[4] We might also think, however, that the distinction between deeds and reasons, and the possibility of doing what is genuinely the right deed for the wrong reason, is clearer when the deed is done as part of an official or institutional role, and in particular that a corrupt judge could still, as it were fortuitously, make a just and proper decision. That is just what Solum wants to deny.

He does not, of course, deny that a corrupt judge could sometimes make a just and proper decision: for a judge who has the vice of corruption – one who is disposed to accept improper inducements, and to allow his decisions to be guided by irrelevant considerations – might not (indeed, probably will

---

[4] More complex is the case in which I overcome my reluctance to visit her from a sense of duty (which would involve recognising my immediate disinclination as morally lacking). Depending on just how the idea of 'duty' figures in my life, we might or might not still be able to see my action as expressing my love and concern for her. See Winch 1972.

not) be corrupted in every case he tries. What Solum does argue, however, is that if a judge is corrupted on a particular occasion, his decision on that occasion is corrupt and "wrong, even if it does, in fact, give the parties that to which they are entitled as a matter of law" (186; see also his remarks on civic cowardice at 187): what might seem to be 'the right decision', because it gives the parties what they are legally entitled to, is rendered wrong by the fact that it is made for the wrong – because corrupt – reasons.

Now we can certainly criticise the judge for his corruption, even if he reaches the legally correct decision, and we can certainly deny him any credit for the correctness of the decision. But I think Solum is wrong to suggest that the decision itself is wrong; that suggestion seems plausible only because he fails to attend to the role of process in constituting 'right' decisions.

Suppose that a judge accepts a bribe to decide a case in favour of one party, and that his decision is directly influenced by that bribe: that is, although he will of course need to find a way of portraying his decision as legally permissible or required, his immediately motivating reason for deciding for A rather than for B is that A bribed him. I agree with Solum that even if we think that the law was on A's side and that A would have won before a non-corrupt judge, there is something amiss in such a case, not only with the judge but also with the decision. What is amiss with the decision, however, is not – as Solum suggests – the judge's corruption as such but the process through which the decision was reached. A judge's duty is to decide the cases that come before her through a process that accords with the requirements of justice – of, we might say, natural procedural justice; and the rightness or justice of her decision depends in crucial part on whether it emerged from a just judicial process. A judge who fails to hear both sides in the case, or decides a case in which she has an interest, might reach a legally correct decision (the decision that would have been reached by a judge whose procedures respected the requirements of natural justice), but her decision is vitiated by the injustice of the process from which it emerged.[5] Similarly, a judge who decides in favour of the party who is legally entitled to win only because she was bribed to do so has failed to observe a basic requirement of natural justice, that she attend only to legally relevant considerations in making her decision; that procedural failure vitiates her decision.[6]

We can see more clearly why what vitiates the corrupt judge's decision is the injustice of the process by which she reaches it, rather than her corruption

[5] On these and other requirements of natural justice, see Pennock and Chapman 1977 and Jackson 1979.

[6] I am not suggesting that we should see judicial decision making as an instance of '*pure procedural justice*' – that we have *no* criterion for the justice or correctness of a decision other than that it was the outcome of a just process; only that the justice of the decision must depend in part on the justice of the process. On the different versions of procedural justice, see Rawls 1972, 85–86, 235; also Resnick 1977.

by itself, by considering a rather different, and less usual, example of judicial corruption. Suppose that a judge is ready to hire herself, in so far as she can carry it off, to the highest bidder: within the limits set by the need not to be found out, she will do her best to fulfil the bidding of whoever offers her the largest bribe; once she has made such a corrupt agreement with the highest bidder, she will as far as she can remain faithful to it. Suppose now that a party to a case she is to try, or a disinterested benefactor seeking to promote justice, offers her a bribe to decide the case in accordance with the require-ments of procedural justice: that is, to attend only to legally relevant consid-erations in reaching her decision. Since that bribe is higher than any other bribe she has been offered in relation to this case, she accepts it and sets herself to decide the case as it should in law be decided; and she reaches the legally correct decision. In this case, the decision is surely not vitiated by the judge's corruption. She is corrupt, and she shows her corruption in the way she goes about deciding this case (for had she not been bribed, she would not have observed the requirements of procedural justice): but her *decision* is not corrupt; it is not 'evil' or 'wrong' (186), since it is a legally correct decision that she reached by following the appropriate and just procedure.

Once we recognise that the justice or correctness of a judicial decision is in part a matter of the justice of the process by which it was reached, we can maintain the distinction between deeds and reasons in this context and deny that the judge's corruption necessarily vitiates the decisions in which it is actualised; we can, that is, still insist that the criteria of justice and correctness for judicial decisions, whilst not independent of the justice of the process through which they are made, are independent of the virtue or vice of the judge.

This is not yet to show, however, that a strictly "virtue-centred theory of judging" (198) is impossible – a theory, that is, according to which the judge's virtue becomes a criterion of the correctness of her decision: for Solum has a further argument for a virtue-centred theory.

4. Virtue and Equity

"A *lawful decision*," Solum holds, "is a decision that would characteristi-cally be made by a virtuous judge in the circumstances that are relevant to the decision"; and a "lawful" decision is a "legally correct" decision (198–9). Such a definition does give virtue a fundamental, rather than a merely derivative, role in a normative theory of judging: instead of defin-ing judicial virtue in terms of legally correct decisions (the virtues are those qualities that a judge needs if she is reliably to arrive at legally correct deci-sions), we define legally correct decisions in terms of judicial virtues.[7]

---

[7] And one could of course do the same with process values: rather than defining judicial virtues as the qualities a judge needs if he is to arrive at his decisions by just procedures, we define just procedures as those that would be followed by a virtuous judge.

Solum thus seeks to invert the more familiar idea that "the notion of a just outcome is prior to and independent of the notion of the virtue of justice" (199);[8] and he argues that we can see the need for such an inversion most clearly by considering cases in which 'equity' is necessary – cases, that is, in which justice, understood as fairness, requires "a departure from the [legal] rules," because the rules, if strictly applied, would produce "unanticipated and unjust results" (205).

Any morally plausible system of law must find room for equity. We cannot hope, that is, to produce a statutory legal code whose articulated rules will be fully adequate to every case that comes before the courts: either the rules will need to be vague enough to leave room for the kind of particularist judgements, the sensitivities to the features of the particular case, that Solum emphasises, or judges will need to have the discretion to depart from the rules when a strict adherence to them would produce serious injustice. That is why the common-law model of case-by-case reasoning, which precisely involves careful attention to the salient features of the particular case, is indispensable even in a codified system of law, although it is unpopular with theorists who yearn after a mythical ideal of legal clarity and certainty.[9]

We might accept too that in at least some cases "the just outcome can only be recognised by a virtuous judge" (199). Solum does not deny that over large stretches of the law anyone with a modicum of intelligence can work out what the law is or requires; after all, if that were not the case, the criminal law could not function as a deterrent. Nor need he deny that in some – perhaps many – cases an intelligent detached observer with no commitment to justice could work out what the legal outcome should be; after all, "detached normative statements" of law can be made by those who do not accept the values that the law embodies, and who might not possess the virtues that judges need.[10] But it is at least plausible that moral understanding and the ability to discern what should be done in difficult situations require moral virtue,[11] and so too that legal understanding and the ability to discern what the legal outcome should be in the kinds of case that might call for equity require the judicial virtues. This is an epistemological thesis, however, which does not *define* the notion of a legally correct decision in terms of the judicial virtues: the idea of a 'just outcome' is still logically "prior to and independent of the notion of the virtue of justice" (199). We might need virtue to discern what justice requires, but what *constitutes* an outcome as what justice requires is not that this outcome is discerned by the eye of virtue.

Solum seems to want to go beyond the epistemological thesis about the

---

[8] See Williams 1980, 196–97 (cited by Solum).

[9] See, e.g., Gainer 1988 and Alexy 1989. On the common-law model, see especially Wisdom 1965.

[10] On 'detached normative statements', see Raz 1979, 153–9.

[11] As Aristotle of course argued: see *Nicomachean Ethics*.

qualities that one needs if one is to *discern* and do justice, to the meta-physical or logical thesis that justice *is*, at least in equity cases, what the virtuous judge would decide. But he offers no argument for this more radical thesis – a thesis that would make his theory truly 'virtue centred' – no argument beyond those that lead us towards the epistemological thesis; and the more radical thesis does not seem plausible.

Its implausibility can be most clearly seen if we ask how a virtuous judge would go about justifying her decision in a hard case – a case in which we might accept that only a judge with the judicial virtues would have been able to discern the just outcome. If the outcome's justice was to be defined, as Solum suggests, in terms of the judicial virtues, a virtuous judge would then be able to justify her decision by pointing to her own judicial virtue: "This is what justice requires because I am a virtuous judge and this is what I decide." Now a judge (or at least one who lacked the further virtue of humility) might indeed ground a claim that we should accept her authority on an appeal to her judicial virtues, just as a doctor might ground a claim that the patient should accept her diagnosis on an appeal to her medical expertise: but in neither case is this to *define* the correctness of the decision or diagnosis in terms of the virtues or expertise of the person who claims authority; nor would either the judge or the doctor try to justify the decision or diagnosis itself – as distinct from justifying the claim that others should accept it – in such terms.

It would be absurd for a judge, in seeking to explain and justify her decision, to appeal to her own judicial virtues as a justification: she would instead identify and explain the relevant, salient features of the case and their relation to legal doctrines and principles that are already recognised in her system of law. This shows, however, that what *constitutes* the justice of her decision or of the outcome that she determines is not her own virtue, as Solum's more radical thesis holds, but the features of the case to which she appeals. In simple cases, what makes the outcome just is not the virtue of the judge but the relevant features of the case: what makes it just, for instance, that the defendant should pay a certain sum of money to the plain-tiff is that this was required by a valid contract between them, or that this would pay for the damage that the defendant had negligently caused. So too in hard cases, although the judge cannot simply apply some existing rule or doctrine; what makes the outcome just must be the features of the case that the virtuous judge can see – and show – to be relevant and dispositive.[12]

---

[12] Solum imagines a judge, questioned by an interlocutor to the point where explanation has to come to an end, saying, "Because that's the way I see it, and I am a competent judge. I cannot say any more than that" (201); and he takes this to support his claim that "virtue is required to explain decisions according to legal rules" (201). But such an appeal to her competence does not explain the judge's decision in the relevant, justificatory sense: it can explain how she came, if she did come, to make a or the just decision in a complex case, but not what makes that decision just or right. The justificatory explanation is to be found in the facts and legal doctrines and principles that she has already cited and discussed; the appeal to her competence is meant to justify not her decision but her implicit claim that her inter-locutor should accept it without further questioning.

Solum's discussion of equity reminds us of the importance of the judicial virtues: a judge who lacks them might not even be able to see what justice requires. It does not, however, lead us towards a truly 'virtue-centred theory of judging', since it does not show that we should, or plausibly could, *define* the justice of outcomes in terms of the judicial virtues. The justice of a legal outcome is still prior to and independent of the judicial virtues – as is shown, finally, by the fact that we can criticise a judge's decision without doubting his judicial virtue. Often, of course, we will rightly ascribe erroneous or unjust decisions to some lack of judicial virtue in the judge – if only he had had more courage, a better temper, or greater integrity, intelligence or wisdom, he would have reached the just decision. Sometimes, however, we can think that the judge got it wrong in a difficult case without therefore supposing that he lacked virtue; what makes some cases hard is precisely the fact that even a virtuous judge can get them wrong.

5. Conclusion

There is a substantial role for an account of judicial virtues and vices in a normative theory of judging: for an account of those qualities that a judge needs if she is to do justice reliably, and of those qualities that will hinder or pervert judicial decision making. Solum has made a start on that account; in developing it further, one question that will need to be tackled is whether there are *distinctive* judicial virtues and vices, or whether judicial virtues and vices are simply ordinary, extrajudicial virtues and vices applied to the particular context of judging.

Solum wants to give virtue a more fundamental role than this, in a 'virtue-centred theory of judging' that makes virtue a *criterion* of just or correct judicial decisions – that *defines* the just or correct decision as one which a virtuous judge would make. I have argued that in this he is wrong. A judge needs the judicial virtues if she is to discern, in hard cases, what justice requires, and if she is to be adequately motivated to arrive at just decisions by a just process: but the justice of that process and of those decisions is not constituted by those virtues.

Department of Philosophy
University of Stirling
Stirling FK9 4LA
United Kingdom
r.a.duff@stir.ac.uk

References

Alexy, R. W. 1989. *A Theory of Legal Argumentation*, translated by R. Adler and N. MacCormick. Oxford: Oxford University Press.

Gainer, R. L. 1988. "The Culpability Provisions of the Model Penal Code."
    Rutgers Law Journal 19: 575ff.
George, R. 1993. *Making Men Moral: Civil Liberties and Public Morality*
    Oxford: Oxford University Press.
Huigens, K. 1995. "Virtue and Inculpation." *Harvard Law Review* 108:
    1423ff.
Jackson, P. 1979. *Natural Justice*. 2nd ed. London: Sweet and Maxwell.
Pennock, J. R., and J. W. Chapman, editors. 1977. *Due Process*. New York:
    New York University Press.
Rawls, J. 1972. *A Theory of Justice*. Oxford: Oxford University Press.
Raz, J. 1979. "Legal Validity." In *The Authority of Law*, 146–59. Oxford:
    Oxford University Press.
———. 1986. *The Morality of Freedom*. Oxford: Oxford University Press.
Resnick, D. 1977. "Due Process and Procedural Justice." In *Due Process*,
    edited by J. R. Pennock and J. W. Chapman. New York: New York
    University Press.
Stephen, J. F. 1967. *Liberty, Equality, Fraternity*, edited by J. White.
    Cambridge: Cambridge University Press. Originally published in 1873.
Williams, Bernard. 1980. "Justice as a Virtue." In *Essays on Aristotle's
    Ethics*, edited by A. O. Rorty, 189–99. Berkeley: University of
    California Press.
Winch, Peter. 1972. "Moral Integrity." In *Ethics and Action*, 171–92.
    London: Routledge.
Wisdom, J. 1965. "A Feature of Wittgenstein's Technique." In *Paradox
    and Discovery*, 90–103. Oxford: Basil Blackwell.

© Metaphilosophy LLC and Blackwell Publishing Ltd. 2003.
Published by Blackwell Publishing, 9600 Garsington Road, Oxford OX4 2DQ, UK and
350 Main Street, Malden, MA 02148, USA
METAPHILOSOPHY
Vol. 34, Nos. 1/2, January 2003
0026-1068

BOOKS RECEIVED

Chrétien, Jean-Louis. *The Unforgettable and the Unhoped For*, translated by Jeffrey Bloechl, Fordham University Press, 2002, 129 pp.

Costa, Claudio. *The Philosophical Inquiry: Towards a Global Account*, University Press of America, 2002, 177 pp.

Cupitt, Don, ed. *Is Nothing Sacred?: The Non-Realist Philosophy of Religion, Selected Essays*, Fordham University Press, 2002, 159 pp.

Deutscher, Penelope. *A Politics of Impossible Difference: The Later Work of Luce Irigaray*, Cornell University Press, 2002, 228 pp.

Goodman, Russell B. *Wittgenstein and William James*, Cambridge University Press, 2002, 212 pp.

Harman, Graham. *Tool-Being*, Open Court, 2002, 331 pp.

Harvey, Irene E. *Labyrinths of Exemplarity: At the Limits of Deconstruction*, State University of New York Press, 2002, 281 pp.

Pompa, Leon, ed. *Vico: The First New Science*, Cambridge University Press, 2002, 302 pp.

Rist, John M. *Real Ethics: Rethinking the Foundations of Morality*, Cambridge University Press, 2002, 295 pp.

Soble, Alan, ed. *The Philosophy of Sex: Contemporary Readings*, Rowman and Littlefield, 2002, 513 pp.

Notes on Contributors

Michael S. Brady is a lecturer in philosophy at the University of Stirling. His current research is focused on the relations between virtue theory and metaethics. He has published articles in a number of journals, including the *Pacific Philosophical Quarterly,* the *Journal of Value Inquiry,* and *Philosophical Quarterly.*

R. A. Duff is professor of philosophy at the University of Stirling, where he has taught since 1970. He works mainly in the philosophy of criminal law, focusing on punishment and on the structures and principles of criminal liability.

Juli Eflin is professor and chair of philosophy at Ball State University. Her research interests include epistemology and philosophy of science. A publication related to her article here is "An Epistemological Base for the Problem-Solving Model of Creativity," in *Philosophia.* She is currently at work on the consequences of askeptical epistemology, its relation to feminism, and the relationships between knowledge and understanding.

Miranda Fricker is a lecturer in philosophy at Birkbeck College, University of London. She edited *The Cambridge Companion to Feminism in Philosophy* with Jennifer Hornsby and has published articles in epistemology, ethics, and social philosophy. She is currently writing a book, *Epistemic Injustice: Power and the Ethics of Knowing,* that explores how relations of power and identity impinge in epistemic practices.

Christopher Hookway is professor of philosophy at the University of Sheffield, where he teaches courses on epistemology and on American pragmatism. He has published books in both these areas, including *Peirce; Truth, Rationality, and Pragmatism: Themes from Peirce; Scepticism;* and *Quine: Language, Experience, and Reality.*

S. E. Marshall is professor of philosophy and dean of the Faculty of Arts at the University of Stirling. Her research interests primarily concern the key points of contact among legal, political, and social philosophy, and she is currently working on aspects of the criminal trial. She is joint editor of the *Journal for Applied Philosophy.*

Marie McGinn is a lecturer in philosophy at the University of York. Her research primarily focuses on the work of Wittgenstein. She is the author

© Metaphilosophy LLC and Blackwell Publishing Ltd. 2003

of *Sense and Certainty: A Dissolution of Scepticism* and *Wittgenstein and the Philosophical Investigations.*

Andrew McGonigal is a lecturer in philosophy at the University of Leeds. His main research interests are in the philosophy of language, aesthetics, and metaphysics. He has articles published or forthcoming in the *British Journal of Aesthetics, Ratio,* and *Religious Studies.*

Philip Percival is a lecturer in philosophy at the University of Glasgow. He gained his doctorate from the University of Cambridge and held a post-doctoral research fellowship at the Hebrew University in Jerusalem before taking up lectureships at the University of Cape Town and various colleges of the University of Oxford. He has published mainly in the areas of metaphysics and philosophical logic, most recently in the journals *Mind* and *Analysis.*

Duncan Pritchard is a lecturer in philosophy and Leverhulme Trust Special Research Fellow at the University of Stirling. He has published widely in epistemology, including recent articles in the *American Philosophical Quarterly, Synthese,* and the *International Journal of Philosophical Studies,* and he is currently in the process of completing a book entitled *Epistemic Luck.*

Michael Slote is UST Professor of Ethics and professor of philosophy at the University of Miami. His areas of special interest are ethics, theory of rational choice, moral psychology, and, especially in recent years, political philosophy. Formerly professor and chair of philosophy and a fellow at Trinity College, Dublin, he is a member of the Royal Irish Academy. He is also a past Tanner Lecturer and a past president of the American Society for Value Inquiry.

Lawrence B. Solum is professor of law and William M. Rains Fellow at Loyola Law School, Loyola Marymount University. He has published articles in numerous journals, including the *Cornell Law Review,* the *Harvard Law Review,* the *Michigan Law Review, Northwestern Law Review, Nomos,* the *Pacific Philosophical Quarterly,* and the *University of Chicago Law Review.* He has written extensively on constitutional theory, legal procedure, and the philosophy of law.

Linda Zagzebski is Kingfisher College Chair of the Philosophy of Religion and Ethics at the University of Oklahoma. Her recent work includes several articles on foreknowledge and free will and on epistemic value. She is the coeditor of two volumes of essays on the virtues, entitled *Virtue Epistemology* and *Intellectual Virtue.* Her current book project, entitled *Divine Motivation Theory,* describes a strong form of virtue theory with a theological foundation.